Remembering Places

Toposophia: Sustainability, Dwelling, Design

Series Editors: Robert Mugerauer, University of Washington, and Gary Backhaus, Loyola College in Maryland

Toposophia is a book series dedicated to the interdisciplinary and transdisciplinary study of place. Authors in the series attempt to engage a geographical turn in their research, emphasizing the spatial component, as well as the philosophical turn, raising questions both reflectively and critically.

Titles in the Series

Mysticism and Architecture: Wittgenstein and the Meanings of the Palais Stonborough, by Roger Paden
When France Was King of Cartography: The Patronage and Production of Maps in Early Modern France, by Christine Marie Petto
Incapacitating Biochemical Weapons: Promise or Peril?, Edited by Alan Pearson, Marie Chevrier, and Mark Wheelis
Environmental Dilemmas: Ethical Decision Making, by Robert Mugerauer and Lynne Manzo
The Timespace of Human Activity: On Performance, Society, and History as Indeterminate Teleological Events, by Theodore R. Schatzki
Metamorphoses of the Zoo: Animal Encounter after Noah, Edited by Ralph R. Acampora
Reading the Islamic City: Discursive Practices and Legal Judgment, by Akel Isma'il Kahera
Spoil Island: Reading the Makeshift Archipelago, by Charlie Hailey
Remembering Places: A Phenomenological Study of the Relationship between Memory and Place, by Janet Donohoe

Remembering Places

A Phenomenological Study of the Relationship between Memory and Place

Janet Donohoe

LEXINGTON BOOKS
Lanham • Boulder • New York • London

Published by Lexington Books
An imprint of The Rowman & Littlefield Publishing Group, Inc.
4501 Forbes Boulevard, Suite 200, Lanham, Maryland 20706
www.rowman.com

16 Carlisle Street, London W1D 3BT, United Kingdom

British Library Cataloguing in Publication Information Available

Library of Congress Cataloging-in-Publication Data

Donohoe, Janet.
Remembering places : a phenomenological study of the relationship between memory and place / Janet Donohoe.
pages cm -- (Toposophia : sustainability, dwelling, design)
Includes bibliographical references and index.
ISBN 978-0-7391-8716-6 (cloth : alk. paper) -- ISBN 978-0-7391-8717-3 (electronic)
1. Memory (Philosophy) 2. Place (Philosophy) 3. Monuments--Miscellanea. 4. Phenomenology. I. Title.
BD181.7.D66 2014
128'.3--dc23
2014014813
ISBN 978-0-7391-9863-6 (pbk

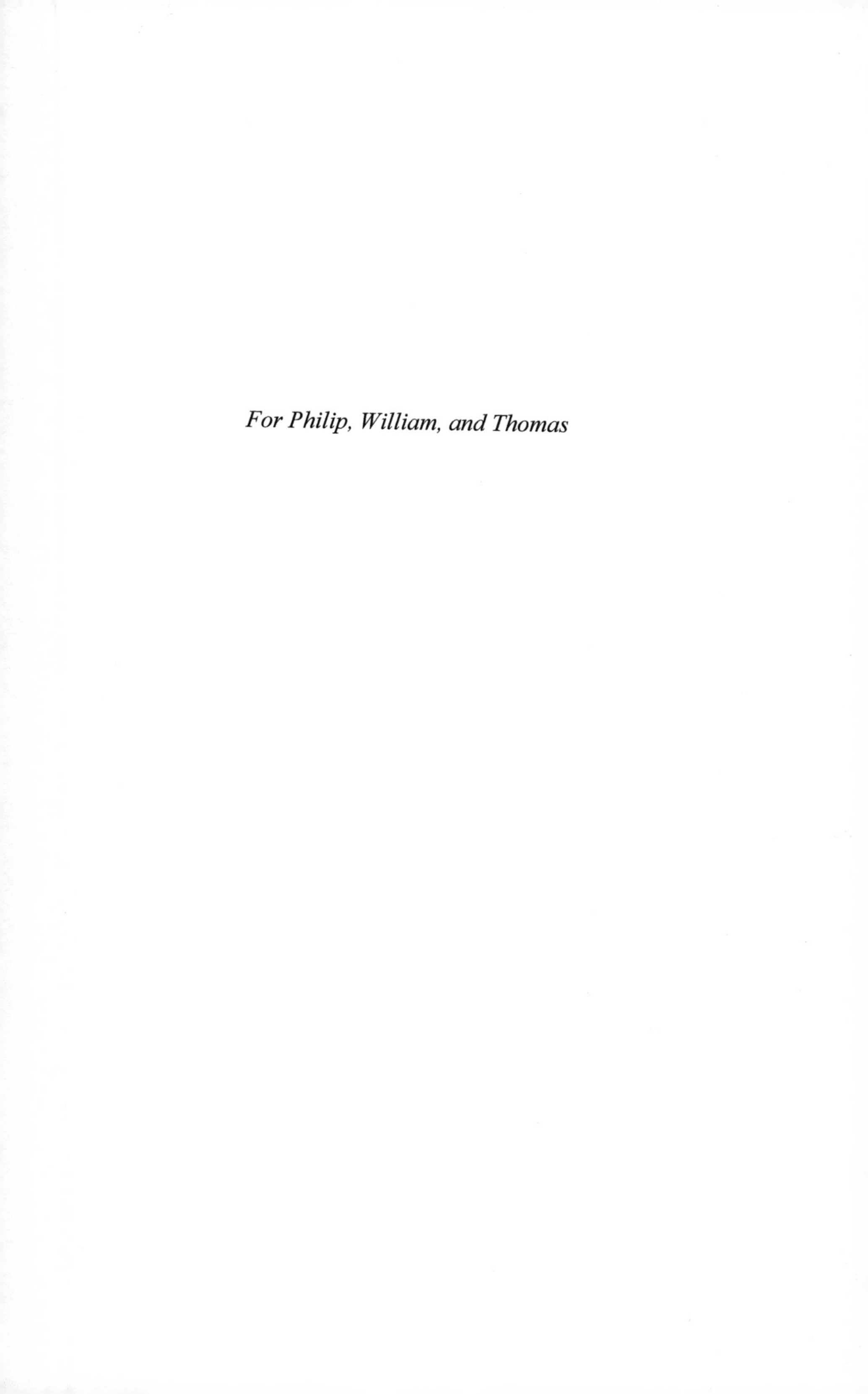

For Philip, William, and Thomas

Contents

Acknowledgements

In my experience it takes many people to write and publish a book and while I take full responsibility for everything between the covers of this book, I could not have completed it without help from others who have my deepest gratitude.

I am grateful to Steve Gish, and Ken and Bernadine Clark for the generosity of allowing me to use photographs from far flung places, and for the generosity of friendship throughout this process.

Many people provided encouragement and support over the last several years without which this project probably would have remained undeveloped. David Seamon's contributions in that regard are especially appreciated. Thanks to Bob Mugerauer, editor of the series, for seeing promise in the project and to the anonymous reviewer whose careful critique made the book better.

Thanks to Jana Hodges-Kluck at Lexington Books for answering my many questions and making the process as painless as possible.

I am particularly grateful to Dennis Keenan, David Vessey, and Jeremy Wisnewski for comments and suggestions on earlier drafts of this manuscript and for the decades of intellectual companionship. What an impoverished philosophical life I would have without them. Thank you to the members of the Society for Philosophy in the Contemporary World, especially Trudy Conway, Joe Jones, and Charlie Harvey for their support and questioning of my work over the years, and for the friendship and collegial intellectual challenges.

And thanks most of all to my husband, Philip, and my two beautiful boys, William and Thomas, for their patience and willingness to put up with me while I was writing, but most of all for helping me to keep it all in perspective. You make it all worthwhile.

Parts of each chapter have been published previously and I am grateful to the editors of those publications for permission to reprint them here in altered form. They are as follows: Part of chapter 1 adapted by permission of the publishers from "The Place of Home," in *Environmental Philosophy*, volume 8, pp. 25–40. Copyright 2011. In chapter 2 parts of sections I and II adapted by permission of the publishers from "Where Were You When . . . ? On the Relationship between Individual Memory and Collective Memory," in *Philosophy in the Contemporary World*, volume 16, pp. 105–113. Copyright 2009. Also in chapter 2, part of section III adapted by permission of the publishers of "The Place of Tradition: Heidegger and

Benjamin on Technology and Art," in *Journal of the British Society for Phenomenology*, volume 39, pp. 260–274. Copyright 2008. Part of chapter 3 adapted by permission of the publishers from "Coming Home and Places of Mourning," in *Resisting the Place of Belonging* edited by Daniel Boscaljon (Farnham: Ashgate, 2013), pp. 171–179. Copyright 2013. Chapter 4 contains versions of three different articles adapted by permission of the publishers from "The Betweenness of Monuments," in *Environmental Hermeneutics* (New York: Fordham University Press, 2013), pp. 264–280. Copyright 2013; "Rushing to Memorialize," in *Philosophy in the Contemporary World*, volume 13, pp. 6–12. Copyright 2006; and "Dwelling with Monuments," in *Philosophy and Geography*, volume 5, pp. 235–242. Copyright 2002.

Introduction

Memory. Tradition. Place. It took me a long time to realize that it is impossible to put these terms into any kind of hierarchical, chronological, or foundational order. In fact, the three terms are so intricately interwoven that it is difficult to separate one from the others. As Edmund Husserl might say, they are distinct, but not separate. Experience is always and everywhere an interweaving of the three. It is this complex web that I hope to be able to shed some light on in the following pages. While it is not difficult to see the connection between memory and tradition, the position of place is perhaps less obvious for place has for so long been overlooked, untheorized, and forgotten. In recent years there has been an increasing interest in place, and even in place in its connection with memory or tradition, but there is much more that can be said and I try to say some of it here.

The importance of place is hard to deny. There are good reasons we take our children and spouses to see the places where we grew up. Seeing the house, the yard, the neighborhood, or the town, and walking around and through them fulfills what would otherwise be constitutionally and narratively impoverished. Likewise, going to the gravesites of ancestors, sometimes many generations past, provides more than simply a mnemonic trigger. These places are imbued with memory and the aura of such places connects us to the past and to traditions, making them present to us.

Places serve not merely as the settings for our lives, but as participants, as vibrant, living aspects of memory, tradition, history, and meaning. Such places are abundant in literature from Combray in Proust's *Remembrance of Things Past* to Sethe's house in Toni Morrison's *Beloved* to the drawing room of Tom Stoppard's *Arcadia.* Places serve not as the borders or containers of memory, but as a palimpsest, a Medieval manuscript in which various writings are visible beneath and through the newer writing upon a linen parchment. The image of the palimpsest works not just for places of memory but for memory itself. Places write themselves upon memory just as memory writes itself upon place. This mutual relationship of change with erasure and with layers of place and layers of memory will be clarified in the following pages through philosophical analysis and phenomenological description.

In this book I investigate the role of place in the production, retention, and reinvigoration of memory, particularly collective memory. I assert that memory is constituted through place and calls us to be more attentive to places in that role. Moreover, I focus on the role of place in the constitution of collective memories and the ways in which collective memories, precisely because they are collective, are frequently inseparable from individual ones. Insofar as collective memory and individual memory are not easy to tease apart, we notice that place is fundamental to both. To see that memory is reliant upon place, is at the same time to see that memory is not simply a stock set of images stored away for recall at will. Instead, memory is reconceived as a many-layered palimpsest of association in conjunction with a similarly many-layered palimpsest of places upon which are written our history, traditions, experiences, and ideas.

I take on this project from a phenomenological perspective, challenging the experience of place as well as the experiences of memory and tradition and the ways in which experiences of one cannot be separated from experiences of the others. The phenomenological method of descriptive encounter necessarily involves us in a hermeneutic interpretation that is required of memory, tradition, and place. The material environment contributes so significantly to memory requiring that it be read in ways that are ever changing just as the narrative presentation of memory must be.

The concept of place will, of course, be developed more and more specifically throughout the book as we investigate how it informs and is informed by memory and tradition. As a starting point, we can say that place is distinct from space. It is also distinct from site. Many geographers define place at its most basic as a meaningful location. We can, however, say more about place than that. Place is not just a setting, but is a concrete, material framework for and participant in human lives. It has a structure that space lacks. It is limited, bounded, and exclusive while space is an unbounded, homogeneous realm.[1] Place grounds space in the order of experience. In other words, place is experienced and space is understood as the homogeneity that is not place and does not have the peculiar characteristics of place. Space is more abstract, lending itself to mathematization and geometry, while place resists such attempts in the way in which it is imbued with value and meaning.[2]

As Aristotle suggests, "everything is somewhere and in place . . . the power of a place will be a remarkable one, and prior to all things."[3] Although everything is in place, humans are not in place in the same way that things are. Place is vitally important for humans in such a way that it cannot so easily be set apart over against humans. When meeting someone for the first time, it is often important to know where that person is from. The person's place of origin is not simply a site as located on a map. It is not even the physical site that is of importance. Instead, the identification of the place a person is from gives a sense of the person even as the person gives a sense to the place. To know a person's place of origin indicates whether that person is like us or not, and if not like us, it often gives us an indication of how that person might be different from us. If we come from the same place, we might have a sense of kinship or camaraderie. Sometimes the place someone is from can be very general, e.g., a country or a state. But place can also be as specific as a street of a neighborhood for defining whether someone is of my gang or the rival gang. Place identifies one with a certain community of people and shapes one's understanding of people and the world.

If people are unable to say where they are from, perhaps because they have moved frequently, we are less comfortable, less able to place them, less able to identify with them. It is not only the sense of origin that is important in asking the question of where someone is from. Place provides a background for the person, a tradition which the person has inherited and which shapes the person even if only through rejection of traditions of the place. It is, then, something (someplace) upon which subjectivity and community are founded.[4] Place is thus exclusive in the sense that it identifies one group over against others, against those not of this place. Having such a distinction between our place and theirs is a necessary distinction, however, since our place could never be ours without that place over against which it is distinguished and from which it is excluded. Our place and theirs belong together co-constituting a world for us all.[5]

Certainly other theorists have noted that place is intertwined with memory. As Ed Casey asserts in *Remembering,* "place is selective for memories: that is to say, a given place will invite certain memories while discouraging others. The fact is that we can't attach just any memories to a particular place . . . place is always definite, and regarding a given place only some memories, indeed only certain kinds of memory, will be pertinent."[6] Gaston Bachelard, in *The Poetics of Space,* is concerned with the transcendence of inhabited space over geometrical space.[7] His phenomenological study emphasizes the subjectivity of place(s) that is grounded in the childhood home. The encounter with the childhood home provides the foundation upon which any other encounter of place(s) is rooted. The place of the childhood home whether it is a hut or a mansion frames the experience of place from then on. Other dwellings are measured by that first dwelling.

In considering places of individual memory, habituated places such as a grandparent's attic full of toys, or the elementary school, or the weekend market square come to mind. These are places where a child would have gone habitually, daily, weekly, or every summer. Such repeated visits make the place familiar. As adults we can recall the hallways of the school, or the smell of the attic, or the crowded feel and oppressive smells of the market square. The places entail those memories. We may be able to conjure such memories as adults in our homes or offices, for example, but the memories are not animated in the same way they would be if we were actually standing in the attic, the school, or the market square. If one returns to any of these places, the school for instance, it may seem smaller than it did to one as a child, but the feel, the sense of it remains the same. The rooms and hallways are interwoven with the memories of elementary school experiences, the desk one sat in, the corner where one was scolded by a teacher, or the music room or gym where one excelled.

Other places are significant for a singular event. These places are less familiar, but still imbued with memory, such as the place where we got married, where one was mugged, or where a parent died. Stepping into any of these places after years of absence, whether a habituated place or a place of a significant event, creates a rush of memories to which the place itself is connected. They are memories that only return due to the sense of the place, the smell, the feel of the air, and the very place itself.

These descriptions may lend themselves to a misunderstanding. Casey and Bachelard have contributed to our understanding of the role of place in individual memory. The descriptions they provide are of places that are important to a particular person, for particular personal experiences and could thus be claimed to be merely subjective. Although they have primarily described places of personal experiences, place should not be thought of as merely subjective space. Place is the foundation of subjectivity in the sense that the subject is always placed, is always in the world, and its being in the world is part of the very structure of subjectivity. The subject, however, is at the same time always with others in the world, so place is always intersubjective. Place is part of the structure of intersubjectivity.[8]

It is not so difficult to recognize the importance of place to individual memory and individual identity, but what of place and collective memory? How does something so personal, become something that is collective? How is place shared? Casey and Bachelard leave us wanting in this regard, for neither of them has much to say about the relationship between collective memory and place. Edward Casey very briefly addresses connections between place and collective memory in an essay about 9/11, but offers no sustained analysis of the role of place in the perpetuation and production of collective memory.[9] Pierre Nora also addresses the relationship between collective memory and sites of memory in his introductions to the three volume work *Realms of Memory* published in France in the 1970s, but not translated for an English audience until the early 1990s.[10] His account fails to accommodate the phenomenological lived experience of places of memory. His descriptions of them are a negative account of the tension between memory and history. What I do here in extending a phenomenological analysis focused on the bodily interaction with specific places of collective memory in the form of monuments and memorials is to offer a much broader sense of place that accounts for its role in the constitution of collective memories.

Space is shared in that many people walk the same streets, visit the same shops, or inhabit the same buildings, but shared space is not always collective place. Shared space can sometimes be transformed into a collective place, but certain criteria must be met in order for this to occur. A transformative event is required to make a space into a place of collective memory. Collective place is responsible for the traditions that we inherit together and has a much more complicated structure than the places of individual memory. Place as foundational for intersubjectivity is foundational for collective memory and the community that shares memory.

Much work has been done on collective memories as the result of narratives that create a collective identity. But such analyses fail to take into account the contributions of the material environment to collective memories. They do not consider that the world, and its places, are part of the constitution of memories and contribute in very important ways to how and what groups remember. While there is growing interest in material place from different disciplines, an in-depth philosophical study of its relationship to collective memory is lacking.

Phenomenological investigations have a difficult time dealing with the idea of collective memory. Memory is most often treated by phenomenologists in terms of individual memory, recollection, and reminiscence. In order to address collective memory, one must have an understanding of what the collective part of that memory is all about. It is necessarily embedded with a phenomenological question of intersubjectivity. At the same time, phenomenological analysis of place allows us to recognize that it is impossible to erase tradition and memory from the landscape and start afresh. Although landscapes can be transformed with new buildings or destruction of old buildings or natural areas, it is virtually impossible to completely erase a city's history and traditions in so doing. We cannot begin with a clean slate because memory and tradition are written on the landscape itself. One glance around a city convinces us of the many layers of sedimented history captured there. The city narrates its past in its buildings, streets, alleyways, parks, and ports. Memories and traditions are layered there much like the geological strata of rock and earth. While it may be relatively uncontroversial to describe the city as a kind of palimpsest, the ramifications of that for collective memory and notions of tradition and history are far reaching. Memory too can begin to be understood as its own palimpsest with some elements being covered over for a time only to be revealed again later while other elements may remain silent.

In the following, I am asking questions of how tradition is transferred through place, and what role places have in the preservation of tradition and history. When considering, in particular, the roles of monuments and memorials, we must think about how their privileged position as places of transference of collective memory must be situated not as a simple position of authority in the construction of collective memories and traditions, but as foci of interpretive systems that provide us with ways to think about our place in the contemporary world. In the age of the subaltern, the forgotten, and the marginalized, a tendency arises to want to throw over the monuments of the past and of traditions in order to hear other voices and to see other colors. One aim I have is to propose a way in which hearing new voices, and celebrating other traditions is part of the constantly changing interpretations of places of the material world. Just as the boundaries of a city change, just as neighborhoods constantly change (not unproblematically), so too do the monuments and memorials that compose the material environment supporting our memories and traditions. Collective memory changes with place as we reinterpret, reimagine, and recollect the images of the past.

I don't think it is difficult to see the influences present in my work. The book begins in phenomenology drawing upon Edmund Husserl's work on lifeworld and developing that thought through Heidegger's understanding of dwelling. This idea of dwelling while not explicitly indebted to Husserl shares the Husserlian genetic phenomenological framework of an embodied being who inherits meaning from its predecessors due to its arising within a world that precedes it and expiring out of a world that continues on. It is here that we begin to see a connection between world or place and inheritance of tradition. The foundational role of the body is enhanced through Merleau-Ponty's work that links body to world so thoroughly as to speak of body as something only to be known through the world. By weaving the notion of memory together with the prongs of body, world, and tradition, we can see how place itself is the connecting tissue of this complex web.

Place theorists such as Ed Casey and Jeff Malpas would not disagree with this notion, I think, but they each develop the connections with slightly different emphases. Casey stakes out a phenomenological position which views Heidegger's claim of being-in-the-world as equivalent to being in a place-world. Malpas, on the other hand, takes up a more purely ontological position with structural overtones, although he speaks of place as prior to the social/cultural and political. My own position is deeply indebted to both Casey and Malpas. We concur on considering place to be a framework through which to understand time and space, but in viewing it that way, we do not establish place on a transcendental level but instead as a material condition for the possibility of experience.

Casey asserts that he and Malpas meet between ontology and phenomenology, between the transcendental and experiential. I find my place in the in-between as well, although where they each focus on one pole or the other of a discussion of the permanence or fragility of place, I find a position in the middle. Malpas focuses on the fragility of place arguing that places are always changing and that place-subjects change as well. Casey, on the other hand, focuses on how place stays the same and provides a foundation for the perduring of the subject. By using a concept of a palimpsest to describe the interconnections between place, body, memory, and tradition, I am drawing attention to the persistence that never remains the same, the continuity within the change. Like a parchment turned palimpsest upon which memory is written and rewritten, erased and covered over with marks that show through and that can never completely be eliminated, so too our bodies and places cannot completely erase the old. The past of the body and places bleeds through, never disappearing altogether.

Like Casey I develop the connection of place to memory through the body, but Casey preserves a border between mind, body, and place that I dissolve. For Casey, the lived body is the *tertium quid* between mind and place. He views the body as separate from mind only overcoming that separation in the felt movement of the enaction of the mind's intentions. Likewise, Casey describes habitual bodily actions as proceeding without consciousness. Habitual bodily movements show us that body and mind are not separated; mind is body as Merleau-Ponty would say. Consciousness is in my fingertips when I play the piano, and in my legs and lungs when I go for a long run. It is in my hand when I automatically reach for the light switch upon returning to my childhood home. Body and place are so intertwined with memory that we cannot separate them off as Casey has done.

The position I am carving out recognizes a horizonal, hermeneutic view of place that represents changes of both place and subject. They both change meaning that every encounter has different horizons even while similarities may remain. So, while Malpas thinks of place as fragile and Casey thinks of place as perduring, the notion of horizon accounts for the limits of the changes that hold place in some kind of stability. Moreover, Casey sees place in its perdurance as "accommodating" an ever-altering self, where I see place and self as mutually accommodating; as place changes, self changes, and memory changes. The mutual interconnected changes do not mean that there cannot be any sense of perdurance, however. Because I consider these elements to function as interwoven palimpsests, the memorial elements, the elements of stability are still poking through the new, still making themselves felt at a bodily level as well as through the hermeneutic process. As much as we might want to think of place as holding memories (both individual and collective) securely and unchangingly, as for example when we erect monuments that we conceive of as permanent, phenomenological and hermeneutic experiences show us otherwise. Places change, memories change, neither is made secure by the other, rather each contributes to further overlay of additional layers of both memory and place upon each other as well as upon one's body. The palimpsest character of place and memory contribute to the palimpsest of the body.

To the extent that I stress the hermeneutic elements in our experience of place, I perhaps align to some degree more with Malpas. Casey disagrees with Malpas's use of narrative in addressing the event of place since Casey sees narratives as fundamentally temporal. I agree with Malpas, however, that to see narrative as primarily temporal is to fail to recognize that any narrative is place-bound.[11] Without place, there cannot be narrative. In so far as the experience of place is narrative and the experience of narrative is place-bound, a hermeneutic approach seems completely warranted. The hermeneutic process is part of what allows for the perdurance within changes that composes the memorial experience of place.

Unlike some other theorists like Edward Relph and David Harvey who draw upon Heidegger to argue for our homelessness, I focus more on the continuity that persists through the change in both places and memory. For Relph our homelessness is in part a result of the changes in mass communication and mass culture that Harvey identifies as consistent with the time-space compression that allows us to travel the globe within hours on an airplane and find ourselves in a completely different culture and place. Time-space compression is also affected by our increasingly technologized interactions through computers and smart phones that can tell us what the weather is like in Verhoyansk while our feet are firmly planted in Atlanta. Both also stress the way in which the homogenization of culture promoted by tourism, disneyfication, and our increasing mobility have diminished our attachment to place and our belongingness to particular places.

I am not trying to deny some of the effects of the time-space compression which certainly is supported by the experience of so many of us. What I am suggesting, however, is that if we recognize the fundamental connections between place, memory, and tradition, and the palimpsestic nature of those connections, we must also recognize that our memories are not static and that the places we encounter, whether habitual or exotic places, are also not static. This is to recognize that place is a porous and elastic notion. So, it does not mean we are homeless, it means that we must ever adjust to being at home and that we can be at home on the shifting sand. Heidegger's inherently romantic ideal of a return to the hut of the black forest fails to account for this shifting as simply the essence of the places we go. Because I am weaving these three intricate notions together memory, tradition, and place, I am piecing together the theoretical foundations borrowing from Heidegger, Merleau-Ponty, Husserl, Ricoeur, Gadamer, and others where it works to do so.

David Seamon also uses phenomenology to focus attention on the bodily engagement in place. He focuses particularly upon movement in order to attend to the essential experiential character of place. For Seamon, the habitual ways in which we are engaged in the world underline the ways in which place is written upon the body. What Seamon provides is an analysis of the way in which even these bodily interactions within place are intersubjective. Although Seamon does not develop the genetic account that Husserl makes possible, he does bring to the fore the connection between the body of the subject and the bodies of others that are constitutive of places together.

I want to take this one step further in looking specifically at monuments and memorials. By using concrete examples, we can see the connections between place, tradition, and memory more clearly. To claim the intertwining of these things is also to claim that there is a kind of mutual constitution of them. To have experiences that are embedded within tradition, as all experiences are, and to remember those experiences or any experiences is to be implaced. At the same time, there cannot be brute place. Place is always caught up with experience and is co-constituted with tradition and memory. Monuments and memorials show us this quite clearly. They are peculiar places that have an important and particular status within our societies and thus warrant special attention. They contribute to the larger discussion by helping us to recognize that what we sometimes think of as permanent actually tolerates a great deal of change and requires a great deal of interpretive activity on our part. Thus, the role of hermeneutics becomes foundational to any understanding of the role of monuments and memorials as places in our world.

These are the issues with which I engage in the ensuing pages. Providing a closer look at the complicated interweaving of memory, tradition, and place through the image of the palimpsest focuses our understanding on the need for a phenomenological and hermeneutic approach to the material environment. Chapter 1 begins with a description of the way in which place and memory are intertwined at the individual level. Bachelard's *Poetics of Space* has provided this kind of phenomenological analysis, but from a much more limited perspective. Bachelard's phenomenology is descriptive and metaphorical while not providing much by way of explanation of the mechanism of the force of home. By using Husserlian phenomenological explanations of homeworld and alienworld, I provide a more detailed account of how home functions as a normative foundation for other experiences of place. While Bachelard focuses much of his analysis on imagination and dream thereby providing a romanticized view of the home, I, in contrast, explore the ways in which the childhood home is foundational in its organization of bodily movement, development of habit, and normative function for all other places of experience. Its role as foundational does not mean that such a foundation is positive. It can be that the foundation is one of abuse or neglect, but those experiences are no less written upon the body and serve as normative than experiences of a happy, caring, safe place of home. By examining the role of the childhood home in establishing for any individual the norm by which all other places are measured, we see the impact of place on bodily comportment and constitution of the lifeworld. This investigation leads to the question of how collective memory and individual memory are related.

Chapter 2 broadens that explanation of bodily comportment and constitution to the construction of collective memory that reflects back upon the impossibility of individual memory being truly private in any meaningful way. Because of the relationship between memory and place, memory is to some degree always ensconced within traditions and thereby collective. For memory to be necessarily intersubjective also means that memory is fundamentally linked to traditions and traditions are linked to place. Places serve traditions in providing pathways of transference across generations. But as we know, traditions are neither unitary nor monolithic, leading to further questions about the dynamism of places and tradition. In an effort to theorize this dynamism, I reflect upon the notion of the palimpsest as a way of capturing how traditions, memories and places all get overwritten by the present in the transference of the past into the future.

Chapter 3 points us in the direction of phenomenological analysis of places of memory in terms of monuments and memorials, but also in terms of everyday places that might hold memory. To this end, we explore the role of mourning in motivating the erection of memorials as an attempt to preserve the past. Mourning is complex and often at odds with the stated intentions of those who erect memorials. This chapter comes to acknowledge that the narrativity of identity and mourning cannot be thoroughly explicated without appeal to place. The places of mourning fulfill mourning in a way that provides credence to our image of the palimpsest of memory, place and tradition.

Chapter 4 provides concrete application of the foregoing chapters to specific monuments and memorials exploring their contributions to collective memory, the role of the dynamism of memory and place in interpreting these memorials, and the call to a hermeneutic process grappling with the inevitable temporality and thus the inevitable change of monuments and memorials. In spite of the fact that monuments and memorials are frequently erected of stone or marble or other durable material, this does not make their meaning permanent and unchanging. To recognize the role of the present in understanding the past and tradition through these places helps us on our way to fully grasping the palimpsestic nature of memory, tradition, and place.

Chapter 5 reweaves the strands that have been teased apart in the earlier chapters. I argue for the need to remember places in our accounts of tradition and memory. By stressing the role of places in producing and supporting collective memories and narratives of collective identity, I also argue for the need for renewal and critique. Place provides continuity across generations. We will see, however, that the dynamism of places undermines any understanding of memories and traditions as monolithic and singular. Instead, the taking up of traditions and collective memories of subsequent generations must be done through a process that involves renewal of those traditions in combination with critique of them. This hermeneutic process calls upon us to think what we are doing. We cannot treat places as static holders of memories nor can we treat memories as containers of the past. We must recognize the palimpsests of memory, tradition, and place.

NOTES

1. Jeff Malpas, "Finding Place: Spatiality, Locality, and Subjectivity" in *Philosophy and Geography III*, eds. Andrew Light and Jonathan M. Smith (New York: Rowman & Littlefield Publishers, Inc., 1998), 24.
2. Although Henri Lefebvre treats this understanding of place as social space and not as subjective place, the more widely used notion of place as described here is what I will be relying upon. For Lefebvre's more nuanced treatment of space see *The Production of Space* (Oxford: Blackwell, 1991).
3. Aristotle, *Physics*, 208b 33–34.
4. Often such identification of another individual trades on stereotypes. This is the less positive and less essential side of the identification that I wish to address here. Apart from stereotypes, the place from which one comes in large part signifies who one is.
5. For more on the notion of the relationship between our place and theirs, see Anthony Steinbock, *Home and Beyond: Generative Phenomenology After Husserl* (Evanston: Northwestern University Press, 1995).
6. Edward Casey, *Remembering: A Phenomenological Study* (Bloomington: Indiana University Press, 2000), 189.
7. Gaston Bachelard, *The Poetics of Space* (Boston: Beacon Press, 1994).
8. Jeff Malpas, "Finding Place: Spatiality, Locality, and Subjectivity." *Philosophy and Geography III* (1998): 21–44.
9. See Ed Casey, "Public Memory in Place and Time," *Public Memory*, edited by Kendall Phillips (University of Alabama Press, 2004).
10. Pierre Nora, "From Lieux de mémoire to Realms of Memory," *Realms of Memory*, edited by L. D. Kritzman (New York: Columbia University Press, 1996), xv–xxiv. And "General Introduction: Between Memory and History," *Realms of Memory*, 1–20.
11. See Malpas, *Place and Experience: A Philosophical Topography* (Cambridge: Cambridge University Press, 1999).

ONE

A Phenomenology of Memory and Place

We usually think of memory in terms of time. We think of it as consumed with the past. Memory is the revitalization of some moment or moments of the past, collecting those moments into the present again. But in so closely associating memory with the past and temporality, we frequently overlook the equally fundamental connection between memory and place. It is not a far stretch to understand that memory is always implaced. A simple thought experiment will point out that it is impossible to remember an event from one's own past without realizing that the event happened in a place however hazy the memory of that place might be. Experience is implaced; memory likewise is implaced. As embodied beings we do not have the advantage of a view from nowhere or a view from anywhere or everywhere. But exactly how place informs our experience is perhaps less clear. In this chapter, we will look at the influence of place upon experience and memory through its association with our embodiment, and with the most fundamental aspects of constitution that arise from an originary place of constitution, our home.

Just as with each memory there is a dual intentionality that focuses on the one hand on the "thing" remembered, while on the other hand on the memory's position within the flow of time, there is a similar association with place. We can remember the place of a particular important event when we focus on that one-time event. We remember distinctly the look of the church where we were married, or the look of the room where we gave birth to our first child. We can place this kind of particular memory in the same way that we can date this memory, very specifically. On the other hand, in terms of repetitive memory, the difficulty of placing a memory such as going to the swimming pool as a child within a particular rather than a general time holds true of place as well. I can distinctly remember the pool to which we went when I was a child, but that pool changed over the years and it is not within my ability to recall each variation in the color of the concession stand or the placement of the deck chairs. The memory is placed, but placed more generally.

Paul Ricoeur reminds us of the importance of place to memory in his *Memory, History, Forgetting* where he explains that place allows us to orient ourselves in addition to providing for our inhabiting. "It is on the surface of the habitable earth that we remember having traveled and visited memorable sites. In this way, the "things" remembered are intrinsically associated with places."[1] This is a primordial level of memory that is prior to the importance of place for historical knowledge according to Ricoeur. "These memory places function for the most part after the manner of reminders, offering in turn a support for failing memory, a struggle in the way against forgetting, even the silent plea of dead memory. These places 'remain' as inscriptions, monuments, potentially as documents, whereas memories transmitted only along the oral path fly away as do the words themselves."[2]

Let us first turn to Edmund Husserl's confrontation with issues of place and space in *Crisis of the European Sciences*. In that text Husserl is careful to distinguish place from space. Space, he thinks, has been compromised by the mathematization of the lifeworld. Husserl provides a description of the mathematization of nature that was occasioned by Galileo's attempts to explain the natural world that exists for us all over against the relative subjective world of each person's experience. Galileo's effort in itself is not misdirected, for Husserl, but the development of the scientific mathematical approach to the lifeworld led to the "surreptitious substitution of the mathematically substructed world of idealities for the only real world, the one that is actually given through perception, that is ever experienced and experienceable—our everyday lifeworld."[3] What this substitution has encouraged is the loss of the sense of place that is the lived arena of human existence. The recovery of the sense of place can only transpire if we take care to be attentive to conceptions of world and place and if we resist attempts to accept the mathematization of the world as self-given.[4] In our vigilance with respect to place we would do well to recognize the richness of the phenomenological method for grasping the lifeworld in its fullness.

Husserl recognizes a paradox of subjectivity with respect to place for he understands the embodied subject to be both "inside" and "outside" of place. The subject is not implaced in the world in the same way a thing is. Where we might think of a thing as contained by the world in the world, a subject is not simply contained in the world. Rather, the subject constitutes the world in which it is at the same time an object. The subject takes up the world in a way that no object ever could. In other words, the subject is both of the world and for the world, in place and "outside" of the place in which it finds itself.

Place, as characterized by Husserl, is the lived, experienced world, what he calls the lifeworld. In order to speak of specific places, or places of memory, an understanding of places "within" the lifeworld must be accommodated. Here, body and memory become involved. The body can be understood to be both spatial and platial for Husserl. Its spatiality is characterized by the fact that my body is the absolute here of my experience of the world. Everything I experience arranges itself around my body and is directed to my body. The spatial body has persistent orientation in the sense of right and left, up and down, before and behind. The body is platial in that its sensations orient it in a place. The body is in a place in the way that it senses and occupies a place.[5] Body, then, is associated with places upon which objective space is founded since it originally experiences place through its own sensations and only subsequently constitutes objective space. The body senses those things that are near it and accessible to it. These places are the ground from which space is constituted. Space is the expansion of the sphere of places constituted around the body.[6]

Turning to the critique that Husserl provides of the mathematization of the natural world will make clear that the space that is described by Husserl as constituted secondarily to place and that is homogeneous and objective is still a space that must be taken up as lived. This presents a complicated picture of the relationship between subjective place that is bodily lived place, and objective space which is also considered lived if taken up appropriately.

But the importance of place to memory is not simply that memory is implaced. It is not just that places provide the backdrop to the action of our lives. Places are not simply settings for experiences. Instead, many places are embodied in such a way that we carry them with us and they inform our constitution of the world. We do not engage in deliberate attempts to remember such places, but they inhabit our memories in the way in which we move through the world. As Ed Casey remarks,

> *in remembering we can be thrust back, transported, into the place we recall.* We can be moved back into this place as much as, and sometimes more than, in the *time* in which the remembered event occurred. Rather than thinking of remembering as a form of re-experiencing the past *per se,* we might conceive of it as an activity or *re-implacing*: re-experiencing past places. By the same token, if it is true that all memory has a bodily component or dimension, the memory-bearing body can be considered as a *body moving back in(to) place.*[7]

Places inform a kind of body memory that can be reawakened if we return to those places, or that characterize our interactions within other places. This is the impact of the homeworld upon our constitution of the surrounding world. Body memory and place memory, then, are not about the past as much as they are about the present and the future.

We cannot limit ourselves to the position that memory is tied up with the body, however. It is also the case that memory is tied up with place. Place bears memory, body bears memory, and memory is thoroughly imbued with place. The three elements can be separated neither with respect to specific memories of unique events, nor with respect to general repeated events, and finally, not even with respect to historical events that are transferred (perhaps as tradition) across generations. In the following chapters I will elaborate upon how this is so. In this chapter, I will focus upon the initial stage of the way in which body and place are interconnected through memory. Subsequently, chapter 2 will shed light upon how such memory can be collective connecting us to other generations and how place informs collective memories.

BODY AND PLACE

Geographer Yi-Fu Tuan tells us that although divisions and measurements of space differ from culture to culture, two things remain constant as fundamental principles of spatial organization and experience, "the posture and structure of the human body, and the relations (whether close or distant) between human beings."[8] In part, what this means is that body and place are inseparable. The fact that we are embodied creatures means that we take up space. But more than that, we inhabit a place through and in our lived bodies. On a basic level we can see the relationship between the body and a particular place of the built environment in the idea of the home. The place we inhabit, be it a house, an apartment, or a tent, is where we say we live. We say "come back to my place." It is a space that is intimate and into which we usually only allow those whom we consider friends or acquaintances. The house is where we develop a certain style of acting in the world. In many ways it reflects our character in the way in which it is decorated and arranged. But the house arranges us too just as any building arranges us, but in a much more fundamental and determinate way.

Anytime we enter a building, we come under its sway. Our movements must be attuned to the building as we find our way down hallways, as we locate bathrooms, etc. The building opens a particular world to us of either work or entertainment or commerce. We are motivated in various ways by the building as well—motivated to look out the windows or not, depending upon whether they are accessible to us; motivated to linger or not, depending upon whether the chairs invite lounging or discourage it. We are often forced, perhaps not merely motivated, to walk the long way through a store past all kinds of goods that might catch our eye, rather than having a straight shot to the checkout aisle with our more meager purchase. We most often are not cognizant of these motivations, but bodily respond to them without really thinking about it. These ways in which we bodily respond to the built environment do not disappear once we step outside. We are in the world in the same way as we find ourselves in the built environment, not only in the way that the built environment includes the sidewalks and streets, light poles and electrical wires, but the ways in which we are motivated by the soft grass in the park or the need to avoid the fire ant hill. These things too we often do with complete neglect of our embodiment. For the most part, we move through the world being buffeted by its pregivenness.

There must be one cautionary word here. We do not want to think of the body exclusively as something that is passively acted upon by the environment. Because the body is a lived body, it is situating as well as situated. For phenomenologists such as Edmund Husserl, Martin Heidegger and Maurice Merleau-Ponty, the body is in the world, but not as water is in a glass.[9] The world and the places we inhabit do not contain our bodies. Body and world are intertwined making place integral to body and vice versa. The body allows us to move in the world, to respond to the pull of things that interest us. As Merleau-Ponty suggests in *Phenomenology of Perception*, "It is one and the same thing for us to perceive our body and to perceive our situation in a certain physical and human setting, for our body is nothing but that very situation in so far as it is realized and actualized."[10] Thus, it is through the body that we inhabit our dwelling places since it is the body that develops the habits and memories that allow it to take up the place of the dwelling. The body is how we get our bearings and orient ourselves in a place. But my own body is also only given to me through the place that it inhabits. As Eva Simms tells us, "the body as mine is given to me not in itself and through the recognition of the boundedness of its skin but as an element in the equation of action space . . . The body becomes predictable in encounters with the things and people of its action space, and particular gestures and experiences repeat and sediment in the flesh."[11]

But what then of the body and memory? The body's movement in places that are familiar to it exhibits the function of memory through and in the body. Familiarity arises because of the bodily memory of how to move through and in a place. If a place is not familiar, we must be more attentive in making our way around obstacles in the place. The more familiar, i.e., the more memory of a place, the more our body can move through the place without our attentiveness. This is why travel to an unfamiliar place can be so exhausting. Familiarity, of course, ranges from that which is quite familiar due to everyday interaction, to that which is mildly familiar because one has been there before a few times or maybe a long time ago, to that which is barely familiar where the place feels familiar, but one can't remember the specifics of the last time one was in the place. That which is familiar does not have to be contemporary. My childhood home is very familiar even though I go there but rarely and it has not been part of my everyday experience for nearly thirty years. There are other places that in spite of some regularity of visit are not familiar. The doctor's office, for example, where I have gone approximately once a year for the last ten years, is not familiar since the layout of the office and the furniture is constantly changing.

Of course, habit plays a role in producing the familiar and habit is the bodily memory that brings what is unfamiliar into familiarity. When a place is familiar, it is not that way because we necessarily remember having been there and can deliberately recollect where objects are in the place. Rather, it is because our body can move through the place with ease. We know also that like the brushing away of dust when one enters a room that has been closed up for a long time, the body memory too sometimes needs to be dusted off. We can have familiarity with a place through the sedimented body memory of that place, but due to the distance from it, the body memory is never exactly as it was. Visiting the grade school playground as an adult can seem very familiar. One remembers quite clearly how far it was from the slide to the swings, but now, in this adult body, the distance no longer seems so far. The memory is written over, and the body is altered. The place is familiar yet different. So while the place has subsisted, it, like the body, has not subsisted in complete stability.

The reverse situation can also be the case. One remembers through bodily habit exactly where the creaky step was and can almost hear it creak when one returns to the place and puts a foot on the step only to discover that the step has been replaced with one that no longer squeaks. This does not destroy the memory, but it does write over it adding another layer of sedimentation. Neither place, nor body, nor memory remain stable because they are all intertwined and all open to changes of habit, changes of body, changes of material environment, and changes of interpretation. The interpretation is as much bodily interpretation as it is memorial or cognitive interpretation.

Ed Casey suggests that body memories are one of the last things that we lose in old age even when memories of other important things have gone. He takes this as an indication of the foundational role that the body plays in human experience claiming, and rightly so, that "absence of body memory would amount to the devastation of memory altogether."[12] Body memory functions in such a way that it does not require deliberate recall. In such cases where we have not engaged in an activity for a long period of time, the body simply "takes over" in performing the activity without our having to willfully recall each movement. When, for instance, a musician sits down to play a song on an instrument that has long lain idle, the musician, assuming she knew the piece of music quite well at one time, can readily play the piece again without having to work hard at remembering it. Instead, the body remembers and moves to play the music. This does not mean that there is not also a cognitive function accompanying this bodily memory. The musician may be recalling the look of the sheet music or thinking ahead to where the music is going, but this is different from the body's movements with the instrument. The difference between these two types of memory is perhaps most evident in the situation where the body has forgotten. In such a case, the musician can read the sheet music and can perhaps even "hear" the music in her head, but cannot smoothly play the music or can only play the music with difficulty, as if relearning the positioning of the hands on the instrument. This indicates that the bodily memory is a pre-reflective experience always accompanying the actions of our daily lives without our necessarily being aware of them. Thus they are always engaging us with our surroundings corporeally and memorially even as we may be engaged at a much more intentional and reflective level. Because the body is three dimensional, it takes up space and is therefore implaced. It is always already implaced meaning all of our actions are likewise always already implaced habitually at a fundamental level. This makes clear that body memory and place memory cannot be separated. We have place memory precisely because we have body memory and we have body memory precisely because we have place memory. This allows us to recognize the importance of home as a foundational bodily memory. The body is how we make a place our own and the central place of our embodiment is our home.

It is no surprise, then, that we think of home in terms of self-identity. It is important to our sense of ourselves and to others' sense of us. Embodied memories function this way because they are multisensory and frequently prelinguistic. This does not mean, however, that they are unchanging. The body serves as a palimpsest of memory in much the same way that place does and in large part due to place. The body can be rewritten to some degree, in the sense that we can work on our bodies through changing our diet and through exercising such that our lived bodies become different. This does not mean that any "older" body is left behind. It means that we have written over certain bodily habits with different bodily habits. Anyone who has dieted understands the difficulty if not impossibility of a complete transformation of bodily habit. This is made all the more difficult because bodily habit is supported by the material place of home. Both body and place affect identity through their mutual material grounding of self.

THE PRIORITY OF HOME

Gaston Bachelard's *The Poetics of Space,* published in French in 1958 and translated into English in 1964, is unique in its poetical treatment of the childhood home. Bachelard's text was revolutionary at the time of its publication due to its suggestion of a relationship between individual memory and place. He provides stimulating descriptions of the childhood home and its necessary role in human dreaming and imagination.

Beginning with the cellars and darker, secretive places of a home, Bachelard explores the impact of such places on the childhood psyche. For Bachelard the home represents the "protected intimacy" of the houses of our dreams as well as those of our reality. He describes it simply as "inhabited space," as "the non-I that protects the I."[13] But it is also more than that for Bachelard. He recognizes that the dwelling place of home is intimately connected to memory. In fact, he understands the home as retaining our past and opening up an immemorial domain. He links this retention of the past with daydreaming insisting that daydreaming makes possible the memories of prior dwellings. As he remarks, "the places in which we have experienced daydreaming reconstitute themselves in a new daydream, and it is because our memories of former dwelling-places are relived as daydreams that these dwelling-places of the past remain in us for all time."[14] The importance of the house to Bachelard doesn't stop there. He credits the house with the preservation of the identity of a human being. Because it is the first world that a child encounters, the hostility of the "external" world is something that is experienced secondarily. The house contains childhood memories especially, for Bachelard, in its many nooks and crannies.

Bachelard does acknowledge that the house is more than a simple repository for memories. It is also "physically inscribed in us. It is a group of organic habits."[15] He explains that the originary house of our childhood is one that would not trip us up on a visit after decades of absence. We would automatically, bodily respond to it as we once did, pulling harder on the door that sticks, raising our hand just the right height for the light switch, and moving about it with the same gestures we used in the past. Again, from Bachelard, "In short, the house we were born in has engraved within us the hierarchy of the various functions of inhabiting that particular house, and all the other houses are but variations on a fundamental theme."[16]

Bachelard is not content with describing the interior of the house. He explores the relationship between the home and the universe, as well as the interior spaces of things within the home—cupboards, closets, chests of drawers and the like. In so doing, he expands the understanding of place to include elements that contribute to making the house a place of memory. He puts the house within the universe in a "dynamic rivalry" where house withstands the attacks of the weather upon it. In this way, the house again exhibits its position as protector. For Bachelard, this so clearly presents the house as something other than a simply geometric form planted upon another geometrical object (the earth). Instead, the house is inhabited space that transcends geometrical space.[17] We may at first be inclined to view the house as a geometrical object. It is frequently box-shaped after all. But Bachelard insists that "transposition to the human plane takes place immediately whenever a house is considered as space for cheer and intimacy, space that is supposed to condense and defend intimacy."[18] Bachelard also explores this dream of intimacy and protection through shells. For him, shells are the natural homes that inspire us to solitude and withdrawal into our own shells of maximum repose.

Bachelard is quite right to have emphasized the role that the house plays in creating the way we constitute the world, and in preserving memory. He has indicated that the house writes itself on the body in a multitude of ways. What Bachelard overlooks is that the house is not static. It is the carrier of a tradition and not just the memories of any particular individual. By focusing on the house, Bachelard has limited his investigation to very personal positions, not acknowledging that such positions can never be without the social and communal aspect that creates generational, historic memory. Bachelard gives precedence to moments of solitude as if those moments are devoid of generational and social elements. They are somehow purified of such elements and can thus produce purely individual memories. In the succeeding chapters of *The Poetics of Space*, Bachelard focuses more and more intently on the intimate spaces of nests, shells, and corners where so many childhood dreams transpire. As he suggests, "if we return to the old home as to a nest, it is because memories are dreams, because the home of other days has become a great image of lost intimacy."[19] I take issue with Bachelard on this point in particular.

Bachelard has romanticized the childhood home. He is clearly writing from a privileged perspective in which the childhood home was stable and long-lasting. Such can hardly be maintained to be the case generally. Whether the childhood home is a hut or a mansion, it is not as static as Bachelard makes it out to be. It is also not necessarily as limited or as comforting as he implies. He refers frequently to it as the home of one's birth, but it is much more in keeping with contemporary views to suggest that it is more likely the place in which one begins to gain object permanence. We, of course, cannot pin this down entirely, but it is the place that establishes the norm for subsequent experiences. The norms of hard surfaces or soft surfaces, an abundance of things or a paucity of them, soothing voices or yelling ones, cold and hunger or warmth and satiety, become established as norms against which all other places are measured.

At the same time, he has represented the childhood home as one of security and protection. While ideally this is the case, it too frequently is not. He writes "The experience of the hostility of the world—and consequently, our dreams of defense and aggressiveness—come much later. In its germinal form, therefore, all of life is well-being."[20] He indicates that the world is the nest for humankind. What this implies, however, is that for each, the beginning is comfort and security while defense and aggressiveness come only after the experiences of that which is beyond the nest, or beyond the childhood home. Such a rosy picture, while seductive, is perhaps not entirely appropriate. To be fair, he does occasionally acknowledge the "offensive" capacity of houses and shells and cupboards, but only in passing and only as exceptional. He completely overlooks that the home could be characterized by need, pain, and degradation.

Bachelard also fails to understand the intersubjective nature of the place of home. His description is one that focuses entirely on the individual and his daydreams. The individual seems utterly autonomous, uninvolved in the often quite complex social arrangements of the household. Even more, Bachelard seems to attribute the daydreams to the house itself, rather than acknowledging the ways in which the house characterizes the daydreams, which indeed, could be nightmares. He universalizes the position of the daydreams thereby denying alternative perspectives. Bachelard has, perhaps inadvertently, privileged the intimate and isolated consciousness. He has, as Joshua Price has suggested, valorized "the solipsistic, or at least the merely solitary thinker. The solipsism of the method finds its correlate in the unitariness of the space so theorized. The general nature of the account, its lack of dialogical play, does not allow it to admit of other voices, perspectives, alternative visions, theories, or accounts."[21] A fuller account is indeed necessary if we are to understand the complex role that the originary home has in establishing one's normative bodily engagement in the world and its impact upon one's memories.

Bachelard has emphasized the places of childhood that preserve and protect memory. He is critical of Henri Bergson for Bergson's remarks that memory is not contained in a wardrobe, or drawer. Bachelard is particularly critical of Bergson's negative use of the drawer metaphor insisting that to view the drawer as mere metaphor is to overlook the use of the drawer as an image that is the product of imagination. The drawer as image can be explored phenomenologically and maintains a spontaneity that metaphor loses.[22] Bachelard's objection is in large part due to the idea that Bergson's rejection of the drawer or wardrobe as container for a memory eliminates the private memory that remains hidden from others or even from oneself. For Bachelard, "every important recollection is set in its little casket. The pure recollection, the image that belongs to us alone, we do not want to communicate; we only give its picturesque details. Its very core, however, is our own, and we should never want to tell all there is to tell about it . . . Surrounding certain recollections of our inner self, we have the security of an absolute casket."[23] What Bachelard does so well is to recount the way in which memory is indebted to place, he takes back in some small degree by insisting that the intimacy of such memory is purely individual. He does not acknowledge that memory itself cannot be so private, so intimate as to be able to have the security of an absolute casket.

For Bachelard the childhood home is about imagination and dreams—functioning psychoanalytically. But the connection between memory and place is much more all-consuming and all-encompassing than merely imagination. Since it is written upon the body and is one's way of being in the world and constituting the world, it is active and foundational, which is not to say that it is completely divorced from imagination and dreams. It is rather to stress that it is less a product of one's own imagination and daydreams and more interconnected with the social elements of the constituted home and the constituting body which cannot be teased apart so easily.

Bachelard has been criticized, by feminists in particular, who suggest that the childhood home cannot always be viewed as such a positive place. It is frequently, and probably more so for women, a place of abuse and fear.[24] Like any other experience of home, this abuse and fear writes itself on the body and establishes a style of constitution that cannot easily be overcome. I agree with much of the feminist critique, but do not think that critique inhibits the claims I am making here about the normative power of home. If home is a place of abuse and fear, then other places will initially be approached from that perspective of lack of safety until one can be persuaded that the place is otherwise. While Bachelard's descriptions may be limited in that they represent a romanticization of the childhood home, they are nevertheless tapping into the normative role that home plays for each of us.

To claim, as I am doing here, that home has a normative power means that encounters with other places, other homes, places of work, or public places, etc., are measured according to the place of home. This does not necessitate that home be a positive place, a place of daydreaming as Bachelard would have it, or a place we wish to return to once we have left it.[25] It means that our bodily encounters in other places are stylized according to the home's normative stylizing of our bodies. Abuse at home writes itself on the body in such a way that places where abuse is not present, particularly places that we might call home, may feel uncannily safe, but also anxiously on the brink of being unsafe. Our default expectation would be that such places are unsafe if our bodies have been habituated to pain and abuse. We may move carefully, unwilling to disrupt another in that place for fear of home-like reprisals. We may shrink from touch, even where touch is caring and loving, due to an expectation of bodily harm. Any place that disrupts that expectation would be experienced as not normal, as bodily awkward.[26]

In spite of describing the childhood home in many similar ways as Bachelard, Ed Casey recognizes the home as a more complete constituting situation. For Casey what is important is the role of the home as hearth, as situation for living, and as a foundation for identity. Who we are has to do with where we are from. We have a tendency to identify ourselves according to the places in which we dwell. Casey adopts this notion of dwelling from Martin Heidegger who describes home in terms of our ability to dwell there. Dwelling is a basic character of being and entails a wish to belong to the environment, to be at home. Further drawing upon Heidegger's notion of dwelling, Casey argues that a building becomes a home from practices of cultivation. Heidegger suggests that "to be a human being means to be on the earth as a mortal. It means to dwell . . . It also means at the same time to cherish and protect, to preserve and care for, specifically to till the soil, to cultivate the vine."[27] At first glance it may seem that Heidegger thinks in order to dwell we need to go back to an era when each of us cultivated the land. He is not taking such a reactionary position.

Heidegger speaks of cultivating in terms of the caring that is related to culture. He is underscoring the inseparability of dwelling and building, but he understands building as the construction of edifices, as well as the cultivation of culture. Both of these activities, constructing and cultivating, are carried out in terms of dwelling. For building is dwelling, being on the earth, and "remains for man's everyday experience that which is from the outset "habitual"—we inhabit it."[28] For Heidegger, then, the quality of human life depends upon how we are able to dwell. This takes Heidegger back to the idea of home. For him, according to Vincent Vycinas, home is "an overwhelming, inexchangeable something to which we were subordinate and from which our way of life was oriented and directed, even if we had left our home many years before."[29] As such, it is fundamental to our identity, to our communal belonging, and is the point of departure for all experiences in the world. Moreover, this home is primordial. Geographer Eric Dardel agrees suggesting that "Before any choice, there is this place which we have not chosen, where the very foundation of our earthly existence and human condition establishes itself. We can change places, move, but this is still to look for a place, for this we need as a base to set down Being and to realize our possibilities—a *here* from which the world discloses itself, a *there* to which we can go."[30] The power of this primordial place seems not to be in dispute, but exactly how does the home function in this primordiality? It is this question that we take up next.

THE STRUCTURE OF THE HOMEWORLD

Edmund Husserl describes the distinction between a familiar here over against an unfamiliar there as the distinction between homeworld and alienworld. Our homeworld is a unity of sense that is manifest in a pregivenness of the things of the world that constitute the norm by which we judge other worlds and by which the pregivenness of other worlds becomes given.[31] In other words, the homeworld structures experience. It is pregiven in the sense that we are not engaged in a conscious constitution of the homeworld or what is most familiar. We engage with it in its familiarity in a kind of absent way. We are not always attentive to it, particularly not as homeworld or as normative. It is the world of our habitualities. Furthermore, it is the world that has written itself upon our bodies in such a way that our movement through this world is structured according to it. The ways in which we move, the givenness of the things of the world are all grounded in our homeworld. As Anthony Steinbock notes, "we actually carry with us the structure of our terrain in the structure of our lived-bodies, in our typical comportment and in our practices."[32] Steinbock speaks of homeworld in terms of terrain. The choice of this word is to stress the actual physical element, not just the cultural practices of a place. The physicality of the world of home has a great deal to do with the cultural practices, the narratives, and the rituals that contribute to our constitution of the world.[33]

However, to say that we live in a physical environment that shapes us is too simple. All people of the same homeworld do not constitute the world in the same way. It is not that the homeworld functions as a rigid structure for constitution. Rather, the homeworld serves as a *ground* in conjunction with our approach to the environment. The environment of a poet is different from that of the profiteer which is different from that of the naturalist, even if they are all experiencing the same place. What they see and how they see it is quite diverse. Where one person may see beauty and is, perhaps, focused on color and light, another may see potential and is, perhaps, focused on structure and accessibility. Where one hears the rich tones of productivity, another hears the noise of conveyor belts and hoists. Implicit in Husserl's notion of homeworld is that this varied constitution of the same environment has to do in part with the normative power of the homeworld.

We become attentive to certain elements of any place due to the habitualities of our homeworld. Again, Steinbock suggests that the familiarity of home "has more to do with the way things in the terrain typically behave, which in turn efficaciously sketches out a range of future comportment, prefiguring this rather than that, highlighting one practice, dimming down another."[34] Things within the surrounding world are thereby colored by the environment. They become "saturated with normative significance" depending upon the practices that compose the environment.

The normative significance also makes itself felt at the level of the lived body. The environment prescribes or calls forth a type or style of comportment towards it. It is not only one's comportment when one is in that particular place; it is one's comportment whether one is in a home environment or an alien environment. It is one's way of being, living, and engaging in the place that is home, but also in the place that is alien.

Homeworld is always co-relative with alienworld and these concepts bring with them the notions of normal and abnormal.[35] While bodily habit, traditions, and rituals are being established through the constitution of the homeworld, that which is not these habits, that which stands over against these traditions, is also being established. In eating with fork and spoon, we do not eat with fingers or bread or chopsticks. At the same time, experiences of alienworlds make the homeworld more explicit to us in its familiarity. Homeworld in its normality can be so close to us as to be unrecognizable until drawn into relief by an alienworld experience.

Consider the quite mundane experience of crossing the street. Until one has gone to a country where people drive on the opposite side of the road, one may not even realize the way in which one's bodily activity is habituated to look first left and then right, for instance, before crossing the street. Once one is confronted with traffic that moves on opposite sides of the street, one realizes that this quite normal bodily habit is in fact dangerous in the alienworld. One can try to change that habit, but it is awkward. Over time it may become easier or even habit, but it is still alien. Even after years of having changed the habit there can be occasions when one "forgets" and reverts to the old ways. There are, of course, degrees of these kinds of differences that make themselves apparent at a bodily level between homeworld and alienworld. But these examples point to the way in which the body in its memory functions as a palimpsest. Older bodily habits may be overwritten by newer habits, but they still can shine through. New habits do not completely do away with older ones.

We can also begin to understand how this influences the constitution of the world. For, in my habit of looking first one direction and then the other before crossing the street, I am also used to constituting a streetscape in a particular way that, at least for me, doesn't include carts, rickshaws, horses, goats, or throngs of bicycles. It is quite possible that when these types of vehicles are on the scene I do not even see them. They are not given to me in my constitution of the streetscape until I am pulled up short by them, or have to jump out of the way of them.

We cannot say definitively when these habits are thoroughly sedimented, but we do know that it happens very early in life. As Yi-Fu Tuan explains, there is tacit knowledge of an alienworld which is necessary for knowledge of one's homeworld. Thus the two are co-constituted. We can also see how this co-constitution transpires developmentally. In considering pregivenness and givenness in terms of developmental issues, we recognize that like most things the depth or intensity of the influence of homeworld can vary from individual to individual. Not all individuals develop at the same rate or with the same specificity. Yet we can see from empirical research that infants gradually acquire a sense of space, and their orientation in that space in the first few months of life. As that sense develops and the infant changes from being primarily prone (at least in

Western cultures) to an upright, mobile being, the foundational experiences get overlaid with the additional evidence of distance and height, expanse and boundaries.[36]

At roughly two to two and a half years old, children are able to distinguish between "home" and "outside" as areas of play. They do not make more specific distinctions than "home" and "outside" and more familiar areas seem to hold more significance for the child, e.g., "here" as opposed to "there."[37] Other kinds of situatedness do not develop until later. As Yi-Fu Tuan indicates, children of four or five are not necessarily aware of how to get from one very familiar place to another since they have not yet acquired the habit of making mental note of the locations of things or landmarks. Child development specialist Arnold Gesell tells us that a child understands "where" at the age of two or two and a half, but that the sense of place becomes more specific as a child gets older.[38]

The constitution of homeworld and alienworld is constantly transpiring while being reconstituted and critiqued. It is a dynamic process of transference of homeworld from generation to generation. It does not behoove us to think of the homeworld, then, as a static norm. It is a way of constituting that is constantly open to the newness of each constitutive act, but each constitutive act stems from the homeworld/alienworld relationship. We are always in the act of generating the homeworld through the repetition and re-constitution of the traditions we take up within the homeworld. And when we encounter some place other than homeworld, its alien qualities are manifest in the environment. Those qualities pull me up short in my habits and reveal to me the normative power of the homeworld.

Homeworld is the place where my body is most habituated.[39] The homeworld is not thereby found to be ethically superior; it is that any other place is more or less alien by relation to and in constitution with the homeworld. I am not at home when I am bodily uneasy, when my habits do not fit, or do not yield the results I expect. This does not mean that the alienworld is lesser or worse. It simply means that it is not home. In fact, I may be all the more attracted to the alienworld precisely because it is not home. It may seem exciting and mysterious, or even more welcoming if my own home is a place of violence or neglect. But this does not change the role of home as home. The homeworld provides a normative power in so far as it is familiar and is the hallmark by which we measure any other place and where our experiences are typical and are in conformity with our bodily expectations.

Homeworld and Normative Power

Husserl speaks of normativity in terms of the "normal" relation between the lived body and the environing world. On this account, normality is not, as it might be for the sciences, exactly the same for all experiencing subjects. Remember the poet, profiteer, and naturalist and their differing constitutions of the same place. The poet sees the beauty and mystery of the forest. The profiteer sees the business opportunity of lumber. The naturalist sees a habitat to be preserved. Since Husserl views the lived body as a constituting element in experience, it must play a vital role in what is perceived as normal and what is alien or abnormal. This means that the blind person's "normal" is different from the seeing person's normal and the 5′ 1″ person's normal is different from the 6′ 2″ person's normal. Normality is a matter of constitution that includes the lived body of each experiencing subject. How, given this highly individualistic sense of normality, could anything be viewed as abnormal?

Abnormality is viewed as a rupture or discontinuity of experience. When I pick up my coffee cup and prepare to take a sip, I first blow on the hot coffee a bit to cool it off. As I tip the cup to my lips, I am startled when my lips encounter a cold liquid. My experience of the coffee cup is disrupted by an unexpected sensation that alters my constitution of the cup as a cup of coffee. The experience is discontinuous. Alternatively, the experience can be disrupted or discontinuous due to an abnormality of the lived body. Abnormality is not determined by reference to some kind of idealized body, but one's own lived body, as when one has a cold, for instance, and can't taste or smell the coffee, or when one has a limb that is asleep and is useless for grasping things or standing upon.

These kinds of discontinuities can be incorporated into a continuous experience by changing one's constitution of the environing world to accommodate them. So, when the cold liquid touches my lips, I do not determine that I was entirely incorrect in picking up the cup as I do every morning. I simply determine that this morning, something is slightly different. I focus my collection of evidence on the liquid in the cup to determine that it is in fact water and not coffee. I set the cup back down and may reach for it again in a minute or two for a sip of water. It has become my "new normal" that allows my experience to be continuous. When I have a cold, my "new normal" is perhaps understanding that I cannot smell things appropriately, or I cannot hear myself speak as I would normally do. For a time, these become the ways in which I constitute my experiences and incorporate them into my normal approach to the world. Usually, my new normal lasts only for a brief time, and I return to the normality of homeworld soon enough.

In some cases the "new normal" is not so easily achieved, as, for instance, in the cases of the phantom limb and the anosognosia that Merleau-Ponty describes in detail in *The Phenomenology of Perception*.[40] For the person suffering from either of these syndromes, the incorporation of a drastic bodily change such as a loss or paralysis of a limb becomes exceedingly difficult and something the person rejects sometimes indefinitely. These persons still attempt to engage in the same projects they would have engaged in before their loss, or they complain of the pain of a limb that they no longer have, but in most cases they relearn their bodily engagement in the world without the use of that limb. To what degree this becomes accepted by them as "normal" varies to a great extent. What these examples underscore is the way the habituated body becomes the foundation for constituting the homeworld. We have yet to question the degree to which that which is alien can be incorporated into home.

If we claim that homeworld is normative, then what transpires for those who are forced out of their homeworld, or who choose to leave their homeworld? What is the experience of the alienworld? Can the alienworld ever become a replacement homeworld? If there is this kind of conception of a "new normal," then would that not mean that any alien world would be incorporated and would eventually become a new homeworld? Interestingly, Husserl suggests that in spite of the multitude of homeworlds, there is still a foundational unified world of perceptual experience—the perceptual world. This is the world of pure perceptual experience and is what he calls the "lifeworld a priori."

All homeworlds are grounded in the singular lifeworld. This, for Husserl, is an eidetic structure that functions as that which is neither experienceable, nor relative, but grounds both the relative homeworlds and experiences thereof. It is not as if in going to London, I have been transported to Mars. Even physical environments that are more radically different from London than small-town Southern United States still share the lifeworld. If we try to think of the most divergent environments we can, elements of a shared lifeworld are still evident. Consider New York City in comparison to Samoa in the South Pacific. In Samoa people live in pole sheds and use sea toilets. There are no automated machines. In New York City many people live in high-rise apartment buildings with indoor bathrooms and the streets are crowded with automobiles. We notice that as alien as New York City would be to someone from Samoa, or as Samoa would be to someone from New York City, elements of a shared life world are still evident. Constitution of discrete objects against a background, and other such basic constitutive elements, remain structurally the same for each. But does this mean that eventually every alienworld simply becomes absorbed into the homeworld?

Can Alienworld Ever Become Homeworld?

We might object to the notion of the homeworld as having normative power by referring to people who are transported to a new place permanently, such as immigrants. People who have lived in a place for several years have often adopted many of the customs and the local language. They have come to respond to the weather, the altitude, and physical aspects of the place much as a native would. Can we not claim that such a place is a new homeworld? Has the alienworld not taken the place of the homeworld and the homeworld become alien? In some ways, perhaps, yes. But not wholesale. Due to the co-relative nature of homeworld and alienworld, the transformation of alienworld into homeworld can never be complete.

The notion of the palimpsest helps us to understand this. The homeworld can be written over by the alienworld, but never without the glimmer of earlier writings that show through in places. The fact that both worlds are grounded in the lifeworld a priori is what makes possible the experience of either of them. If the alienworld were not grounded in the lifeworld a priori it simply would not be able to be experienced as world. The lifeworld makes it possible for me to experience the alien and perhaps even to "feel at home" abroad, but the home abroad will only ever be measured as "homelike" because of the asymmetry of the originally co-relative relationship between homeworld and alienworld.

This conflict between homeworld and alienworld is manifest in material ways, not just in the narratives, the traditions, and the myths of a cultural world.[41] Having grown up in the United States in the state of Nebraska, my alienworld is my current home in the state of Georgia. I have lived in Georgia for over ten years—long enough, one might think, to get used to the Georgian ways. And perhaps in some respects I have. Parts of my homeworld have been overwritten. I now drink sweet tea, understand the best way to eat grits (although I still don't like them—my homeworld shows through here), and recognize a good biscuit when I see one. I can occasionally be heard to use the phrase y'all, and to focus my ideas for beach vacations on Florida. But the surrounding world still feels alien.

In Nebraska I enjoyed digging in the dirt as a child. Each spring we would make tours of the yard looking to see which bulbs were coming back, getting excited at the first signs of growth. We did very little in the yard, actually—just enough to keep the rose bushes blooming, a few tomato plants alive, and the irises and lily-of-the-valley in shape. In Georgia, the climate and landscape are very different. The air in Georgia is alive with growth. It weighs heavily upon one's skin. Rather than coaxing things to grow in the yard, I am constantly hacking away at bushes, brutally pulling up plants as they sprout anywhere and everywhere. It is impossible to *keep things* from growing.

Not only have my approach and my habits had to change, but the way in which I conceive of myself and the surrounding world has had to change in quite radical ways. I can no longer view myself as the encourager and care-taker of nature. I am instead virtually at war with nature. Being interested in a sustainable garden requires constant vigilance against the natural tendencies of my garden. Likewise, the world is no longer constituted as the neutral territory of a Nebraska yard, but is the overwhelming and even dangerous realm of my Georgia naturescape.

With a yard full of seventy foot pine trees, we live with the anxiety that a tree will come down in a storm and smash our house or worse yet, kill us in our beds as has happened to a neighbor. In Nebraska, trees are a luxury, not a danger. The Georgian world is alienworld as a landscape, not just as a cultural background.

Will Georgia ever become my homeworld? I think not. I will continue to develop ways to cope, but it will always be in co-constitution with the more primordial and normalizing experience of my Nebraska homeworld. While I now pull weeds automatically when I find them in the yard, this new bodily habit is not entirely natural to me. There will always be something a bit uncanny about it. The pull of the homeworld will always be there even if it is covered over in some places by new habits formed in the alienworld. Homeworld is not just about the traditions that get translated through myths and stories; it is about the embodied relationship to an environing world.

We cannot so blithely separate the cultural from the environmental, since the cultural is frequently what it is precisely because of the environmental. Skiing is very much a part of the cultural world in Colorado with the equipment, the language, and the traditional events that surround it. This is not so in Georgia for very obvious reasons of environment, climate and thus culture. On the other hand, gardening for native Georgians is a mark of one's belonging. Not so in the mountain towns of Colorado since it is almost impossible to get garden vegetables to grow.

The homeworld is not better than the alienworld. Nor is the alienworld better than the homeworld. In many cases, where one *feels* comfortable may in fact be a place completely opposite from the homeworld, but such is the case in large part due to the experience of the homeworld. If the homeworld is a place of danger and anxiety or abuse, then one may in fact be more comfortable in the alienworld, but the alienworld is still judged on the basis of the homeworld. Homeworld is formative for the ways in which we constitute the surrounding world generally speaking since it is formative for one's bodily habits and style of constitution.

In our contemporary situation where we are much more mobile than in ages past, we might wonder whether home still has the kind of pull it used to have. Without the permanence of the childhood home, the argument seems weakened. In fact, the homeworld is no less of a pull than it used to be. It is a matter of how expansive we consider the homeworld to be. Consider the military family that moves with regularity from base to base across the world. It is not uncommon for a child of a military family to be moved every two years. While it is true that this kind of mobility would mean a different house structure for a child, it does not mean that each new home is completely foreign. There are organizational systems of a home that remain in place regardless of the physical structure and those organizational systems frequently involve the physical space. For example, the drawers in the kitchen, while not in exactly the same places in each house, are organized in the same relative way. Knives are near the cutting boards, which are near the stove. Cups and glasses are in the upper cupboards while pots and pans go in the lower cupboards. The physical space regulates the body even if there are variations from house to house.

Even completely nomadic groups retain organizational and physical aspects in spite of their moves. The yurt is placed on high ground overseeing the grazing land and oriented towards the sun in the same way each time, the positioning of things within the yurt remains the same. The fact that nomadic peoples carry their yurt with them, in fact, makes it quite a stable home in spite of the constant moving of the tribe. Roughly the same holds true for carnival workers. In most cases they travel in their own mobile homes and park them in each new town where they will erect the carnival for a week or so before moving on. In spite of their separation from any particular place, they have a homeworld that is their mobile home. The nomadic tribe or the migrant farm workers follow roughly the same rotation through places year after year following the herds or the crops and however minimal their belongings, these are used to make any place in which they reside a home. Such homes, like brick and mortar homes, leave their mark upon the bodies of their inhabitants. Homeworld, then, is more or less expansive.

Having discovered that the homeworld is so fundamental to the embodied nature of human existence, to our ways of perceiving and knowing, we naturally wonder what this means for memory. Why should it matter that the homeworld has this kind of normative effect for perceiving and knowing?

MEMORY AND PLACE REPRISE

If memory is so intimately tied to body and place, then how is it that we can forget? Body memory establishes for us the normal and the abnormal, and is our way of constituting the world which would seem to preclude the possibility of forgetting. The image of the palimpsest helps us to understand how these kinds of memory function together.

The body is written upon and its habits develop from infancy on. It is not that these habits are unchanging, not that the body becomes a stable and impermeable vessel for who we are. Instead, the body in its interactions in place becomes written upon and rewritten upon layer upon layer upon layer. Sometimes the earlier layers are manifest and sometimes they are so covered over by other layers of habit as to become unknowable, unidentifiable, or forgotten. To be forgotten does not mean that they are totally lost, however. We are occasionally surprised by responses we have to places or the bodily reactions we have to things that bring back floods of memories or even glimmers of memory that we would never have been able to recall willingly. Try as we might, we may not be able to remember the name of a person from our past until confronted by a bodily mnemonic trigger: a smell, a taste, a song.

As Ed Casey reminds us, "even persons (i.e., the very beings who are the sources of separation anxiety) are experienced and remembered primarily as persons-in-particular-places: 'Crawford at Asheville,' 'Dan at the Handcraft Center,' 'Tunie in Topeka.'"[42] This relationship between people and places will become fundamentally important in later chapters when we begin to think about mourning and commemoration. People who are familiar to us are closely connected to places we inhabited with those people; memories are intimately tied both to the places and to the groups that support the memory, as we will see in chapter 2. The loss of such people frequently threatens the loss of memories and motivates a desire to return to the places we shared in an effort to mourn, to remember, to memorialize those people. We also mark places where people have died as part of this effort. Places are not isolated, individual places; they are communal, collective places that cannot escape the collective memory of them.

Like place and memory, identity is also a palimpsest, never static, never closed, and always changing. It is overwritten in some areas, erased in others. Because memory is so diffuse and disparate, the identity that should follow from a stable memory is also diffuse and disparate. We want to think that by embedding memory in place we are securing it not only for ourselves and our contemporary society and culture, but perhaps more importantly for future generations. We are passing along to them the sense of who we are and what we stand for, but in so doing, we frequently fail to realize that the place itself changes and that any monument or marker we may erect at that place will carry with it and reflect the reading of those who view it. The meaning is caught in the strands of the web which shift and shimmer in the breeze. It is not static, it is not secured, it is open to reinterpretation, reinvention, and not simply repetition. As we learn from Maurice Halbwachs, "There are as many memories as there are social groups."[43]

What I have shown in this chapter is that place is written upon the body creating one's style of constitution. Memory is also written upon place making the homeworld foundational for constitution of all further experiences of the world. The threads are intertwined since homeworld is foundational for one's constitution and for one's embodied way of being in the world while, at the same time, home carries within it the memories of one's manner of being.

Place is not, as Casey and others have claimed, a container for memory. Memory and place are intertwined in such a way that each serves the other with a stability that is not stable. Casey suggests that "requisite to any full understanding of memory of place is thus a recognition of the way in which place itself aids remembering. It does so precisely as being well suited to contain memories—to hold and preserve them."[44] Casey draws upon Aristotle's use of the Greek *periechon*, meaning container as the "action of place." He describes place as having a "unique power to hold in or keep in," to serve as a boundary, to hedge against dissipation. He sees place as having a persistence, as being able to be re-entered both through memory and bodily. Place, he claims, has the capacity to "hold its contents steadily within its own embrace."[45] It is clear from these few lines that Casey is aiming at the stability and enduring nature of place vis-à-vis memory. But here is precisely where I take issue with Casey. While we do return to places sometimes for the sake of memory, and while the body remembers the places as we see in the examples above of remembering bodily where the light switch is in automatically reaching for it, we also see in other examples that will be elaborated upon later, the way in which the places change bringing us to a sense of the loss of the memory, or a sense of the uncanniness of being in a place that is not what we remember it to have been. Such experiences indicate the way in which some memories persist even as the place persists, but others do not. The experience is more about the intertwining of body and memory and place than it is about the stability of one of the poles of this intricate web. Thus I appeal to the notion of the palimpsest. Place, memory, and body function as palimpsests, written upon repeatedly from differing perspectives at different moments with different salient themes and values layered one upon the other. Some of those layers can be uncovered and viewed again from a new perspective while others are forever covered over or erased. Some make themselves felt without being able to be fully uncovered while others are glaringly obvious. To think of place as a stable container for memory is to do a disservice to both concepts. Neither place nor memory is stable. They require a hermeneutic approach that can lead to a much richer understanding of our relationship to a past and to place.

NOTES

1. Paul Ricoeur, *Memory, History, Forgetting*. Translated by Kathleen Blamey and David Pellauer (Chicago: University of Chicago Press, 2004), 41.
2. Ricoeur, *Memory, History, Forgetting*, 41.
3. Edmund Husserl, *The Crisis of the European Sciences and Transcendental Phenomenology* (Evanston: Northwestern University Press, 1970), 48.
4. Husserl, *The Crisis of the European Sciences and Transcendental Phenomenology*, 47.
5. See Edward Casey, *The Fate of Place* (Berkeley: University of California Press, 1997), 219.
6. Casey, *The Fate of Place*, 219.
7. Edward Casey, *Remembering: A Phenomenological Study* (Bloomington: Indiana University Press, 2000), 201–2.
8. Yi-Fu Tuan, *Space and Place* (Minneapolis: University of Minnesota Press, 1977), 34.

9. For more on their notions of body, see Edmund Husserl, *Ideas of a Pure Phenomenology and Phenomenological Philosophy*, Vol. 2, especially sections 36–44, pp. 152–170; Martin Heidegger, *Being and Time*, pp. 79–80; and Merleau-Ponty, *Phenomenology of Perception*, especially Part I, pp. 90–92.

10. Maurice Merleau-Ponty, *Phenomenology of Perception*. Translated by Colin Smith (London: Routledge Press, 1962), 340.

11. Eva Simms, *The Child in the World* (Detroit: Wayne State University Press, 2008), 42.

12. Edward Casey, *Remembering: A Phenomenological Study* (Bloomington: IN, Indiana University Press, 2000), 147.

13. Gaston Bachelard, *The Poetics of Space*. Translated by Maria Jolas (Boston: Beacon Press, 1994), 5.

14. Bachelard, *The Poetics of Space*, 6.

15. Bachelard, *The Poetics of Space*, 14.

16. Bachelard, *The Poetics of Space*, 15.

17. Bachelard, *The Poetics of Space*, 47.

18. Bachelard, *The Poetics of Space*, 48.

19. Bachelard, *The Poetics of Space*, 100.

20. Bachelard, *The Poetics of Space*, 103.

21. Joshua M. Price, "The Apotheosis of Home and the Maintenance of Spaces of Violence," *Hypatia*, 17 (2002): 51.

22. See Bachelard, *The Poetics of Space*, 74ff.

23. Bachelard, *The Poetics of Space*, 85.

24. See, for example, Joshua M. Price, "The Apotheosis of Home and the Maintenance of Spaces of Violence," 39–70.

25. For a more contemporary perpetuation of this kind of Bachelardian view see Kirsten Jacobson, "A Developed Nature: A Phenomenological Account of the Experience of Home," *Continental Philosophy Review* 42 (2009): 355–373. Jacobson describes the home in terms of daydreaming, security and relaxation. I do not claim such to be the case. Familiarity does not necessarily mean comfort or security. The home does write itself on the body in terms of the body's development of habits and a style of being in the world, however, and on this point Jacobson and I agree.

26. What this also draws into question is the predominant view of home as a place of refuge, a place "inside" that fends off the "outside." By using notions of embodied normativity, we can recognize that what becomes normal habituated embodied being for one is not at all the same for another and it may not be at all a secure "inside." The language of "inside" and "outside" leads to misunderstanding as does the language of security and refuge when speaking of the home place. It is home through its normative power by being the foundation that is most primary for our embodied habitual being in the world. It is a position of familiarity, but this does not equate to refuge, safety, or other romanticized notions.

27. Martin Heidegger, "Building Dwelling Thinking," *Basic Writings*, (London: HarperPerennial (2008), 349.

28. Heidegger, "Building Dwelling Thinking," 349.

29. Vincent Vycinas, *Earth and Gods* (The Hague: Martinus Nijhoff, 1961), 84, as quoted in Edward Relph, *Place and Placelessness* (London: Pion, Ltd., 1976), 39.

30. As quoted in Relph, *Place and Placelessness*, 41.

31. Anthony Steinbock, *Home and Beyond: Generative Phenomenology After Husserl* (Evanston: Northwestern University Press, 1995), 154. Husserl explains that pregiven refers to those things that exercise an affective pull upon us while that which is given is such that we are attentive to it in a more active way. We focus on a thing, we pay attention to it meaning it is given to us. See Edmund Husserl, *Analysen zur passive Synthesis. Aus Vorlesungs-und Forschungsmanuskipten 1918–1926*.

32. Steinbock, *Home and Beyond*, 164.

33. Notice that homeworld can equally apply to those who are homeless, those who are nomadic, or those who have varying degrees of static homelife. It does not only

refer to the semi-permanent structure of a house. Military children, for instance, who do not stay more than two years in any one place have a kind of moving homeworld since, for them, we could say the built environment has a certain precedence because it is more static—the military base remains largely the same even though the bases may be in various corners of the world.

34. Steinbock, *Home and Beyond*, 165.

35. Husserl does not mean normal and abnormal to carry any ethical significance here. They carry normative significance simply in terms of one's habituated engagement with the world.

36. Tuan, *Space and Place*, 20–33.

37. Tuan, *Space and Place*, 25.

38. Arnold Gesell, et al. *Vision: Its Development in Infant and Child* (New York: Paul B. Hoeber, 1950), 121, as quoted in Tuan, *Space and Place*, 210.

39. Again, homeworld is not necessarily a place of comfort in the usual sense of the term. In cases of abuse or neglect, the body is habituated to the abuse and neglect such that a place of safety, a place devoid of abuse, feels strange or fragile, as opposed to the "usual" feeling of anxiety or fear or pain.

40. See Merleau-Ponty, *Phenomenology of Perception*, 84–102.

41. In *Crisis of European Sciences*, Husserl focuses precisely on this notion of narrative and language in the transference of homeworld across generations. There are also elements in that text, however, that allude to the primacy of place. Those elements have generally not been the focus of secondary-source commentary and are the elements I would like to focus upon.

42. Casey, *Remembering*, 195.

43. As quoted in Stephen Legg, "Contesting and Surviving Memory: Space, Nation, and Nostalgia in *Les Lieux de Mémoire*," *Environment and Planning D: Society and Space*, 23 (2005): 494.

44. Casey, *Remembering*, 186.

45. Casey, *Remembering*, 186.

TWO

From Individual to Collective Memory

If place is written on memory and memory is written on place, then what we frequently think of as our own individual memories need to be reconsidered in light of the embodied nature of memory and place. We often have the impression that our memories are a private box of keepsakes. We do not think of memory as necessarily something that ties us to other people or that can be easily shared. We readily make a distinction between my memories and yours and acknowledge that even if we remember the same event, our memories are not truly shared in any deep way. Certainly, there are people with whom we share a past, our siblings, for instance, or old friends, but we conceive of that past as something objective that has been shared, some event we each experienced from our own perspective. While we know that the picture is not quite so simple and that our lives are interconnected with the lives of others, it is still difficult to give up the notion that my memories are my own and that they are quite distinct from what we might call collective memories. In the following pages I will explore the way in which our memories are, in fact, never truly our own. To pursue the question of what collective memory is and how it is possible, I will examine how collective memories are transferred across generations, and written on the world. I will provide a phenomenological investigation of collective memory which will show, just as we saw with individual memory in chapter 1, that collective memory is not strictly or even primarily constituted through narrative, but depends in large part upon its connection with place and its association with bodily memories. We will see three kinds of collective memory here. There are those of a particular unique event shared with others, those that are general and representative of repeated similar events that become lumped together, and those that are historical memories of events that were not actually experienced but have been passed along. Each kind of memory is intersubjective and collective as we will see.

MEMORIES AND INTERSUBJECTIVITY

To tease out these relationships, we begin by examining how memory is intersubjective at a very basic phenomenological level. It is not readily apparent that phenomenology would be able to claim that memory is intersubjective. For, if experience is fundamentally grounded in the subjective, it would seem that memory, too, would be subjective. Indeed, in his *Memory, History, Forgetting,* Paul Ricoeur argues that Edmund Husserl's conception of memory is part of what he calls the "tradition of inwardness."[1] He claims that Husserl can be favorably compared to Augustine when it comes to the issues of interiority, memory, and time. Ricoeur focuses his analysis on a shift of thinking that takes place in Husserl's text *Phenomenology of the Consciousness of Internal Time.* Husserl moves from thinking of memory in terms of its objective relation to an enduring object to considering the constitution of temporal flow without consideration for the "object-oriented intention." This means that Husserl deals with temporality in terms of the isolated subject's own temporal flow and not with its relation to any other subject's temporality.[2] Ricoeur's concern, by contrast, is with the "confrontation between private remembering and public commemoration."[3] His argument is that Husserl, in describing the self-constitution of the temporal flow of internal time-consciousness, limits any attempt that might be made to speak of an "us" or to accommodate an "other who is always already implied in the solitary consciousness of self."[4] Ricoeur does not find the Other in the Husserlian account of memory. As far as he is concerned, the Husserlian transcendental consciousness proves to be solitary, making the prospect of collective memory impossible. Ricoeur attempts to overcome the isolation of the subject by accounting for collective memory through narrative. But, as we will see, narrative is not enough.

Furthermore, while collective memory for Ricoeur is something that is primarily transmitted through narrative and is thus initially a discourse with oneself that transpires through the language of others, what we began to see in chapter 1 and what I will elaborate upon here is that what we think of as private, individual memory is often only made possible through a collective/historical memory that is transmitted through something more fundamental than narrative. Just as individual memory is connected to place and body, so the transmission of collective/historical memory transpires through place as something that makes narrative more meaningful and collective memory possible.

Phenomenology is frequently charged with being too subjective, or solipsistic. Husserl's early writings on time consciousness address phases of the ego's experience that are formal and schematic. They deal with the ego as itself formal and not as a concrete individual ego with its own history. The ego is understood to be apart from a world that carries its own history with it. This means that the ego is in many ways alone, not in a shared world. Intersubjectivity must be derived from the ego's experience, rather than being foundational to it.

Ricoeur, like so many scholars of phenomenology, has mistaken the *Cartesian Meditations* as Husserl's last word on the issue of intersubjectivity, the issue of the Other. For Ricoeur, the *Cartesian Meditations* is linked with the conception of shared memory insofar as it attempts to work its way out of the focus upon an analysis of memories that depends upon the self-constitution of a temporal flow as the product of a solitary ego. He acknowledges that "the negative" or absence is part of Husserl's analysis from the beginning through concepts such as *Phantasie*, and the remembered, which attempt to bring into presence that which is absent. However, Ricoeur thinks that Husserl's descriptions of these elements essentially nullify them in ultimately reducing them to acts of an ego within which is constituted that which is foreign. Ricoeur's recurring question is, "if we deny the internal negativity of self-consciousness, is this not secretly denying the primordiality of our relation to what is foreign in the egological constitution of self-consciousness?"[5] Ricoeur graciously suggests that perhaps an investigation into Husserl's concept of intersubjectivity as it is presented in the Fifth Cartesian Meditation could provide an avenue for a phenomenology of common memory.

In Husserl's Fifth Cartesian Meditation, the move from the ego to the Other is one that transpires via analogical apperception. Husserl describes the necessary reduction to a sphere of ownness where we recognize that all constitution stems from one's own consciousness. The sphere of ownness is the founding stratum, the "essential structure, which is part of the all-embracing constitution in which the transcendental ego, as constituting an Objective world, lives his life."[6] Since the Other is not immediately accessible to the ego as the ego is to itself, a different, and mediate, mode of appearance must make experience of the Other possible. This is what is called "making co-present" or "appresentation."[7] It is most easily explained by analogy with the front and back of an object. The front of a house is immediately presented to me as I stand looking at it, while the back of the house is appresented, made co-present while not immediately perceivable. The perception of the back of the house can be fulfilled in that I can walk around the house and have the back of it immediately presented to me. Appresented aspects of a thing need not be fulfilled, however, such as the interior of my computer, which is appresented in my immediate experience of the computer keyboard and functioning screen.

Such mediateness applies in distinguishing the Other from the ego in terms of the Other's body. If the Other were immediately presented, there would be no way to differentiate between the ego and the Other. However, appresentation, otherwise called analogizing apperception, is necessary to make the body of the Other an animate organism. Transferring the sense of 'animate organism' from the immediately perceived animate body of the ego to the body of the Other takes place through analogy. Because the body of the Other is similar to the ego's own body, the analogizing apprehension is possible. The ego understands the Other's body to be a body like its own and therefore to be an animate organism, a body with a consciousness.[8]

This association of the ego and the Other indicates that "*ego* and *alter ego* are always and necessarily given *in an original 'pairing,'*" which means that ego and alter ego are "given intuitionally . . . in the unity of a consciousness"[9] through a passive association in which they are constituted as a pair. The Other is constituted as foreign or not me, but is at the same time constituted as being analogous to me and thereby apperceived as an ego over there.

The notion of collective memory depends upon a notion of collective experience that is entirely indebted to this idea of intersubjectivity through analogous apperception. It is a derived intersubjectivity which would mean that the collective memory that is grounded upon it must also be derived. What is misunderstood is the manner in which experience itself can be collective. This relates back to the phenomenological issue of intersubjectivity which can be described, and is described by Husserl in texts other than the *Cartesian Meditations*, as the way in which any ego can recognize itself as intersubjective at its very core—the ego, in other words, is never alone.

Phenomenology has taught us that all experience is characterized by intentionality. What is often overlooked is that intentionality is not restricted to the egoic act, but transpires intersubjectively in the sense that the object of experience is almost never experienced as there for me and me alone. Because of the horizonal and perspectival nature of experience, experience itself can be understood to be intersubjective. The fact that the experience is perspectival and that I can only see the table, for instance, from this perspective at this particular time also allows us to say that I am aware of the other perspectives of the thing that can be available to others in different places, with different views of the thing. The actual presence of an Other is not required; it just indicates that no experience can happen without placing me amidst others, even if they are absent others. In this manner the thing itself can be understood to be objective.[10]

Without this recognition of the intersubjective aspect of the object, I would be stranded in a two-dimensional world of my own thought objects. Any experience allows us to recognize that subjectivity is never isolated, never without others. It also allows us to see that intersubjectivity is itself grounded in a shared world.

Ricoeur's specific claim is that Husserl contributes to the "tradition of inwardness." The claim reveals a slippage in Ricoeur's understanding of the distinction between immanence and transcendence as being associated with inwardness and outwardness, allowing him to assert that Husserl's position limits his ability to speak of intersubjectivity. It is quite clearly not the case for Husserl that such a connection can be made. Immanence and transcendence are linked to the essence of intentionality, and thus to consciousness itself. This does not mean that there are two realities—one the reality of the phenomenon that is immanent to consciousness after the reduction and another that "really" exists outside of consciousness. The phenomenon of experience is the real or actual world regained after the reduction as lived experience, not as something inward over against an outwardly real world.[11]

Specifically in Husserl's later writings there are two distinct ways in which he speaks of the intersubjective nature of subjectivity. First, he identifies what he claims as the deepest level of the ego, calling it the streaming-living present. What is important about this discovery for our discussion is that this deepest level makes possible an explanation of the identity of the ego that entails a description of historical sedimentation at the level of *hyle*.[12] This means that the ego begins to develop through the passive sedimentations coming from a pre-constitutive level. There are sedimentations of the ego, then, which are not the result of the ego's constitutive activity but are the result of a social foundation of convictions and habitualities that an ego inherits. These are the kinds of bodily habitualities that form one's style of constitution from a very young age as we saw in the previous chapter.

Secondly, the personal identity of an ego from birth to death requires the Other in order that the ego can be constituted as a human being with a memory. Without the Other, the ego cannot constitute itself as a human, nor can it fully constitute its identity through memory. It can only constitute itself as a presently constituting consciousness with a limited past and a limited future, certainly not with a birth or a death and not as a historical being. This means that the position of the ego in a human community requires the Other since the ego can only truly be a person within the community of Others. Even the ego which presently constitutes its surrounding world is an already communalized ego, in the sense that there is no possibility for constituting the surrounding world outside of an already inherited tradition which shapes the human ego as a member of a community. What this shows is that collective memory is necessary, but also that collective memory is grounded in a shared world.

Ricoeur describes the overlap between individual memory and social or collective memory in terms of language. This serves his purposes of focusing on narrative as constitutive of identity through memory. For him, memories are a kind of discourse that one initially has with oneself. "What is pronounced in this discourse occurs in the common language, most often in the mother tongue, which, it must be said, is the language of others."[13] Moreover, this discourse connects one with the larger community giving one a sense of one's own history. As he suggests, collective memory "is held to be a collection of traces left by the events that have affected the course of history of the groups concerned, and that it is accorded the power to place on stage these common memories, on the occasion of holidays, rites, and public celebrations."[14] In placing on stage the common memories, the identity and memory of any single individual is also affected.

This focus on the narrative approach reveals a limitation in Ricoeur's approach that will be made more explicit later. It arises from an inattentiveness to the bodily elements described in chapter 1—elements that are in large part dependent upon material environment or place and are already intersubjective.

THEORIZING COLLECTIVE MEMORY

Ed Casey, in his book *Remembering,*[15] also deals with memory primarily through narrative. Even when describing the role of reminiscing, which is the only kind of memory he identifies as being with-others, he uses the language of narrative. For Casey, however, the narrative does not happen independently. It must often be prompted by something—a *reminiscentia,* as Casey calls it. The *reminiscentia* is not simply documentary evidence of something and in fact frequently could not serve as documentary evidence. It is, rather, something that prompts recollection, often involuntarily, simply through its representation of a former time. For example, I recently played a compact disc of kid's music for my own children to listen to. This disk had been a gift, so I was unfamiliar with the music. Suddenly, however, as the notes of a song began, I was transported back to my grade school classroom. I didn't even know that I knew the song, and had not heard it in over thirty years. It was in no way any kind of documentary evidence about my childhood. Instead, it transported me back to a particular place of my childhood. I was seven years old again and in my second-grade classroom. Certain feelings accompanied this memory and a sense of the light and smell of my second-grade classroom returned to me. I telephoned my sister and together we reminisced about our shared childhood. That reminiscence would not have happened without the prompting of the song that had until that moment been completely lost to my memory. True, I could have simply reveled in the discovery of a childhood tune on my own, but the memory was brought to more fullness through discussion of it with my sister since it was a memory we shared of our childhood. Still, on my own, the particular sounds, like Proust's famous madeleine, returned me to a place of memory and a memory of place that was shared.

Maurice Halbwachs also makes clear that memory is never strictly my own, never isolated from others, and never truly private. To explain this he provides a description of walking through London. On such a walk, Halbwachs insists he is never alone, never experiencing the city on his own, but is always accompanied by the architects and city designers, as well as Dickens whom he read as a child, and the painter who had originally conducted him around the city. He fits himself into all of these groups as they help with his remembrances on his perambulation. As he writes, "I can still feel the group's influence and recognize in myself many ideas and ways of thinking that could not have originated with me and that keep me in contact with it."[16]

This perspective on collective memory also helps us to understand certain kinds of gaps in our memories. It is frequently the case, as Halbwachs points out, that upon the conclusion of a semester and the beginning of a new semester, the names of the students in a class with whom a professor was so familiar become lost to her. During the semester each student's name is readily present when the professor encounters that student on campus and the professor knows precisely where that student sits in the classroom. When the semester is over, however, and the professor is confronted with a whole host of new faces of new students, the names and sometimes even the faces of most of the former students become lost to her memory. For Halbwachs this is a direct result of the loss of the communal aspect of memory.[17] The association with the group that supported the memory has been severed. Had the professor remained in contact with the group of students, the ability to recall their names could have persisted. Some of those students can be recalled either because they are associated with another group with which the professor is also associated, say philosophy majors, or students who request recommendations. Without the group association, however, the memory is lost.

Beyond this kind of mnemonic support that the group provides, there are other ways in which memories are supplied by others. I recollect events that might be on the fringes of my memories, but I claim them to be my own because they have been described to me by others as my own. For instance, my husband recalls the voyage on a ship from England to the United States when his family immigrated to this country. However, this voyage happened when my husband was only eleven months old, an age when babies, we are told, are not capable of sustained memory. My husband's memories, then, most likely arise because he has heard the voyage discussed many times by family members who have described the reactions he had as a baby to the event. In recollecting this event that has been experienced by others or that has been described to him as his own childhood experience, he relies mostly upon others' memories of their own experience of his experience. In some respects, then, such events of one's own historical period are not known any better than events of a historical period of a different generation. These memories, of course, differ from the memories of things that one has experienced and remembered oneself only in the degree to which they can be recalled. They are memories mediated by the narratives of others, but perhaps more importantly, they are not as completely associated with a particular place.

Collective memories are not necessarily limited to what we have experienced together. There are cultural collective memories that link us to a history, a heritage, a collective past. These collective memories are perhaps somewhat more problematic than the type of collective memory we have just been exploring. They are not constituted memories and connect us with others in ways that are not easily described through direct constitutive activity. They function at a more passive level.

If we think about the role of collective memories of history, what is immediately apparent is that such memories are not necessarily memories in the strict and egoic sense of the term. We remember events that have taken place in our nation's history, but we remember them not necessarily due to particular experiences that we ourselves have had. Instead, we remember them because of newspaper articles and the testimony of people who did actually experience those events.

Individual memories become sedimented because of collective/historical memory. Consider the common refrain of those who can recall where they were when President John F. Kennedy was assassinated, or when the wall came down in Berlin, or when the Oklahoma City bombing took place. We are familiar with the question "Where were you when you heard . . . ?" In most cases, what one was doing or where one was is only remembered because of its association with this historical event.[18] The personal memory of grading papers or fixing dinner would have long faded away had it not been marked by the historical event of the same moment. We remember it because it becomes part of the fabric of society and the groups with which we engage are interested in it.[19]

For Husserl, the sedimentation of collective memory points to the unity of one time and place for us all. He suggests in his last published work, *The Crisis of European Sciences*, that "the constitution of every level and sort of entity is a temporalization which gives to each distinctive meaning of an entity in the constitutive system its own temporal form, whereas only through the all-inclusive, universal synthesis which constitutes the world do all these times come together synthetically into the unity of one time."[20] Husserl explains this world as being a lifeworld that is common as we saw in chapter 1. It is the "intersubjectively identical life-world-for-all [that] serves as an intentional 'index' for the multiplicities of appearance, combined in intersubjective synthesis, through which all ego-subjects are oriented toward a common world and the things in it, the field of all the activities united in the general 'we,' etc."[21] These two statements make clear that the lifeworld, a place, serves as the foundation for common experience, common memory, the 'we.'

These explanations of collective memory indicate the various ways in which our memories are not exclusively or even primarily our own. Memories, even those we think to be private, connect us with others. Frequently this connection is apparent through the narratives that provide support for our identity as members of a community. It is equally important to recognize the ways in which collective memory cannot be separated from individual memory. The memories of any individual are never simply one's own. They are always remembered within the context of a collective tradition that serves as the foundation for the significance and shaping of any individual memory. We can understand the subject to be communal and to be connected to history and traditions because of the intersubjective layer of all experience. The recollections of any individual are never understood to be private recollections. They are not entirely dependent upon the narratives of the community either. Halbwachs writes, "the collective memory . . . encompasses individual memories while remaining distinct from them. It evolves according to its own laws, and any individual remembrances that may penetrate are transformed within a totality having no personal consciousness."[22]

Even Ricoeur acknowledges, "One does not simply remember oneself, seeing, experiencing, learning; rather one recalls the situations in the world in which one has seen, experienced, learned. These situations imply one's own body and the bodies of others, lived space, and, finally, the horizon of the world and worlds, within which something has occurred."[23] Ricoeur charges Husserl with an inability to accommodate the world pole due to the prominence of the epochē in Husserl's methodology. He does not account for the ways in which Husserl reasserts the priority of the lifeworld in his later published and unpublished manuscripts. But what Husserl indicates, and what is perhaps not so readily acknowledged by other theorists, is the role that places have in those connections with the past and with others.[24]

What is prevalent in these theories of the connection between individual and collective memory is that they hinge upon narrative. They assert that the stories we tell provide the foundation of memory that continues beyond a particular generation or even across that generation. I continue to suggest that it is not the narratives alone, but that the narratives themselves are dependent upon the much more subtle ways in which place is created and organized. Commemoration is not simply a story. It is an event that transpires in a particular place which is itself important to the securing of the memory.[25] Monuments as locations of commemoration involve us bodily as we move around them as places in the world. We write these stories on the landscape. The stories in themselves are reinforced by the event and the place of created memory. Some of these stories become traditions to which we as members of a group adhere.

So, while I do not disagree with Ricoeur's focus on narrative as the explanation for the fundamental structure of time-consciousness manifest in the discourse that I have with myself, it seems that Ricoeur has failed to take account of the fundamental role of places to collective memory. He has failed both in reference to his critique of Husserl's analysis of memory, but also with reference to our everyday experience. In many respects places function independently or perhaps more primordially than narrative in the promotion and preservation of memory. Places are not strictly thought of in terms of narrative, but can be seen to be a link between the individual or egoic memory and the collective memory making the concept of egoic memory itself something questionable. Thus, the final stage of what I would like to claim here concerns the role of the world in establishing and maintaining collective memory. The role of places is vital in creating connections between individuals and the groups with which they share memories.

I indicated earlier the two ways in which memory is intersubjective on Husserl's account. The role of the world in each of those ways is important. First, I know I am with others because of the other perspectives of a thing of my experience. In other words, because I have experiences in a world I can know there are others. The world becomes foundational for intersubjectivity. Secondly, at the level of the streaming-living present, the ego develops through sedimentations connecting the ego to other generations. This happens in a world that is part of those sedimented habits. What I inherit is not worldless, but is very much a culturally transpiring world from which I acquire habitual approaches and attitudes. I learn to look for cars when crossing the street, not sheep and buggies. I habitually go in the door on the right and to pass on the left because these are worldly, bodily behaviors that I have inherited from my culture. These may seem like mundane examples, but they have ramifications for the ways in which I think about the world and for the memories that we share.

Moreover, the *reminiscentia,* which Casey speaks of as conducive to remembering-with, is frequently not a thing, but a place where something of our past has transpired. And even if it is not a specific place, the ability to reminisce without putting into place that which we are recollecting is rare if not impossible. When speaking with my sister about the song from our childhood, we each remembered the school building where we first heard the song and in being transported back to our past, we could "feel" the ambiance of that particular place. Moreover, if I ask a group of people who get together once a year, at a conference for example, to engage in a reminiscence of the last time they were together, they might recall the papers they heard and the conversations they had. They will most likely remember the particular room in which they met, or the hotel where the meeting was held. Of course, they may each recall that room or hotel differently, due to individual perspectives and experiences, but nonetheless, they will recall the room. Even the things that they only vaguely recall, such as the restaurant where a compelling discussion of the death penalty took place, are still recalled as having taken place in a place whether it was Mexico or North Carolina or Pittsburgh or Chicago, they can't be sure, but it seems to matter in some way in helping them to recall the discussion more clearly. The places make the narratives of collective memory more immediate.

The difference between the narratives of the attacks on the World Trade Center on September 11, 2001 and the experience of actually visiting Ground Zero is remarked upon by those who visit the site. Consider too the difference between reading Holocaust narratives and actually going to Buchenwald or Auschwitz where so many were slaughtered. Or, consider the difference between telling your children about your own childhood home and taking them there. The narrative experience is brought to life by the place of the original activity.

There are also constructed places, such as monuments or memorials, which are deliberately produced to evoke the collective memories of a group and to transfer those memories across generations. Narratives are brought to life by such constructed places that serve as reminders, invoking a memory that may not be one's own, but becomes part of the collective memory in which each of us participate.[26]

THE PLACE OF TRADITION

It is difficult to think about collective memory without thinking about the role of traditions. Traditions are of all sorts: family traditions, community traditions, national traditions. Frequently traditions are treated as inviolable, carrying with them the assumption that they have remained unchanged for generations, or even that things have simply always been this way. In fact, traditions are constantly changing with each generation and are not nearly as monolithic or singular as we often presume.

A completely traditional belief is one which is accepted without question, often without acknowledging the acceptance, but merely thinking that the belief is not traditional, but true. It is accepted because it has "always" been accepted by "my kind." This sets the past in a position of authority that moves beyond experiential authority to sacred authority. The unreflective attachment to what has been given by this authority is associated with fear of that authority and with the desire to be connected to the past. This leads to the unthinking repetition of an attitude or perspective of the past.

At the other end of the spectrum, the compulsive rejection of traditional beliefs is not necessarily indicative of an engagement with critical appraisal of those traditions. It is often fomented by simple drive for individuality, which in itself does not necessarily constitute an original response to tradition.[27] It reflects a misunderstanding of the complex relationship between historical memory, community, and identity.

A position between these two extremes can be preserved through acknowledgment of the role of created place(s) with respect to community and collective memory. Inheriting traditions or historical memories cannot be understood as simply taking up a whole from the past, nor is any tradition itself a unified way of approaching or understanding the world. For some, tradition is to be adhered to simply because it is tradition, for others tradition is oppressive and must be rejected or overcome, and for still others tradition is carried along without recognition or acknowledgment. Nevertheless, each generation is the recipient of and participates in many traditions be they religious, cultural, political, national, or familial. Traditions range from such mundane prescribed activities as, say, shooting off fireworks for Independence Day, to fundamental attitudes like racism or liberalism.

It is clear that tradition cannot be understood simply as a collection of links in a chain that can be traced back to a certain origin. There is, rather, an interrelation between the new and the old that complicates the concept of tradition. There is a tension between wanting to preserve tradition, the importance of remembering, and wanting to disrupt tradition in order to encounter something new. Place, as providing for the inheritance of historical memory in particular, has an important role to play in this tension between preservation of the old and openness to the new.

In this section, I wish to explore the role of traditions and their relationship to place. Edmund Husserl, Martin Heidegger, Walter Benjamin, and Hans-Georg Gadamer reveal a concern for traditions and indicate a role for place that has not, as yet, been fully appreciated. Husserl, Heidegger, and Benjamin all remarked upon the presence of a crisis in European tradition in the early twentieth century. They identify the crisis as intrinsic to tradition, but also as being exacerbated by the modern technological society of the time. The crisis is subsumed by the concerns of everyday modern existence and the need for a response to the crisis is forgotten, or deferred. Later in the twentieth century Gadamer takes up the issue of tradition as an avenue towards recuperating the human sciences in light of the scientific, technological sway over our thinking.

In the following sections I will elaborate upon the paradoxical character of tradition as explicated by the first three of these philosophers. I will draw out the way in which each of them understands the relationship between tradition, technology, and place. They see this relationship as an opening for being able to think through the connection between collective memory and place in such a way that collective memory is not seen to be a monolithic imposition upon individual memory, but is understood within the context of the palimpsest of memory, tradition, and place.

I will begin with a comparison between Benjamin and Heidegger since they are most directly addressing the technological situation of the early twentieth century as they find it. They address the possibility of salvation from that crisis in terms of an alternative to technological thinking that can be provided by artistic/poetic thinking that is not reduced to aesthetic thinking but is a different breed entirely. They are rethinking the aesthetic vis-à-vis tradition and technology revealing an emphasis on place and its role in the transferring event of tradition. I highlight this relationship between artistic/poetic thought and place in an effort to more sharply exhibit the role of place with respect to tradition.

Tradition is brought into relief as a question for these three philosophers through their analysis of the role of technology in modern life. While none of them wholly demonize nor wholly valorize technology, they are similar in their recognition that in technology there is a certain elimination of place that has complex ramifications for tradition. It is this threefold relationship that I would like to focus on in order to develop the ways in which Husserl, Heidegger, and Benjamin may inadvertently share a respect for place and its importance for tradition and for a way of thinking that cannot be reduced to aesthetics or to calculation. We will see that Gadamer, too, shares this respect for place, but in a different enough way that we will discuss his position separately.

Heidegger and the Crisis of Tradition

Heidegger's presentation of the crisis of tradition has to do with the myopic view of modern science; a view that limits our ability to come to terms with the history of ontology. This theme dominates much of Heidegger's later work. He frequently argues that science is forgetful of the ways in which Being is open to questioning. He relates this forgetting to the dominance of modern technology. Heidegger describes modern technology as depending upon the calculability inherent to science that allows for the manipulation of objects. But modern technology is different from just any technology. Technology is fundamental to our being in the world and as such is not wholly destructive. Rather, there are many ways in which tradition is only possible because of technology. What Heidegger means by technology, then, is something quite broad, applying to a great variety of beings in the world. Technology is not something new, but for the world to be dominated by the instrumental thinking ushered in by modern technology is new. Modern technology has created a world wherein no particular technological device can necessarily be viewed as wholly bad, but where the technological has appropriated everything and has organized it into a singular totality. The world itself has become technological. In this way, it is no longer a system of tools to be used by humans, nor is it any longer merely one way of thinking among others. It has become the very way the world itself appears.

In the use of technology, an object, the tool, places restrictions upon its user in terms of the range of ways the tool itself can be used. The user is required to adapt to the tool. The more complex the tool, the more restrictive it is of its user. In order for one to compose an article on the computer, one must learn the position of the computer keys. The movement of one's hands must conform to the position of the keys. The user conforms to the tool rather than the other way around. This applies not only to what we might call advanced technology, but also to simple technology, simple tools as well. Of course, in order to use Heidegger's famous hammer, one's hand must conform itself to the handle of the hammer, but the hammer could also be used in a myriad of ways, or could be used to hammer any number of things. It is less restrictive of its user.

The computer, on the other hand, requires certain activities from me in order to get it to perform its function. I must position it where the sun does not shine too directly on the screen, for instance, so that I can read what is presented there. I must enter passwords in order to access the files I need. I must strike certain keys in a particular order to open the proper files. I must learn sets of commands, and pull-down menus. My language is altered to include not only new vocabulary like website, internet, and wifi, but also new meanings for old words like "surfing," "mouse," and "scrolling." If the hammer breaks, I can see precisely where it has gone wrong even if I cannot fix it. If the computer breaks, however, I am at a complete loss. Its complexity frustrates any attempt I might make to discover the problem.

The difference of modern technology for Heidegger is that in its specificity and narrowness, it reduces the nearness of things.[28] This is not due to particular "advances" in technology, or particular technological devices. It is instead a result of the very essence of modern technology itself which Heidegger calls "enframing" (*Ge-stell*).[29] Enframing is what allows things to be understood as "standing reserve" meaning that things are thought to be there for our use, not only establishing a kind of secondary status for things and world, but also establishing the subjectivity of knowledge. All of nature becomes merely resources for a subject. Ultimately this means that even we ourselves become resources. The impact of this way of knowing, this relationship to things is that the world is approached as resource and is thus dominated, taken control of. It is not approached through the openness of the question.

The results of this kind of elimination of the question are profound. If the world is viewed as standing reserve, knowledge is reduced to a calculative approach to it. Truth is nothing more than the correctness of results of investigation. Inquiry is limited to determinations of this correctness.

What is lacking, according to Heidegger, is the *aletheic* nature of truth, and the openness to that truth that comes through *poietic* thought.[30]

The crisis of tradition for Heidegger is the scientific elimination of an approach to tradition that allows for the openness of the question. That elimination is the consequence of a lack of places for a kind of forgetting and remembering. The authentic place of tradition must be the place of the gap of difference that allows what is handed down to be forged into something new. The technological approach of the modern era eliminates this openness to the questioning of Being. As Jeff Malpas has suggested, "It is the apparent 'neutrality' of technology and its inability to recognize any mode of questioning that is not itself framed from within technology as such that is part of what leads Heidegger to talk of ours as 'the age of the complete questionlessness of the essential' and 'the total unquestionableness of all things and of all contrivances.'"[31]

The unquestionableness is what constitutes the contemporary crisis of tradition. The era of modern technology results in what Heidegger calls the "flight into tradition." In "The Age of the World Picture," he writes, "the flight into tradition, out of a combination of humility and presumption, can bring about nothing in itself other than self-deception and blindness in relation to the historical moment."[32] A flight into tradition is characterized by a calculation and investigative manner of taking up tradition rather than the openness that allows the historical moment to reveal itself in its historicality. In other words, the flight into tradition is often as acceptance of tradition for tradition's sake and as the truth, the way it has always been, as opposed to an open recognition of the historicality of truth and the world that is preserved in the gap of difference. In creative questioning Heidegger finds the possibility of "safeguarding" into truth the incalculable, the unrepresentable. To represent the world is to make of the world a picture and such picture character makes the world an object for which the human can be subject and which the subject can manipulate and calculate.

The crisis brought on by the role of modern technology poses a threat to the place of tradition. If thinking technologically reduces all things to the status of entities that can be manipulated and calculated, this means that even those places where tradition is transmitted become places of calculation. Heidegger identifies these as places like the ancient Greek temple, the Van Gogh painting of the peasant shoes, or the cottage in the Black forest. In technological thinking these places are approached as historical objects that can be carbon dated, analyzed, calculated, rather than approached as places where tradition transpires, where a world is opened up, or where we can dwell. To approach such places technologically constitutes an erasure of the conflict between world and earth and thus "poses a threat to the site of tradition."[33] For Heidegger sees the rift between world and earth as a necessary function in the worlding of the world. Modern technology attempts to free the world from the earth and in so doing destroys that necessary conflict that keeps us in mind of tradition.

Heidegger contrasts modern technology and its issuing in of crisis with the salvational position of art, poetry, and non-discursive thought. In so doing, he indicates an alternative to the technological way of knowing. He does not advocate giving up technology or retreating from technology, but indicates that there must be a different approach to technology that does not succumb to its domination. As he suggests in "The Question Concerning Technology," "the merely correct is not yet the true. Only the true brings us into a free relationship with that which concerns us from its essence."[34] The alternative arises in part because of the opening of a place for thinking, a place that is non-calculative and allows for non-calculative thought. Heidegger focuses on place as the truth of Being, as the event that takes place. Poetic dwelling preserves the "proper measure" with respect to places.

Heidegger acknowledges this approach to thinking in "The Origin of the Work of Art" where he addresses the theme of tradition through the analysis of the work of art—a spatial non-representation of tradition. In this essay from 1935 Heidegger provides a description of an Ancient Greek Temple. The temple does not *represent* anything according to Heidegger, but it is doing the work of gathering around itself a unity of "birth and death, disaster and blessing, victory and disgrace, endurance and decline."[35] This gathering opens up the world of an historical people. It allows us to return to that world, however the "view remains open." The world that is revealed through the place of the temple is "never an object that stands before us and can be seen." It is rather the "ever-nonobjective to which we are subject."[36] Heidegger explains further that the world entails places where the "decisions of our history that relate to our essential being are made, are taken up and abandoned by us, go unrecognized and are rediscovered by new inquiry."[37] He distinguishes such places from mere earth and the relation of world to human as distinctive from the surroundings of plants and animals. Heidegger claims that a work of art makes "space" for the spaciousness of worlding that transpires in the world. What this means is that places are important precisely in being places that establish a world. It is through the work of the work of art that a place is opened for the world of the work of art to shine forth. For Heidegger this world is the "self-opening of the broad paths of the simple and essential decisions in the destiny of a historical people."[38] In other words, it is a historical world that is revealed as the destiny of a people. The places are where human decisions are made, where human activities transpire, and where world is created. They are places of tradition.

Furthermore, in "The Question Concerning Technology," Heidegger warns that the danger of technology is homelessness. In other words, technology threatens us with loss of place. This threat of homelessness

Heidegger understands as a loss of the world as a dwelling place for us. This loss of place is also related to the displacement of the work of art that loses the quality of its presence insofar as it is limited to the space of its exhibition. "The work of art opens up a dwelling place that transcends the exhibition setting."[39] But if we view the painting only in terms of the space that the content of a painting occupies, we overlook the place that is opened up by that content itself. A world is made available to us through the work of art. The artwork does not merely represent something or someplace, it opens up a place that is incalculable, unmanipulable. It is a place of dwelling.

Heidegger wants to (re)place art thereby reinforcing its saving power. Art's saving power comes in the form of the ability to warn us of the essence of modern technology and the danger that it poses. Beyond warning us of the homelessness that looms large through modern technology, however, art also has the ability to demonstrate to us the possibility of dwelling, or the possibility of a different conception of place.[40] He writes in "The Question Concerning Technology" that "because the essence of technology is nothing technological, essential reflection upon technology and decisive confrontation with it must happen in a realm that is, on the one hand, akin to the essence of technology and, on the other, fundamentally different from it. Such a realm is art."[41]

Furthermore, in "The Origin of the Work of Art" Heidegger explains that the "fixing in place" of truth through the work of art must be thought as the "letting happen" of truth rather than the willing or the enframing that marks the modern era. The work of art reminds us particularly of this relationship to the emergence of truth as a letting happen over which we do not have calculative control. It is a way in which we can dwell in the world as opposed to the way in which we conquer it. If we consider again the temple that Heidegger describes, we see how it opens a place of dwelling. Recall that Heidegger describes the temple as a thing that unifies the paths of birth and death, disaster and blessing that are the shape of our destiny. The "all-governing expanse of this open relational context is the world of this historical people."[42] The place of the temple brings us to mindfulness of birth and death, disaster and blessing, and the destiny of human being and the world, our historical world. The place of the temple saves us from calculative thinking by recalling us to our place in the world. By bringing us to dwell in our world with a mindfulness of our historicality, it provides a response to the crisis of tradition.

The issue is that when modern technology dominates, there is a poverty of place. In its calculative approach modern technology relates to locations in space that are demarcated by coordinates and quantitative descriptions. Such a calculative approach cannot accommodate places. They are not accessible. Places cannot be distinguished one from another on such an account. The locations that modern technology identifies cannot reveal the truth of the world for we do not dwell in coordinates. Our lives do not transpire simply in locations. We live in a world of different places the differences of which are incalculable.

In "Art and Space" Heidegger again reinforces this idea by suggesting the importance of the relationship between the work of art and place. He initially questions the role of the scientific conception of space indicating that such a conception varies greatly from the conception of space consequent with art. "Art and scientific technology regard and work upon space toward diverse ends and in diverse ways."[43] He stresses in this particular article that the event of truth is where places happen. The "clearing is releasing of places."[44] Place here is not the objectivity of a being present at hand, nor is it the being of beings, nor is it the scientific ideal space. Neither are places merely subsets of the overall scientific, technological space. Rather, places are the places of the "worlding of the world," of the coming to pass of the Event (*Ereignis*) of Being.

So, the crisis of tradition is really two-fold. It involves an alienation from place, an elimination of the place that is required to combat the second aspect of the crisis, which is a limitation of an attentive thinking that allows for the openness of questioning. The distinction between scientific thinking and the *aletheic* thinking of unconcealment is the difference between calculating a location and allowing a place of truth to emerge by being open to things as they are. The computer, described above, limits one's ability to be open to the thing as it is due to the way in which it dictates its own use, thereby preserving its instrumentality. The poetic thinking that Heidegger describes is not necessarily literary, but is thought in terms of an event (*Ereignis*). The work of art is the prime example of such an event because it allows for the rethinking of truth in terms unrelated to a metaphysics of representation, disrupting the categories of knowledge, correctness, or adequacy. The work of the work of art is the work of the event of truth. Art is thus not thought of in terms of aesthetic categories, but in terms of *poiesis*, in terms of an experience. This means that we cannot easily identify any technology as negative and any work of art as positive. Not all art works allow for *poietic* engagement and not all technology prohibits it. Heidegger has shattered the aesthetic categories at the same time that he has shattered the technological categories. Instead, what matters is the setting into work of the event of being, which takes place in a place that is roomy enough for thinking. For, it is place that makes the saving power of *poiesis* possible.

As we proceed to an analysis of Benjamin, I would like to call our attention to the three ways in which I will show the similarities between Benjamin and Heidegger on these issues. The first is with respect to the crisis of tradition. Both authors acknowledge a crisis and although they have different understandings of tradition itself, they recognize that there is a crisis. The second has to do with the necessity of a new kind of thinking for overcoming the crisis. And finally, the third is about the role of place in *poietic* thinking as a response to the crisis of tradition. This is vital to our overall project as we will proceed in the next chapter to an analysis of monuments and memorials as places where tradition is produced and transferred. We will be asking about such monuments in their role of preserving tradition, and transferring tradition across generations.

Benjamin and the Crisis of Tradition

Benjamin too uses the work of art as a way of approaching our relationship to tradition and its crisis. Although Benjamin viewed tradition as a more destructive force than Heidegger, it is possible to think of Benjamin's position in conjunction with Heidegger's approach as it has been described above in terms of the necessity of making way for a different kind of thinking than the tradition of modern technology promotes. "The Work of Art in the Age of Mechanical Reproduction," also written in 1935, takes on many of the same themes as Heidegger's text and works through the relationship of tradition to the visual (spatial) presentation in the work of art. Unlike Heidegger, however, Benjamin is more critical of tradition, although it can be argued that Benjamin also recognizes the paradoxical aspects of the remembering and forgetting that characterize tradition. He focuses, though, on what he deems to be the destructive character of tradition. It is not possible to have an authentic relation to tradition within tradition. It can only come with the Messianic cessation of tradition. Benjamin sees tradition as devoid of redemptive power due to its relationship to the individual subject within time. The only redemption that Benjamin is willing to recognize, the only gathering together of history he acknowledges, is one that takes place in Messianic time, outside of historical time or tradition. This eliminates the possibility of an authentic historical subject.

Both Heidegger and Benjamin understand tradition as the neutral medium of transmitting the past to the present that is rife with risk, particularly in the modern era.[45] The risk is always one of inauthenticity at the site of tradition—inauthenticity due to the impossibility of embracing the past without imposing a will upon it, and without making it something it isn't. Tradition as the act of handing over is a process of destruction. The past cannot be accessed as past, so to bring it into the present is the only possibility for making it accessible and yet, in bringing it into the present its pastness is destroyed and it is inevitably altered. So for Benjamin, the destruction of the past is necessary, for without it, nothing could be transferred across generations. Tradition works precisely by distancing its objects, making them inaccessible as past by bringing them into the present. Technology, in freeing an object from its place within tradition by making it infinitely reproducible, goes one step further by destroying the distance thereby allowing for at least the illusion of control. But for Benjamin this is not necessarily a negative result. Like Heidegger, then, Benjamin understands technology as having an effect of destroying both the possibility of nearness and the possibility of distance. Just as for Heidegger, the work of art has a peculiar place because it is the site where it is possible to acknowledge the destruction of tradition, the irretrievability of the past, and therefore the historicity of truth.

Benjamin is concerned with the work of art in its reproducibility because he wants to grasp how the work of art can be understood in relation to tradition. Technology, in allowing for the reproducibility of works of art, eliminates the "cult value" of the work of art and replaces it with an "exhibition value," thereby eliminating the distance that the "cultic" work of art maintains from its viewer. Because of the singularity of the work of art in its non-reproducibility, it remains aloof from the vast majority of people, hidden away in museums or private collections accessible to the elite, or at least only accessible for limited viewing within the confines of the museum. Technology, in allowing the work of art to be infinitely reproduced destroys the distance and challenges the cult value by making the object able to be reactivated in any variety of particular situations, not only in one, singular, original work.[46] Benjamin acknowledges that every work of art is reproducible, but the mechanical reproduction of the work of art "represents something new."[47] The magnitude of reproductions that mechanization makes possible means that the work of art can proliferate in endless places.

The rise of photography and film allows for the transmission of all works of art and thus has a profound effect on how such works of art make themselves felt in the public sphere. For the reproduction of the work of art is not the work of art itself and the difference between the two must have an impact on the influence of the work of art on the public. But reproducibility has become altered with the introduction of the mechanical. With respect to manual reproduction, the unique original work of art has a particular provenance, which is, of course, lacking in mechanical reproduction. Such provenance is the deciding factor in determining the authenticity of a work of art.

Authenticity, then, has a position independent of reproducibility. But enter mechanical reproduction and this question of authenticity and provenance becomes greatly altered. Copies of originals can be present in situations where such would be impossible for the original. Perhaps the most obvious example of this is recorded music that allows one to hear the performance of a piece of music without having to be in the recital hall. But also, the moving picture brings to the screen visions of Notre Dame Cathedral, Stonehenge, or a rock concert. This places the authenticity of the reproduction into question and thus the authority of the object is affected. In affecting the authority of the object, there is at the same time a limitation on authority generally, which has rebounding effects on the authority of subjectivity.

Benjamin insists that

> The authenticity of a thing is the essence of all that is transmissible from its beginning, ranging from its substantive duration to its testimony to the history which it has experienced. Since the historical testimony rests on the authenticity, the former, too, is jeopardized by reproduction when substantive duration ceases to matter. And what is really jeopardized when the historical testimony is affected is the authority of the object.[48]

Benjamin takes this quite seriously as is evidenced in a footnote where he insists that a provincial staging of Faust makes it possible for a viewer to engage with the tradition of the play in ways that the film fails to do.[49] It is important to keep in mind that for Benjamin, tradition is destructive. The authority of the object is what establishes the distance between viewer and object. It is maintained through a tradition that proposes that object as having magical qualities, what Benjamin calls "aura."

Tradition gets lost in the preponderance of reproductions. By creating a plurality of copies and allowing the copies to "meet the beholder or listener in his own particular situation" there is a "shattering of tradition" which contributes to what Benjamin identifies as the "contemporary crisis."[50] The cult value of the work of art which relates it particularly to a place and a time, a tradition, is replaced by an exhibition value which allows the work of art to be divorced from a particular place and time in order to be exhibited everywhere. Not only does this have an impact on cultural heritage and its transmission, but it also affects the way in which the world is experienced. It is at the same time destructive of the aura of the work of art.

For Benjamin, the aura of natural objects is "the unique phenomenon of a distance, however close it may be."[51] These particular conceptions of nearness and distance are temporal as well as spatial. The unique work of art is uncapturable in its entirety. It surpasses all attempts to completely and exhaustively experience or understand the work. At the same time, however, aura depends upon representation since the only way there can be a feeling of distance is if there is something close at hand. The work of art makes allusion to something uncapturable through something experienced in the first place. There must be something familiar in order to recognize the distance. So the aura of the work is something that points beyond the work itself. Thus the aura has an element of indeterminacy as well as an element of transcendence to it.[52] Benjamin suggests that "you breathe the aura of those mountains of that branch"[53] by which he means that one is merely receptive, taking it in the same way one takes in a breath.[54] This receptivity is in contrast to the kind of inattentiveness that is characterized by the response to film images and which will be addressed later in this section.

The contemporary decay of aura is a result of mechanical reproduction that makes art available to the masses. As he writes in *The Arcades Project*, "For the decline of the aura, one thing within the realm of mass production is of overriding importance: the massive reproduction of the image."[55] That means it is also the result of the "increasing significance of the masses."[56] The masses desire to "bring things 'closer' spatially and humanly and endeavor to do this through grasping at the thing through reproductions."[57] The masses want to have the Monet print hanging on their living room wall. We want the Eiffel Tower key chain, and the Statue of Liberty snow dome. The desire for these kinds of reproductions contributes to the destruction of the thing's aura according to Benjamin. It "is the mark of a perception whose 'sense of the universal equality of things' has increased to such a degree that it extracts it even from a unique object by means of reproduction."[58] For Benjamin, this is not the elimination of place; it is the establishment of place on different grounds. Benjamin's interest is in the new place formed for a different kind of perception, a different kind of thinking than the authority and tradition of the work of art allowed.

Because Benjamin understands the uniqueness of the work of art to be related to its position within tradition, then the reproduction of the work of art, which destroys spatial distance, also destroys its position within tradition. The position of the work of art as bearer of tradition is also changed by the fact that the more reproducible it is, the more the focus is on its exhibition value as opposed to its cult value. Howard Caygill suggests that "for Benjamin, what is viewed in the film is the 'handing over' of an object not by tradition, but by technology; in it the subject matter cannot be distinguished from the way it is presented. What is delivered by technology is above all its mode of delivery."[59] The movements of images in the film are not the movements of the viewer, but the movements of the camera, which never brings itself into view. This alters the audience's relationship to that which it is viewing. The audience is placed in a position of detachment, which allows the audience to take on the role of critic. This is related to the demise of aura due to the distance created by technology. "The aura which, on the stage, emanates from Macbeth, cannot be separated for the spectators from that of the actor. However, the singularity of the shot in the studio is that the camera is substituted for the public. Consequently, the aura that envelops the actor vanishes, and with it the aura of the figure he portrays."[60]

For Benjamin, the unique work of art absorbs the spectator into its place, its world, whereas the reproducible work of art is absorbed by the spectator. "The film with its shock effect meets this mode of reception halfway. The film makes the cult value recede into the background not only by putting the public in the position of the critic, but also by the fact that at the movies this position requires no attention. The public is an examiner, but an absent-minded one."[61]

Benjamin's claim of absent-mindedness should not be assumed to be acquainted with a lack of thought or a kind of mindless acceptance. What Benjamin is trying to get at here is a different kind of attention to works of art than tradition would usually dictate. He notes that the shock effect of film is something that "hit[s] the spectator like a bullet, it happen[s] to him." But again, Benjamin reminds us that this does not lead to utter passivity in the face of the constantly moving images of the film. Instead, it requires of the spectator a "heightened presence of mind" in order to cushion the blow of the shock.[62] In order to make sense of a film, the viewer needs an ability to synthesize the streaming images. This activity of synthesis, however, is not something that the viewer is engaged in deliberately or masterfully. Instead, it happens to the viewer as the continuous replacement of one image with the next prevents the viewer from having time to contemplate any one frame. The series of images is constantly reshaped and revalued as further images provide a framework and reference for the film as a whole. This kind of hermeneutic engagement with the film means that the film cannot ever be made to come under contemplation in its entirety.

So for Benjamin the increased availability of the work of art has "produced a change in the mode of participation."[63] Benjamin compares the kind of absent-minded participation with the experience of architecture. While other art forms come and go, the need for shelter has remained constant. Architecture, thus, can serve as a model for the kind of artistic experience Benjamin wishes to draw upon in describing the distraction of the masses. The fact that what Benjamin is ultimately appealing to is the experience of place should not be lost on us. Our appropriation of places happens through habit. We most often do not stand before places in contemplation. We are engaged in the world in a tactile, habitual way and in such a manner we gradually become accustomed to new constructions of our surrounding world. We encounter our world through a different kind of thinking. "Reception in a state of distraction, which is increasing noticeably in all fields of art and is symptomatic of profound changes in apperception, finds in the film its true means of exercise."[64] If we try to think this in more Heideggerian language, in order to see the comparison, we might say that the distracted form of thinking that Benjamin is describing here is the kind of thinking that allows things to be what they are instead of forcing them, through the contemplative power of our thought, to become what we wish them to be. In apperception, what comes to the fore is the periphery as opposed to the center.

Thinking Heidegger and Benjamin Together

At first blush it seems that Heidegger and Benjamin have completely opposing views. Heidegger sees the work of art as enveloping the spectator into a world and allowing the spectator to make contact with a tradition. For Heidegger it seems this is the soteriological role of the work of art whereas for Benjamin that role preserves aura and closes off precisely the kind of thinking Heidegger suggests it makes possible. How is it that we can reconcile these thinkers on this account?

Like Heidegger, what Benjamin is interested in is not the object of the work of art, but the work of art as an event. This requires thinking of the work of art not in aesthetic terms, not in terms of its provenance and authority, but in terms of the challenge to the authority of the object, which is the flip side of a metaphysics of subjectivity. Benjamin, like Heidegger, is concerned to disrupt the logic of presence and absence, and the linear temporality of the origins of a work of art that give it clout vis-à-vis tradition.[65]

While one can read Heidegger's account of the opening of the world of the work of art as still tied to a more traditional notion of the work of art where the subject is absorbed into the work, Benjamin's notion of the spectator as absorbing the work does not necessarily have the opposite effect of Heidegger's. Both thinkers view the interaction between the work [*techne*] of the work of art and the viewer/subject as a "happening," an "event" that is a place for thinking. Both thinkers, then, move beyond the work of art as mere representation to the work of art as a place where the openness of questioning can occur. While Benjamin views this position of the work of art as being made possible through technology, Heidegger sees the work of art as a possible response to technology. Both philosophers, however, view technology as having a destructive relationship to tradition, although Heidegger lays this at the feet of modern technology exclusively. Benjamin differs from and is critical of Heidegger's position regarding tradition in that Benjamin wants to stress the destructive nature of tradition in relation to history and subjectivity. These differences do not undermine the attention that both thinkers pay to the spatial element of the transmission of tradition. For Benjamin, "the configuration of the site of tradition is no longer determined by the play of presence and absence, nor consequently can the work of art be viewed any longer in terms of aura, for 'even the most perfect reproduction of a work of art is lacking in one element: its presence in space and time, its unique existence at the place where it happened to be.'"[66] For Benjamin the response to the technologization or the reproducibility of art is fundamentally political.

Finally, Heidegger and Benjamin see technology as having taken over the place of tradition. They argue that if technology determines our experience of space and time we will be confronted with a crisis that can only be overcome through a renewed sense of perception and thinking. That renewed sense would allow us to experience the world through an attentiveness and openness that makes it possible for the world to come forth rather than forcing the world to appear through a calculative approach.

For both philosophers, there is a recognition that traditional forms of understanding the relationship between the subject and its experienced objects are misaligned. The subject is not master of its experiences, or its objects of experience. Technology has revealed on the one hand the tendency to think of the subject in such terms but has also challenged the idea of the subject to the point where we must reconsider the relationship between the subject and the world in terms of the event of truth.

Both of these approaches will become fundamentally important as we consider the role of monuments and memorials in the transference of traditions across generations. As places that can be experienced both aesthetically and calculatively, we will have much to consider.

Husserl and the Crisis of Tradition

Edmund Husserl also recognizes a crisis of tradition. He sees the crisis as stemming from the mathematization of the world where critique is necessary and salvational. He characterizes the crisis as "a radical life-crisis of European humanity."[67] In *Crisis of European Sciences,* Husserl suggests that philosophy, too, is in a state of crisis. He argues that the crisis is due in large part to the forgetting of origins, which means accepting methods and values as self-evidently given with no understanding of their embeddedness within history or tradition. This forgetting does not exclude the philosopher, who, as an inheritor of a tradition, can also be culpable. Husserl describes Europeans of the 1920s and 1930s as feeling the emptiness of their cultural values and a collapse of the order to which they had become accustomed. They were being inundated, as far as Husserl was concerned, with the false solutions of irrationalism, anti-humanism, anti-universalism, and naturalism, not the least of which was Nazism. The natural sciences were failing to provide an adequate response to the crisis due to their alienation from the lifeworld. It is no small thing to see that Husserl understands the crisis in terms of the place of the lifeworld.

The mathematization of the world, as far as Husserl is concerned, began with Galileo and has continued to such a degree that we no longer understand lifeworld, but conceive of world and the things of the world solely as mathematical, calculable objects. As Husserl suggests, "through Galileo's mathematization of nature, nature itself is idealized under the guidance of the new mathematics; nature itself becomes—to express it in a modern way—a mathematical manifold."[68] Galileo ushered in a kind of thinking that mathematicians and mathematical physicists of the modern era embrace. It is a kind of thinking that moves entirely in the "sphere of symbolism, far removed from intuition."[69]

The problem is not with geometry itself, but with the way in which the geometrized and mathematized idealities have replaced the intuitive surrounding world. Geometry deals more and more exclusively with geometrical idealities. This means that its ability to say anything meaningful about the lifeworld becomes more and more restricted. As Husserl describes, "this arithmetization of geometry leads almost automatically, in a certain way, to the emptying of its meaning. The actually spatiotemporal idealities, as they are presented firsthand in geometrical thinking under the common rubric of 'pure intuitions,' are transformed, so to speak, into pure numerical configurations, into algebraic structures."[70]

The reason this is possible is that we take up tradition without the appropriate effort to revitalize the originary foundations. In other words, what Galileo discovered has become so much a part of the fabric of the way in which we view the world that we take it for granted that it is the way the world is. We forget that such a view is historically grounded in discoveries made by Galileo that have since been broadened by other scientists and applied to the surrounding world of life in such a way that we are no longer aware of them. There has been a "surreptitious substitution of the mathematically substructed world of idealities for the only real world, the one that is actually given through perception, that is ever experienced and experienceable—our everyday lifeworld."[71] This substitution has been passed along to all subsequent physicists and has worked its way into the broader society such that it is understood to be self-evident. But it is no more self-evident than any other tradition. It is a "garb of ideas" that "encompasses everything which, for scientists and the educated generally, *represents* the lifeworld, *dresses it up* as 'objectively actual and true' nature."[72]

So, like Heidegger and Benjamin, Husserl recognizes that there is a crisis of tradition that is linked to a way of thinking about the world that covers over or obscures alternative ways of thinking. Where Heidegger and Benjamin link this to technology, Husserl links it to a mathematization of lifeworld.[73] Heidegger, too, recognizes that theoretical physics makes modern technology possible, so traces the roots of the crisis also to a mathematized perception of the world. While Heidegger and Benjamin see salvation in the possibilities of art to demand or call forth *poietic* thought, Husserl finds that salvation in the possibility of critique. He suggests the critical attitude as one that allows us to call into question our sedimented convictions as well as our inherited convictions. What is required is a project of renewal that entails a peeling away of layers of sense in order to come to an understanding of the sedimented sense that has been passed along through tradition. The process of questioning back after the origins of thinking helps to uncover the forgotten aims and forgotten relationships of thinking to the lifeworld. It points out the complex relationship of the individual consciousness to its inherited traditions of meaning. It would help us to understand that all "objective" scientific thought is initially grounded in a lifeworld that is not an idealized mathematical entity, but is the world of (inter)subjective, perceived everyday life.

Any critical attitude that we adopt cannot be taken up from outside of any tradition. We must always do so from within a tradition since any position is taken up from a human perspective that is always historical, and thus always influenced by some tradition or other. From a position within a tradition we can take on an attitude of responsible renewal of the tradition rather than naïve acceptance of the tradition. The position of critique suggests that we are open to the traditions that have been handed down to us through our surrounding world and community, but that we are also capable of rejecting those traditions or bringing new understanding to those traditions thereby overwriting the tradition and layering a new understanding upon it. Renewal aims "to make vital again, in its concealed historical meaning, the sedimented conceptual system which, as taken for granted, serves as the ground of the individual's private and nonhistorical work."[74] While individuals may engage in renewal and critique independently, it is also an intersubjective process. Husserl makes clear that the role of renewal and critique is "not only to reawaken the chain of thinkers, the social interrelation of their thinking, the community of their thought and transform it into a living present for us but, on the basis of the *total unity* thus made present, to carry out a *responsible critique*, a peculiar sort of critique which has its ground in these historical, personal projects, partial fulfillments, and exchanges of criticism."[75] By taking on the renewal of traditions, we move out of a passive acceptance of them to a position of freely renewing them that allows for the possibility of responsible critique.

Husserl, then, like Heidegger and Benjamin, links the crisis of tradition to a way of thinking and particularly to a way of thinking about place. The recognition that thinking is deeply related to place is underscored by all three theorists. Gadamer's position in relation to a crisis of tradition is similar and his attempt at a solution is to rely upon a metaphor of place to grasp how we can retrieve tradition while still maintaining the openness of questioning.

Gadamer and the Crisis of Tradition

Gadamer argues in *Truth and Method*, that tradition is a fundamental part of all human inquiry including both the modern physical sciences and the human sciences. The modern physical sciences have attempted to free themselves of the biases of tradition in order to attain absolute objectivity. Gadamer argues that such an attempt is not only futile, but contributes to the sense of a crisis of tradition. Biases need to be understood, instead, as the starting point for all inquiry. One must know something in order to ask further. Finding oneself within a tradition that has preceded one and that one has inherited from prior generations does not prevent one from understanding, but is the very condition of the possibility of understanding even if that understanding is misunderstanding due to a certain blindness based on that tradition.

In the opening of Part II of *Truth and Method,* Gadamer explores the Heideggerian notion of fore-meanings. They are described as our projections of the meaning of a text that are anticipatory in nature. They may originate in prior experience or in traditional approaches that have been handed down from prior generations. Any reading of a text involves expectations as soon as an initial meaning becomes apparent in the text. For Gadamer, as for Heidegger, this engages one in a hermeneutic circle in that one's expectations can be revised based upon what one encounters in the text, while what one encounters is in part colored by one's expectations. This constant cyclical movement is the hermeneutic process of understanding. The reader's task is in part to approach the text with an eye to examining the legitimacy of the fore-meanings that she projects. Without the foundation of tradition that informs one of what to expect (fore-meanings), inquiry could never begin.

The difficulty, of course, is in making sure that one is not blinded by one's own fore-meanings. Gadamer insists that this requires questioning oneself as well as the text, but also requires being attentive to the alterity of the text. For, as he suggests, "The important thing is to be aware of one's own bias, so that the text can present itself in all its otherness and thus assert its own truth against one's own fore-meanings."[76] The text is responsible for pulling us up short should we expect something of it that is not there. In confronting something that does pull us up short, we are forced to modify our expectations bringing them into line with the text itself, thereby allowing the truth of the text to speak.

Drawing upon Heidegger, Gadamer specifically addresses the way in which the focus upon ridding ourselves of all prejudices, which was ushered in by the Enlightenment and is the cornerstone of the physical sciences, is detrimental to the poetic. The Enlightenment privileges reason over tradition, giving reason the authority of arbitrating truth. In so doing, it denigrates the *mythos* of tradition. Gadamer writes that "It is now said, not that poets tell lies, but that they are incapable of saying anything true; they have only an aesthetic effect and, through their imaginative creations, they merely seek to stimulate the imagination and vitality of their hearers or readers."[77] What is troubling to Gadamer is that tradition has lost its authority in being aligned with mere imagination. The authority has been given over to science.

Gadamer also recognizes how the physical sciences have contributed to mathematization of our world. He elaborates upon the way in which contemporary physics has assumed the existence of a world in itself according to which various creatures construct their own worlds. The biological universe is derived from the physical universe. This may seem obvious or even inconsequential to us, but for Gadamer the result is that it "constitutes a new kind of inquiry." That new inquiry is behavioral biology which makes possible a conception of the human perception of the world as simply a special case of a much more complex mathematized structure. He likens this to the way in which we perceive the world of bees today. They way in which bees perceive the world orienting themselves through their sensitivity of ultraviolet light is a special case based upon their particular capacities, but the world of the bees and the world of the humans are just aspects of the much more complicated, mathematized true world.[78] In thinking of the world as being-in-itself, the sciences posit the world as something over against which there must be an investigator. "For even a world equation that contained everything, so that the observer of the system would also be included in the equations, would still assume the existence of a physicist who, as the calculator, would not be an object calculated."[79] In other words, physics, which posits a world-in-itself, also seems required to posit a view from nowhere, or at least a view from outside that world. It fails to recognize the place-boundedness of the human being in any true understanding of the world.

Insofar as the human relationship to the world is not characterized by objectivity, neither is it merely relative to any particular. The relationship is linguistic. "For to live in a linguistic world, as one does as a member of a linguistic community, does not mean that one is placed in an environment as animals are."[80] Instead, it involves one deeply in one's own way of being through the linguistic tradition that one has inherited. Use of language is not restricted to calculation. We each use language in our own unique way just as we take up traditions through a process that makes them our own. That process is what Gadamer is outlining as the hermeneutic process. If all understanding begins with biases, and reading, or any inquiry, takes place through a circular hermeneutic movement between the inquirer and its object, then the insights one gains from this process are constantly modified and redeployed in gaining deeper understanding.

Still, it is no coincidence that Gadamer sees the crisis in terms of our relationship to the world. In our everyday encounters in the world, we confront things from a particular perspective that is supported by our fore-meanings and traditional understandings that he refers to as horizons. His use of the concept of horizons is a recognition that we are always embedded within not only a specific time of history, but within a particular place, a cultural place that informs our understanding in its connection to language. Gadamer understands this in terms of the variety of lifeworlds (we might in keeping with Husserl say homeworlds) that characterize the way in which we see the world. The horizons that Gadamer will subsequently describe in his hermeneutic approach are platial horizons as much as they are temporal horizons. "one look at such fields of investigation as ethnology or history informs us that spaces and times produce highly different life-worlds in which highly different things pass as unquestioningly self-evident."[81]

Saying that we are so deeply indebted to tradition does not mean that we must simply take it up without resistance to it or revolutionary attitudes towards it. We can only have resistance or revolutionary attitudes in so far as we are taking up traditions to begin with. The relationship between tradition and world is highly important for Gadamer insofar as he conceives of humans as having a relationship of freedom from environment and towards a world which is linguistically constituted. Traditions themselves are part of any encounter with anything new. Thus, Gadamer establishes the notion of horizons to describe the encounter between tradition and newness.

Not surprisingly, for Gadamer just as for Heidegger and Benjamin, part of the corrective to the crisis of tradition as posed by the sciences is a return to or recuperation of art and aesthetic consciousness. Like Heidegger, Gadamer sees the work of art as having the capacity to open us to a world, but that openness is one that is inseparable from our own horizon. While we may be able to transpose ourselves to some degree into that which is other, we cannot position ourselves outside of our own horizon. Through aesthetic consciousness, however, Gadamer believes we learn to see better. We learn to view the work of art in terms of its own horizons, recognizing that it has been painted in a particular time and for a particular place. The work of art is able to show "us a world that is there for itself and as such."[82] Like Heidegger, Gadamer conceives of the experience of a work of art as the experience of something emerging from the artwork; a truth emerges. The person experiencing the work of art is by no means passive, however. Instead, one tarries with the work of art. It is a "tarrying that waits and preserves in such a way that the work of art is allowed to come forth . . . what comes forth 'addresses us' and so the person who is addressed is as if in conversation with what comes forth."[83] The work of art engages the viewer in a conversation that resists the calculability of scientific discourse. It is not a work that can be approached scientifically, "with a measuring tape in one's hand," or "through the number of its computer bits."[84] The dominance of the scientific discourse has created a situation of "homelessness and placelessness to art and to the artist" which is due to the loss of the "presence of the past in the present [that] belongs to the very nature of the human mind."[85]

When Gadamer speaks of horizon, he defines it as a "situation" that "represents a standpoint that limits the possibility of vision." He asserts that horizon is essential to the notion of situation. Gadamer is quick to insist that we cannot transpose ourselves into another's horizon without mistakenly setting that horizon up as something closed, as something that encloses a culture. This, he claims, is merely an abstraction. It is the case, however, that the horizon is "something into which we move and that moves with us. Horizons change for a person who is moving. Thus the horizon . . . which exists in the form of tradition, is always in motion."[86] It seems to me that Gadamer is approaching a concept of palimpsest with the idea of the movement of horizons. In one respect, the horizons are not radical losses of what has come before, but they are still open to that which is new. It is not a far step from that idea to the idea that the new is layered over the tradition in such a way that the tradition is not lost.

Husserl's concepts of homeworld, alienworld, and lifeworld seem to function in the background for Gadamer here. For, the horizons to which he refers are horizons of place as well as horizons of time. He suggests that we do not transpose ourselves into alien worlds that are completely unconnected with our own, but that both homeworld and alienworld depend upon one great horizon that moves beyond the frontiers of any particular world. Any particular moving horizon is one which determines lives as heritage and tradition and is something we are never without. Gadamer reminds us that "There is always a world already interpreted, already organized in its basic relations, into which experience steps as something new, upsetting what has led our expectations and undergoing reorganization itself in the upheaval."[87] Recognizing that we always already find ourselves in a world of tradition that precedes us means that any encounter with what is new or different transpires initially according to what is understood as opposed to what is misunderstood. Again, Gadamer says, "Misunderstanding and strangeness are not the first factors, so that avoiding misunderstanding can be regarded as the specific task of hermeneutics. Just the reverse is the case. Only the support of familiar and common understanding makes possible the venture into the alien, the lifting up of something out of the alien, and thus the broadening and enrichment of our own experience of the world."[88]

We find the connection between Gadamer and place in his response to the crisis of tradition. For Gadamer, we need not resort to scientific method in order to be able to speak of truth. Truth and meaning arise in the fusion of horizons between reader and text, inquirer and subject. This allows one to hold on to tradition and allow it a position of authority, without being blinded by it or adhering to it at all costs. Instead, because Gadamer understands those horizons to be constantly moving and shifting it allows us to understand our relationship to tradition as one of openness and constant reinterpretation, or in Husserlian terms, of renewal and critique. The place of tradition is not only where the world of tradition is opened to us through a work of art as it is for Gadamer, Heidegger, and Benjamin, but also the place where we encounter tradition as well as that which is open to inquiry—the horizons of ourselves and our world.

Tradition and Place

The crisis as we have seen it presented by these four philosophers has to do with the technologization and mathematization of the world as well as the focus of the scientific method upon objectivity. We have seen that Benjamin and Heidegger have each developed a nuanced response to this technological age. While they each recognize the ways in which technology has challenged and undermined tradition, neither of them calls for a simple return to tradition nor a simple rejection or embracing of technology. Instead, they have called for a renewed relationship to thought that happens through the work of art, through *poietic* thought. Gadamer, too, responds with an appeal to the poetic. The poetic opens up a world. As Gadamer puts it, "It does not describe or signify an entity, but opens up a world of the divine and human for us."[89] While Husserl does not go so far as to embrace the work of art, he too calls for a different kind of thinking through the advocacy of renewal and critique of tradition that does not take the mathematization of the world as self-evident.

All four philosophers see modern technology, science, and mathematization (which for Gadamer is about the reliance upon scientific method) as participating in a crisis of tradition. That crisis is one that is manifest in a calculative approach to the world that precludes a kind of questioning that is fundamental to tradition. This presentation of tradition is one that indicates a necessity of openness and questioning that maintains the vitality of tradition in creating an event of truth. For Benjamin, Heidegger, and Gadamer alike the event of truth can be grasped more readily through the work of art than through modern technology, while for both philosophers the work of art is understood not in purely aesthetic terms but in terms of its openness to questioning. Again, Husserl also sees the necessity of an openness to questioning in the form of critique. Gadamer uses the platial metaphor of horizons to bring us to the position of seeing how we can take up tradition while at the same time be open to critique and modification of tradition. The relationship of place to these questions, albeit subtly presented in each thinker, is essential. They all adhere to a notion of the event of truth that takes place in a place. Such places are those that resist manipulation and calculation. They are the incalculable, the poetic that make possible the openness of the question, that allow for dwelling on this earth.

What strikes me as fruitful here is what can be said about the role of place in tradition. Each philosopher appeals to the place of the event of truth. This place is one where tradition transpires in an open way that engages with questioning. It is a place that does not give tradition the power of domination, nor does it fully deny the importance of tradition, but it opens tradition to the questioning that makes possible the recognition of the event of truth and the historicality of human beings.

We saw in chapter 1 that the link between memory and place on an individual level frequently transpires through bodily experience. When we elevate this to the level of collective memory, the produced places of the world are effective not only in preserving, but also in producing, collective memory. The concrete examples provided in the upcoming chapters will give some insight into the ways in which and the reasons why we need to be constantly vigilant in our attentiveness to our experiences of the world around us. The kind of thinking that is demanded by many phenomenologists in the response to our everyday experiences is paramount not only in the production of places of collective memory, but in our experiences of those places as well.

To that end, we must come to terms with *how* such memories get transferred from generation to generation, as well as why place is so important and effective in the transference of tradition. Public monuments and memorials are examples of such places where transference of tradition transpires. They contribute to collective memory. An analysis of their contribution reveals how events of the past and communal responses to such events are transferred through generations. The monument can be conceived as an event of openness that allows for the transference of tradition itself. It is the happening of the transference of tradition. It is something that is written on the earth that creates a world and a place. An encounter with the monument is an encounter with an unconcealment of tradition that can only take place from within a world that is at the same time partly constituted by that tradition. But the meaning of monuments is dynamic. The transference of the tradition they inspire is not some closed system, but is open to renewal by current generations. For instance, monuments in the Midwest that were originally erected to celebrate settlers' conquests over Native Americans and the advancement to the Pacific Ocean are viewed differently now than when they were first erected. The traditional view of Native Americans embodied in them has by no means disappeared entirely, but it has become altered in the recognition that they are inaccurate representations of Native Americans. Likewise, we now recognize that such monuments fail to acknowledge the atrocities that Native Americans suffered at the hands of conquering Europeans.[90] Tradition is sedimented in the experience of these monuments. As each generation approaches the monuments and buildings that make up its public space, there is an alteration in the way such monuments reveal themselves. As part of a human environment, the monument is never actually viewed or understood statically and in isolation. It achieves its meaning within the context of a world that is written upon by it, but also writes the history of the monument itself.

Places of commemoration—monuments, for example—take up a place within this tension between renewal of the tradition and critique of the tradition. They are important in the preservation of memory and thus tradition; they provide a locus for collective memory and preserve that memory in a somewhat permanent manner through marble or stone, for instance. But this does not explain the entirety of the relationship to tradition through place. Traditions do change; they are not static. Thus, the relationship between tradition and place must be understood in a hermeneutic fashion. The past and the present confront one another in the place of monuments or places of memory. The monument allows for retention of the past in its depiction of a past event, hero, or ideal, but because the experience of the monument is in the present and projects itself into the future, there cannot be a complete retrieval of the past. The old beliefs coexist with the new and each generation modifies the beliefs of the previous generations that are presented in that place.[91] The renewal and critique, the *poietic* event of truth, is something that can happen in the place of monuments and memorials. Let us consider this more carefully in the following chapters.

NOTES

1. Paul Ricoeur, *Memory, History, Forgetting*, trans. Kathleen Blamey and David Pellauer (Chicago: University of Chicago Press, 2004), 109.
2. *ibid.*
3. Ricoeur, *Memory, History, Forgetting*, 111.
4. Ricoeur, *Memory, History, Forgetting*, 115.
5. Ricoeur, *Memory, History, Forgetting*, 117.
6. Edmund Husserl, *Cartesian Meditations*, trans. Dorion Cairns (The Hague: Martinus Nijhoff, 1977), 125/93.
7. Husserl, *Cartesian Meditations*, 139/109.
8. The residue of Husserl's earlier theory of empathy as a re-presenting is evident here although the language is more refined and precise. Husserl has provided the appropriate distance between the ego and the Other, so that the Other's empathized anger does not become the ego's anger.
9. Husserl, *Cartesian Meditations*, 142/112.
10. Even in cases of hallucination when someone might be aware that her hallucination is not shared, this does not discount that she is still within a shared intersubjective world. While the hallucinator has the sense of experiencing something that is unique to her, the *awareness* that she is hallucinating, means that she recognizes that there is a shared world separate from the hallucination, and that this shared world is understood to be objective.
11. Jane Chamberlain, "Thinking Time: Ricoeur's Husserl in *Time and Narrative*," *Journal of Philosophical Research* 27 (2002): 292.
12. *Hyle* is the Greek term for matter. Husserl uses it here to get at a very fundamental brute sensory experience.
13. Ricoeur, *Memory, History, Forgetting*, 129.
14. Ricoeur, *Memory, History, Forgetting*, 119.
15. Edward Casey, *Remembering: A Phenomenological Study* (Bloomington: Indiana University Press, 2000), 110.
16. Maurice Halbwachs, *The Collective Memory*, trans. Francis Ditter, Jr. and Vida Yazdi Ditter (New York: Harper and Row, 1980), 24.
17. Halbwachs, *The Collective Memory*, 30.
18. I'm not suggesting here that these memories are infallible because they are supported by the community. Nor am I suggesting that they remain ever the same. Because we think of memory as a palimpsest, even these memories are open to change

and are rewritten and sometimes completely covered over. What is at issue here is the fact of remembrance at all and the association of that remembrance with place. The memory might not remain were it not deemed important socially and the place of the memory is linked in importance. It is important to us for the memory to be emplaced even if we unknowingly remember differently at different times.

19. Halbwachs, *The Collective Memory*, 61.

20. Edmund Husserl. *The Crisis of European Sciences and Transcendental Phenomenology*, trans. David Carr (Evanston: Northwestern University Press, 1970), 169.

21. Husserl, *The Crisis of European Sciences and Transcendental Phenomenology*, 172.

22. Halbwachs, *The Collective Memory*, 5.

23. Ricoeur, *Memory, History, Forgetting*, 36.

24. Ed Casey speaks of memory-frame and worldhood in the context of remembering, but for Casey it seems quite clear that the place of memory is treated as simply a frame, the worldhood is the setting or the scene for the memory. This is too limited a notion of the role of place in memory. Place is not simply setting, but is intimately tied up with what is remembered and is fundamental to the memory. This is not to say that there can't be some places that do simply serve as setting, but place is generally more foundational to memory than merely as setting for action or object of memory. See Casey, *Remembering*, 68–69.

25. Due to the palimpsestic character of memory and tradition, sometimes these places of memory change. This helps us to underscore that we are concerned here with the phenomenological sense of place in its association with memory and not so much with a strictly geographical place. Memory is co-constituted with place, and sometimes this coincides with a geographical place, but not necessarily always with exactly the same geographical place. We may even be wrong about the place that is associated with the memory, but this does not destroy the co-constitution of memory and place or our sense of the place as imbued with the memory.

26. Halbwachs refers to these two types of memory as "autobiographical" and "historical" memory. He is careful to make clear that these two types of memory cannot so easily be distinguished one from the other. They are intimately intertwined. See Halbwachs, *The Collective Memory*, 52.

27. For more on tradition, see Edward Shils, "Tradition," *Comparative Studies in Society and History* 13 (1971): 122–159.

28. For this notion of "nearness" see Jeff Malpas, *Heidegger's Topology: Being, Place, World* (Cambridge: MIT Press, 2007).

29. Martin Heidegger, "The Question Concerning Technology," *Basic Writings*, ed. David Farrell Krell (London: HarperPerennial, 2008), 324.

30. See Babette Babich, "The Essence of Questioning After Technology: Techne as Constraint and the Saving Power," *Journal of the British Society for Phenomenology* 30.1 (1999): 107.

31. Malpas, *Heidegger's Topology*, 291.

32. Martin Heidegger, "The Age of the World Picture," *The Question Concerning Technology and Other Essays*, trans. William Lovitt (New York: Harper and Row, 1977), 136.

33. Howard Caygill. "Benjamin, Heidegger and the Destruction of Tradition," *Walter Benjamin's Philosophy*, eds. Andrew Benjamin and Peter Osborne (London: Routledge, 1994), 22.

34. Heidegger, "The Question Concerning Technology," 313.

35. Martin Heidegger, "The Origin of the Work of Art," *Basic Writings*, ed. David Farrell Krell (London: HarperPerennial, 2008), 167.

36. Heidegger, "Origin of the Work of Art," 170.

37. *ibid.*

38. Heidegger, "Origin of the Work of Art," 174.

39. Kathleen Wright, "The Place of the Work of Art in the Age of Technology," *Southern Journal of Philosophy* 22 (1984): 577.

40. For more on this see Kathleen Wright, "The Place of the Work of Art."

41. Heidegger, "The Question Concerning Technology," 340.
42. Heidegger, "Origin of the Work of Art," 167.
43. Martin Heidegger, "Art and Space," trans. Charles H. Seibert, *Man and World* 9 (1973): 3.
44. Heidegger, "Art and Space," 6.
45. Caygill, "Benjamin, Heidegger and the Destruction of Tradition," 27.
46. Walter Benjamin, "The Work of Art in the Age of Mechanical Reproduction," *Illuminations*, ed. Hannah Arendt, trans. Harry Zohn (New York: Harcourt Brace & World, 1969), 223.
47. Benjamin, "Work of Art," 220.
48. Benjamin, "Work of Art," 223.
49. Benjamin, "Work of Art," 245 fn3.
50. Benjamin, "Work of Art," 223.
51. Benjamin, "Work of Art," 224.
52. Yvonne Sherratt, "Aura: The Aesthetic of Redemption?" *Philosophy and Social Criticism* 24.1 (1998): 33.
53. Benjamin, "Work of Art," 225.
54. Willem Van Reijen, "Breathing the Aura—The Holy, the Sober Breath," *Theory, Culture & Society* 18.6 (2001): 31–50.
55. Walter Benjamin, *The Arcades Project*, trans. Howard Eiland and Kevin McLaughlin (Cambridge: Harvard University Press, 1999), 337.
56. Benjamin, "Work of Art," 225.
57. *ibid.*
58. *ibid.*
59. Caygill, "Benjamin, Heidegger and the Destruction of Tradition," 27.
60. Benjamin, "Work of Art," 231.
61. Benjamin, "Work of Art," 242–43.
62. Benjamin, "Work of Art," 240.
63. Benjamin, "Work of Art," 241.
64. Benjamin, "Work of Art," 242.
65. Krzysztof Ziarek, "The Work of Art in the Age of its Electronic Mutability," *Walter Benjamin and Art*, ed. Andrew Benjamin (London: Continuum Publishing, 2005), 214.
66. Caygill, "Benjamin, Heidegger and the Destruction of Tradition," 23.
67. Husserl, *The Crisis of European Sciences*, 2.
68. Husserl, *The Crisis of European Sciences*, 23.
69. Husserl, *The Crisis of European Sciences*, 24.
70. Husserl, *The Crisis of European Sciences*, 44.
71. Husserl, *The Crisis of European Sciences*, 49.
72. Husserl, *The Crisis of European Sciences*, 51.
73. Heidegger also links it to a mathematization of lifeworld in his 1936 essay "What is a Thing?" For him, the mathematization of the lifeworld is deeply connected to the rise of instrumental thinking with modern technology. For the relevant sections, see Martin Heidegger. "Modern Science, Metaphysics, and Mathematics," *Basic Writings*, ed. David Farrell Krell (London: HarperPerennial, 2008), 267–305.
74. Husserl, *The Crisis of European Sciences*, 73.
75. *ibid.*
76. Hans-Georg Gadamer, *Truth and Method*, translated by Joel Weinsheimer and Donald G. Marshall (New York: Crossroad Publishing Company, 1992), 269.
77. Gadamer, *Truth and Method*, 274.
78. Gadamer, *Truth and Method*, 415.
79. Gadamer, *Truth and Method*, 452.
80. Gadamer, *Truth and Method*, 453.
81. Gadamer, *Philosophical Hermeneutics*, 189.

82. Hans-Georg Gadamer, "The Artwork in Word and Image—'So true, so full of being!' (Goethe)," *The Gadamer Reader: A Bouquet of his Later Writings*, edited by Richard Palmer (Evanston: Northwestern UP, 2007), 111.

83. Gadamer, "The Artwork in Word and Image," 114.

84. Gadamer, "The Artwork in Word and Image," 116.

85. Gadamer, "The Artwork in Word and Image," 120.

86. Gadamer, *Truth and Method*, 304.

87. Gadamer, *Philosophical Hermeneutics*, 15.

88. *ibid.*

89. Gadamer, *Truth and Method*, 470.

90. Consider the larger-than-life, boldly painted statue of Pocahontas that stands at the entrance to the town of Pocahontas, Iowa, or the grave of Sitting Bull in Mobridge, South Dakota. Memorialization of Native Americans has changed a great deal in the last fifty years from demonization and infantilization to much more respectful representations of them and educational presentations of their history. Both kinds of memorializing are creative of a collective memory of Native Americans.

91. Barry Schwartz, "Social Change and Collective Memory: The Democratization of George Washington," *American Sociological Review* 56 (1991): 234.

THREE

Collective Memory, Place, and Mourning

In the first two chapters we have seen the impact of place on the body and on the act of constitution. We have also seen how memories are thoroughly intersubjective and how place allows for the transference of memories and traditions across generations. What we have yet to discuss is the way in which place is important in maintaining the community and how mourning as an act of the community in its loss is connected to place. Mourning, of course, is also individual, but we demand its public expression and we use the earth as a part of the process of mourning by deliberately marking the earth, or by returning to places of the past. In so doing, we express our understanding that places hold the past. We need to explore how places hold the past and what transpires when we mark places of death or mourning as well as what transpires when places are destroyed or when we become separated from them.

It is easy to understand that collective memories are linked to place. The cafeteria or a favorite hangout locates the memory of college pals and their shared times. At a college class reunion, the pals could make a pilgrimage to the cafeteria or hangout to relive the shared moments. Some place like an army camp, tent, or battlefield holds soldiers' memories and the bank holds the memories of survivors of a holdup. The soldiers' memories and historical memories have an additional aspect in that they are events that are often publicly commemorated, deliberately publicly remembered. They are prone to places that are created specifically for the purpose of remembering together, for the purpose of creating collective memory. Other places of collective memory are less deliberately created, but come about because they are places where collectively important events took place. They "take place" *in* a place that subsequently becomes *the* place for the collective memory. Such places are often marked for the sake of perpetuating a collective memory or as places where collective memory is created.

If a place already has a privileged position with respect to collective memory, then what possible need is there to embellish (or perhaps denude) a place by the erection of a place marker? Place markers such as monuments, memorials, and living museums like battlefields, or preserved farmsteads, are those built, or produced places. Do they serve a different function than the "unmarked" place? Created places are deliberate ways of transferring tradition across generations, of writing tradition and memory on the world.[1] Building has the role of transforming space into place by the creation of an environment that is human and deliberate. It provides for the inheritance of tradition, and the transference of historical memory. But we need to explore how these deliberately-built memory sites function.

OF MEMORY AND MOURNING

On July 28, 2008, Toni Morrison dedicated a bench by the road in Charleston Harbor, South Carolina near Sullivan's Island. The bench was something she had worked a long time to have erected to mark the gateway to the New World for the American slave trade. In keeping with her novel *Beloved,* which arose from Morrison's need to commemorate slaves and their history, Morrison remarked in an interview in 1989, "There is no suitable memorial, or plaque, or wreath or wall, or park or skyscraper lobby. There's no 300-foot tower, there's no small bench by the road."[2] Now Morrison, and the rest of us, have that bench by the road. But how does such an object help us to remember and to mourn? Clearly, Toni Morrison is not interested in the bench by the road for her own sake only. She is interested in the role that the bench by the road can play for all of us in producing and sustaining a collective memory of the uncounted, unmemorialized, forgotten millions that slavery defaced. She wants the knowledge of the slave trade to be transferred across generations by making it a part of the material world.

Monuments and memorials are places deliberately constructed for purposes of remembering. They are erected in memory of someone as a marker of that person's life on the occasion of his or her death. In an effort to come to grips with why we conceive of monuments as important in the effort to remember those who have died, I would like first to think through the process of mourning, particularly collective mourning. With the help of Jacques Derrida, we will look at the relationship between mourning, memory, and places of mourning—sites of death, cemeteries, monuments, and memorials. We will use Derrida's texts to come to terms with how he thinks we fail in mourning, then consider the way we engage in collective mourning and whether it suffers the same failings. Third, we will consider the places of monuments and memorials, their contributions to mourning, and whether those contributions help us to understand mourning.

What Is Mourning?

Many of us recognize that we have a duty to the dead.[3] We seek to redeem the dead or seek justice for the dead who may have been forgotten by history. Toni Morrison is seeking to do just that in erecting a bench in honor of those who died on the Middle Passage. Through mourning we are supposed to be able to lend a voice to the dead, to give them presence in their absence. Derrida corroborates by claiming that mourning the dead is a form of bearing witness.[4] For Derrida, bearing witness is "an ethical or political act, for today and for tomorrow."[5] Erecting monuments and memorials, then, is in part an act of mourning and as such participates in the perpetuation of the narrative of a life. Mourning's connection to memory is tied to an Other in the hermeneutic gaze of the self and the present. We bear witness in the immediacy of the present. For Derrida the work of bearing witness is to make the Other present to ourselves which means that the act of mourning, the work of bearing witness, must fail for we cannot make the dead present again. Derrida stresses that we must attend to the Other in this act as wholly Other, in the Other's singularity.[6]

Derrida attempts to bear witness to the uniqueness of each relationship with many friends in eulogies, letters of condolence, and funeral orations. In publishing many such writings, Derrida "has tried to respond to a singular event, a unique occasion, with words fit for the friend—words that inevitably relate life and friendship to death and mourning."[7] But here we are confronted by the question—how in the singularity of the relationship between Derrida and Paul de Man, Michel Foucault, or Louis Althusser could Derrida possibly express publicly that relationship in its uniqueness and singularity? How could such mourning, memorializing, and commemoration take place publicly without distortion, without desire for effect, and without destruction of the very uniqueness it aims to recognize? The symbolization of the friendship through commemoration makes the friendship itself political, underscoring the impossibility of mourning.

Derrida recognizes that mourning presents a dilemma for the living since it has two aspects: possibility and impossibility. The *possibility* of mourning consists in interiorizing the dead and recognizing that anything that we can give the dead can only be in us, the living. In his essay "The Deaths of Roland Barthes," Derrida suggests that even while his thoughts are *for* Barthes, they "will no longer reach him." Derrida's words are like the words of every funeral oration, every gathering in the name of the dead, every monument to the departed in that everything said of the friend or even to the friend "remains hopelessly in us or between us the living" such that "All we seem to have left is memory."[8] Yet, the memory is what we the living can continue to share between us of the dead Other.

The *impossibility* is the awareness that the Other is Other and more particularly so in death. The Other is inaccessible and has an uncompromising alterity that cannot be altered by my mourning. This means that we are unable to remember the dead as she was. Death is an abyss between us which confirms the absolute difference of the Other. In life that difference is one with which we can be in relation and we can understand that relation as in part constitutive of ourselves. In death, however, we realize that we are incapable of allowing the Other a position in relation. The Other becomes only a matter of my memories of the Other. Mourning, in its impossibility, can acknowledge only the lack of relation, and the absence that results from death.

In many of his letters and eulogies, Derrida makes clear that he conceives of the death of the friend as the cessation of a relation which has played a constitutive role in the sense of self. Without the continued relation with one who has died, the shared vocabulary of our relation is ruptured and the memories that we shared are no longer shared, but now "interior" to me alone. No doubt there are others with whom we shared experiences and memories and those others can help to support my memories of the one gone, but there is a difference in quality, a difference in the support of those memories. There is a gap left by the one who is no longer in relation with us, but who is divided from us by the chasm of death.

In his funeral essay for Jean-François Lyotard, Derrida writes that any kind of personal testimony with regard to the dead "always tends toward reappropriation and always risks giving in to an indecent way of saying 'we,' or worse, 'me.'"[9] He warns that mourning always harbors the danger of narcissism. In mourning a friend's death we frequently are tempted to take pity upon ourselves. We express our mourning in terms of part of ourselves that has also died with the friend never to be recuperated because it is how we were only with the friend. Or, we suffer what Paul Ricoeur recounts in *Living up to Death* as a kind of anxiety at our own continuing existence. He speaks of it as "The make-believe of Death [that] . . . becomes indiscernible from the 'bare anxiety of living' in its aspect of 'chance.' The *luck* of tragedy according to Martha Nussbaum. Why my child? Why not me? To survive, like anyone without merit, hence also without any fault."[10] We suffer in that we are left to bear witness.

Finally, Derrida speaks of the infidelity that inevitably comes with mourning any singular death. For in each singular death that we mourn, we are infidels to the other singular deaths we have mourned and will mourn. No singular death can be the death to end all death. We will mourn others and in mourning others, we risk infidelity to the singularity of any death. While death may be universal, it is also the ultimate marker of individuality. Each death is, just as each subject, distinct.

For Derrida there are primarily three ways, then, in which mourning is impossible. First, it risks denying the singularity or alterity of the Other often by reducing the Other to my own memories of the Other, and sometimes reducing the Other to a symbol. Second, it risks a kind of narcissism in our concern for our own selves and our perceived loss or our own tragic continuing existence. Finally, it risks infidelity to the Other in the plurality of Others whom we attempt to commemorate or memorialize. The subjectivity of mourning, then, is that we cannot mourn the Other in the Other's absolute singularity. We have a tendency to reduce the Other to an interiority of our own memory of the Other which, of course, can never give vent to the vastness of the singularity of the Other. At the same time, our mourning of the Other cannot be separated from our own anxiety about our own death as well as our anxiety about our own continuing existence.

But perhaps the concern here is slightly misdirected. For if the mourning is truly to be between us, the living, then the rite of commemoration or the memorial serves its purpose in acting as a place or event of collective memory between us, and a way of preserving that memory for the future. It provides a presence of the Other. The continuing narrative of one who has died also needs its place. Perhaps by embedding the memory of the Other in stone, we escape some of the failings of mourning. How then for the possibility of collective mourning?

Collective Mourning

If individual mourning of a unique and close relationship is impossible, we can hold little hope that collective mourning will be any more successful. How do we mourn collectively? Let us consider a recent event that we might think of as calling for public, collective mourning. Consider the December 14, 2012 Newtown, Connecticut shooting by a teenager with automatic weapons of twenty elementary school children and six adults in the school building. The public in its fascinated horror demanded of the Newtown families who lost loved ones that they mourn publicly. We demanded, as we so often do in such tragic cases, that they speak to the media outlets and express their grief. We expressed to each other our shock and grief for the families affected. Why? As Camus would say, we were bored. It has been our "little transcendence, [our] aperitif."[11] We wrap it up in the language of collective mourning suggesting that we are all horrified and that we all mourn the loss of those twenty-six individuals, and yet those twenty-six deaths became a rallying point for a political agenda on both sides. We did not hesitate to use those deaths to promote gun control or the placement of armed guards in every school. The very public response to these deaths facilitates the failure of mourning. We fail in all three ways that Derrida has outlined: we fail to honor the singularity of each of those twenty-six deaths, we reduce the dead to symbols of political ills, we immediately reduce their deaths to something "like Columbine," and we wrap ourselves in concern for the safety of our own children or school children generally.

We might also consider an event that could reasonably be held to have had more public impact, such as the destruction of the World Trade Center on September 11, 2001. We could say that 9/11 was a terrorist act directed at the United States and we as citizens suffered because of it. The United States was momentarily brought to its knees in shock and trauma. Our demand that we are traumatized, that the act be politically symbolic, robs those who lost loved ones of their mourning. If the possibility of mourning is, as Derrida suggests, about mourning the singularity then the families and friends of those who died were prevented from doing so because they were prevented from bearing witness since others wanted to bear witness in their place. But when those others do so, it is not witness to the singularity, it is merely symbolic. Imagine the President of the United States standing at the site of ground zero expressing his outrage. It was a symbolic gesture that was not about making the Other present in her Otherness. We cannot attempt to make the unknown others present, cannot even attempt to bear witness in our utter ignorance of them. We must leave that to those who experienced their singularity and allow them to serve out their duty to their loved one in whatever way they can.

So often collective mourning reflects our boredom. It reflects our desire to be attached to a tragedy for the sake of self-concern. Or, we might say it leads either to the symbolic use or the political use or both of the dead whom we claim to mourn. It suffers the same impossibilities that Derrida ascribed to individual mourning. Collectively, we cannot honor the singularity and alterity of an Other. Collectively, we concern ourselves with the political ramifications of the loss and the anxiety that accompanies being those who remain and are, perhaps, responsible for attempting to prevent the same kind of thing from happening again. Collectively, we are infidels to the unique deaths of unique Others.

What, then, is the relationship between collective memory, collective mourning and the work of monuments? Do monuments assist us in the work of mourning? Why do we traditionally expect the embeddedness of the dead in a place and why do we return to such places as an act of mourning? Given the tension between the intersubjectivity of our memories and the impossibility of mourning the Other as a unique Other, how do we understand the role of place, tradition, and memory with respect to death? How does the failure of mourning apply to place, to monuments of stone and simple grave stones that we erect in memory, to commemorate or memorialize?

PLACES OF MOURNING

In terms of constructed place, graves and cemeteries are perhaps among the most common. These kinds of places are constructed as part of the Western tradition of mourning. It raises the question why we believe that place is an important part of mourning. It seems to be important in ways beyond the erecting of a stone marker in a graveyard or a place to lay to rest a loved one since we visit those places. We return to graves of ancestors, we visit memorials to fallen soldiers. And even though we perhaps do so less now than in ages past, we seem to believe there is some value in doing so.

Returning to the Cemetery

If we consider the notion of our infidelity to the Other in mourning, we can query how any one monument can do justice to the deaths of those it memorializes or even to the war, battle or event it memorializes. Monuments, like graves, are repetitions and in their repetitions appear their infidelity. How can the statue to the soldiers of Iwo Jima inspire in us the memory of the singular soldiers whose loss we should mourn when those soldiers are not only merely symbolic in the monument itself, but are also repeated in the soldiers standing near the Vietnam Veterans Memorial and the Korean War Memorial and so many World War I Memorials in each little town across the United States and Europe? Each of the deaths associated with these wars and with the generations of these soldiers is singular. No death is the same, no war the same, no life lived the same and in many respects they are all radically and completely different. On what grounds, then, do we lump them together, speak of "the war dead" and "The greatest generation" without violating the singularity and uniqueness of each?

But for so many military families, it is conceived as an honor to bury a loved one in a military cemetery, especially Arlington Cemetery where all the graves are lined up perfectly and each looks exactly like the other. Yet, we mark the grave with a name and a rank to identify this soldier as opposed to any other. We know that name and rank does not encapsulate the individual's life. It does not reveal to us the more-than-soldier, the father, the piano player, the business school failure, the pasta lover. Likewise, the existence of the national monument to the symbolic dead soldier is not adequate to any soldier's singularity. No grave or memorial ever could be and to ask it to be is to expect too much.

It must be that we expect something else of graves and memorials such that we continue to erect them. Karsten Harries suggests that "The grave gestures toward the solidarity of mortals, even as it shatters such solidarity by facing each individual with his or her own mortality. . . Bringing us home to ourselves, [the] grave at the same time lets us feel homeless in the everyday with all its familiar cares and concerns, bids us attend to the essential: our one death-bound life."[12] As Derrida has reminded us, these monuments are always between us the living. They cannot be "for" the dead. And yet, we seem to erect them for the dead. Is the impulse one of attempting to exteriorize that which can only be interior? Is it a move to create a place that belongs to all of us and is outside of any one of us? Is it an attempt to concretize what can otherwise be only the faulty palimpsest of memory?

If this were truly the case, then it seems that any grave would do. And to a point, perhaps any grave will do. Simply entering a graveyard can be an opportunity for reflection on the meaning of death or the meaning of life. Graveyards are often beautiful, manicured, places that are peaceful and removed from the busyness of the everyday. But we normally do not go to graveyards for the simple effect of them. We may, of course, go for the aesthetic effect, but we most frequently go to visit the grave of someone in particular, someone we knew, maybe someone famous, or someone related to us or our family.

Recently, for example, my family returned to my husband's country of birth, the United Kingdom. We spent two full days visiting sites of family heritage, the birth home of his father, and the graves of grandparents and great grandparents. In many cases these were not people my husband had ever met, but it was important to both he and his parents that our two young sons should see these places. It gives one the sense that these graves were not placed for those who died, but for those of us who live so that we may have a place to go in order to contemplate the loss as well as the heritage—what has been received from these people whom we have never met. In cases of people we knew, the grave serves as a kind of mnemonic device of our loved one and our time together. But for ancestral graves, to visit the grave is to call to mind the family connection, to place one in contact with a community of others—both those others who also visit the grave, the other living relatives, but also those others whom Al Lingis describes as "those with whom we have nothing in common."[13] This foray to the grave of ancestors connects us with those of our family in our living, but also provides for a community of all in death, a community beyond clan and nation, beyond creed and race to the community of mortal beings.

It is not just cemeteries to which we return, however. We often make pilgrimages to places of our past in memory of the deceased or to get in touch with our heritage by "returning" to places we have never actually been before. Visiting such places allows us to form a connection to the places of our ancestors, thereby helping us to incorporate the family heritage into our own narrative. But how indeed does that happen?

Returning to the Death of Our Past

In his Memoir *Running in the Family,* Michael Ondaatje describes his return to his native home of Sri Lanka motivated by the death of his father who gasped the word "Asia" at his death. Ondaatje comments that his journey home to the places and people of his past was due to his desire to "touch them into words."[14] This return to a place rife with memories is coupled with the narratives that are shared about his family and his ancestors. Even in the absence of the people, the place calls them to mind and the memories come unbidden. It is this spontaneous connection between place and narrative, between memory and mourning that I would like to investigate here.

Ondaatje is not alone in the desire to return to a place of memory to retrieve narrative as an act of mourning. Journeys home are often made to bear witness to the dying and as pilgrimages in the aftermath of death sometimes for burials or the commitment of ashes. Cemeteries become places we return to in memory of those who have gone before us, to whom we are indebted for our traditions. But also, people frequently want to be buried in their native country or their hometown. Cemetery plots are purchased well in advance for all members of a family to be buried in adjoining plots no matter how far flung their lives may be. These homecomings are not the typical picture that is presented of a romantic association with home, or the joyous reunion of family. They are often fraught with pain, uneasiness, and loss. They are *always* uncanny.

Normally when we think of narrative in terms of self-identity or communal identity, we think of it in terms of providing unity for a fractured temporality. The narrative organizes and clarifies our temporal experiences. What is not so frequently remarked upon is that the narrative also organizes our spatial experiences. With every narrative plot, there is a narrative setting. Plot does not just happen, it happens somewhere. And the somewhere, insofar as it structures our knowledge also structures our plot which means that the setting is not merely something objective from which we are separated. The plot doesn't just happen in a place, it happens in this particular place which is just as important and influential for the experience and the memory as anything else. The places of experiences are living elements of those experiences which is why they can serve to make those experiences present in their absence when we replace ourselves in them. Our habitual places structure our knowledge insofar as they provide us with an embodied style of being in the world that manifests itself in the constitutional act in such a way that certain things are salient while others are dormant. This is a way of constitution that includes the valuation of the salient which is why it is salient. Such constitutional factors are passed along from generation to generation in the place and because of the place. The stories we tell, then, have to do with how the world is constituted and what we know of the world cannot be separated from how it is constituted. Narrative helps us to organize the spaces and places in which we find ourselves according to what aspects of those places make themselves felt by us.

This does not get passed along unchanged, nor does it remain unchanged even for an individual, however. Just as with every narrative there is an element of mimesis involved, so too with narrative there is a platial re-setting that occurs. According to Paul Ricoeur, any narrative transpires with a gap between the living of an event and the narrating of the event. The telling is not the living, the living is not the telling. But in the telling a particular perspective is taken up vis-à-vis the living such that the telling can only be performed from an already pre-formed position, style, and genre. This can be said, too, of the place of living and can, thus, explain part of the reason for the importance of returning to ancestral or childhood places. The narrative can reveal place and the place can reveal narrative.

As Jeff Malpas suggests, "The past cannot be prised away from the places—that is, from objects and persons as they interact within particular spatio-temporal regions—with respect to which that past is established. This is so with respect both to the past that can be recounted as part of a personal biography and to the past that is articulated through communal narrative and history (and neither, of course, is wholly independent of the other)."[15]

The recollection of the past that often takes place through places is frequently romanticized—we wish to recapture, nostalgically our past through a visit to grandma's old house or the old school we used to go to, but it is important to recognize that pilgrimages can also take place to sites of trauma or tragedy. Such pilgrimages are hardly nostalgic, but play a slightly different role in perhaps incorporating the trauma into one's narrative of self or more concretely into the communal narrative. We can read of Eastern Europeans who were chased from their homes during the Nazi era who return to see the places they were forced to abandon. The act of returning to the place serves as a way of reincorporating that bit of the past into a more unified narrative of self.[16]

The return to places of the past or the pilgrimage to places of heritage or even to places once important to a lost loved one cannot entirely reconcile us with the loss. They can, however, contribute to a kind of knowledge of someone or a relearning of one's past that takes place through the narratives that are inherently connected with the places. This means also that the experience of loss is inseparable from the experience of place. In returning to a place, we do not recapture that person with whom we shared the place, nor do we recapture the time. Because it is mimetic there is a gap between the living of it and the re-encounter with the place. What we do is contribute to the narrative experience of ourselves. It is to come face to face with the march of time, with the loss of a younger self or a loved one, and which are always juxtaposed with the movement away from the place, into old age, into change. Again, as Malpas notes "Not only, then, do the places and spaces of human dwelling change and disintegrate, but those places and spaces are themselves disclosed only through processes that bring change and alteration in their wake—indeed, such places and spaces are disclosed only in relation to movement, agency and, one might say, to change."[17] Change of place is change of self and change of self is change of place.

Cemeteries have pretensions to a life eternal, which is an attempt to deny the change we have just been thinking through. Some even think of cemeteries as the preparatory ground for bodily resurrection. If such is the case, however, we fail to recognize the ways in which to be who and what we are is to be creatures who are in place, for whom places characterize our identities and our very experiences. To escape being in place is to cease to be human and to seek to return to one's homeland to be buried or to say goodbye is a matter of acknowledging the place-boundness that composes the narrative of one's self and cannot be separated from the loss of place that also composes the narrative of one's self. Thus, we turn to the uncanny, the way in which being bound to place creates for us a paradoxical sense of homelessness.

Should we simply abandon gravestones and monuments as failures? They are after all simply that-they fail to singularize, they fail to do justice to the unique Other, they fail to mourn or to remember. What then do they do that makes them worth having? What I would argue is that monuments in their relationship to the earth and to the world allow for the hermeneutic process that can make us aware of the impossibility of resisting memory, of the inevitability of subjectivity, and of the present towards the future. They can make us attentive to the changing landscape of nation, of war, of heroism, of family. Monuments allow us to recognize the palimpsest of memory that is transcribed onto the palimpsest of the earth and that calls for the careful hermeneutic approach that requires us to acknowledge that which cannot be made present, cannot be interiorized, and cannot be symbolically captured in stone. While the monument can be a stand-in, it cannot be a replacement. It points out to us, if we are attentive, our own forgetting, our own inability to make the past present, to project our present into the future, and to stop the layers of time, memory, and stone.

So while the impulse for monuments is about maintaining the past in the present there is an effort to preserve that past in the image of the present. We construct the memorial for our time that will last for all time. The messianic time of Benjamin and Derrida, however, is for the future when the present too will pass on into something new and different. Monuments are not static and in their dynamism, they suffer, or perhaps celebrate, reinterpretation by others for whom the mourning is even further removed.

Perhaps what our monuments and memorials are achieving is not so much about mourning, but as Derrida might say opening up the possibility of a political space of accommodation. He stresses in his essay on Lyotard, that the Athenians used the funeral oration as a "foreclosure of mourning by lifting death up, sublating it in the fulfillment and glory of the 'beautiful death,'"[18] We can see the same functioning in monuments and memorials of our own time. This places the monument within the political context instead of simply the context of mourning. And here we return to the subjectivity and the hermeneutic moment of the experience of any monument. For what the monument speaks of is both the time when it was erected as well as of our own time. It draws forth memory and marks a time and place of both the then and the now. It is the inscribing of an event. For in spite of the death of the Other of the grave or the Others of the monument or memorial, here we stand at this event of viewing the memorial and in this event we are thrown back upon our own subjectivity in projection towards the event of future generations who will mourn us and will understand the monuments and memorials in light of the political elements of their own time. The repetition of the event is both the event of death and the event of witnessing and mourning the death which is no less genuine in bearing the marks of our own future death within it. This is our responsibility to the dead as well as our responsibility to the living and the yet to come. The palimpsest of memory that is grounded in the palimpsest of place is what makes this possible.

What we have seen here is that we mourn without knowing. We mourn without awareness that mourning is impossible. We mourn in an attempt to secure ourselves and not really for the Other at all. This is what Derrida describes as our narcissism and it is in part why our mourning fails to be mourning and why our monuments fail to be about the past and are instead about the present and ourselves. What this calls forth from us, however, is a particular attentiveness to the hermeneutic process of engaging the past through our present in the recognition of the palimpsest of memory, place, and tradition.

So, while on the one hand monuments and memorials are utter failures that idealize or make merely symbolic the Other while failing to recognize our own role in the preservation and production of memories of the Other into the future. On the other hand, we should not stop erecting them because of this failure. Instead, we should erect them in our efforts to bear witness and to preserve memory while always taking care to be as attentive to the idealizing, interiorizing, and infidelity that happens even as we deposit an external marker on the earth. We must engage in the possibility of the impossible as Derrida might say or, as Heidegger might have it, we must think what we are doing.

Constructed Places or Lack of Place

We have seen that, in spite of their failure, it is not unreasonable to construct a place specifically to remember those who have died and we do so often as a matter of course. In the case of collective mourning through memorials, we realize that they are quite often not constructed at the site of death, but are constructed in public places where they serve to reinforce not only public, communal values, but to emphasize our collective loss. We are inclined to wonder whether there are other differences, however, between the monuments and memorials that are erected in the town square and its equivalent, or the places that are deliberately (or not) left unmarked. Such places as District 6 come to mind, but so do places in the deserts of Arizona where Mexican labor seekers die hungry and alone in the desert.

Why is it that Toni Morrison thinks a bench is so necessary as a reminder of those unnamed millions who died on the Middle Passage? Unlike other memorials, a bench does not identify particular persons by name. It does not even seem to invoke our discomfort since benches are meant to provide comfort as a place to sit. But Morrison's impulse is not strange; it is the impulse to provide a place for those who are otherwise placeless. It is meant to provide a place of memory for those who would otherwise be unremembered. Like the War Memorials of the public squares, the bench memorials (for there are roughly ten of them in the United States and France) must function as interruptions of the everyday fabric of our environment. They cannot mark the actual places of death; they cannot even mark the places from whence all those Africans came. The fact that there is no place for the victims of the Middle Passage is both the cause and the effect of the lack of collective memory of the event. Having been separated from their originary place, the slaves had no foundation upon which to create their communal recollection. At the same time, the lack of support for their community on U.S. soil restricted their ability to create a place here to allow for the preservation of memory. In being separated from place they are also separated from their narrative support. Narratives that do exist are impoverished due to their lack of place, thus identity and tradition are weakened.

How much different it would be if there were a kind of Ellis Island equivalent for those who came across the Middle Passage. What kind of heritage might have been preserved there that could be transferred across generations. What Toni Morrison's benches attempt to do is to provide a beginning place for those narratives, to give support to the community identity that can be buffered by those places. That community is dispersed, so the places too must be dispersed.

On the other hand, what does the lack of constructed place mean for District 6 which was deliberately allowed to remain fallow without a publicly constructed place?[19] District 6 was a neighborhood in the center of Cape Town, South Africa. It was a thriving residential neighborhood originally inhabited from the 1870s by immigrants and former slaves as well as Malay people. By the 1950s the neighborhood was still thriving and lively with a wide variety of peoples living there. It was populated mostly by colored people but also included Malays and black residents as wells as whites and Afrikaans. These divergent populations lived in harmony and the neighborhood was prosperous. Apartheid policies, however, dictated that interracial neighborhoods needed to be dismantled because they led to conflict and strife. Thus, in 1966 the apartheid government declared the area a whites-only zone and began the removal of its residents relocating them in most cases to the Cape Flats Township. By the mid-1980s roughly 60,000 people had been removed from District 6 and the houses bulldozed. Bowing to international pressure, the apartheid government was never able to develop the land. For over twenty years this prime real estate in the middle of Cape Town was left undeveloped and for many served as an ever-present reminder of the horrors of apartheid and as a way of mourning the tragedy of the destruction of a vibrant community.[20] This mourning is not about mourning the specific people necessarily as it is mourning the community and its place. The place that supported the community was destroyed and the community dissipated because of it.

Another constructive example is the destruction of the ancient Buddhist statues in Bamiyan, Afghanistan. The Taliban blew them up in 2001 as a deliberate act. One statue was the tallest of its kind in the world reaching a height of 175 feet. It was a standing Buddha carved into the side of a cliff and dated back to the sixth century. The dynamite reduced the statue to a pile of rubble. In defiance of international calls to preserve the statues, the Taliban committed what has since been called a crime against culture. Although the Taliban claimed that all they had destroyed was rock and that the motivation of the destruction was to remove any pre-Islamic elements within their society, and finally that the statues were false idols that are prohibited by the Islamic faith, the fact that they felt the need to destroy the statues speaks of a different motivation. The destruction indicates the power that the Taliban attributed to them in the passing along of a Buddhist tradition. In spite of their denials, the Taliban recognized the power of this place as a preservation of the culture of Buddhism.

Since the initial destruction of the Buddhas in 2001, work has begun to rebuild the statues by mixing the original pieces that had been shattered by dynamite with modern materials. There is much controversy surrounding this project as many believe that the two stalls in which the Buddha's stood ought to remain empty as a monument to the brutality and the fanaticism of the Taliban.

This example shows us that in spite of the change to the place which was in fact quite radical, the place itself is still deeply marked with the tradition now of Buddhism and of the Taliban. The earth carries both traditions forward layer upon layer. The narrative alone of the Silk Road and its importance to Buddhism, or the destruction of the statues and what that means about the Taliban is supported and enhanced by the physical place of Bamiyan, Afghanistan. The community of the Taliban is supported by this place as is the community of Buddhists worldwide. This is what was acknowledged by those who protested the destruction of the monuments. It is also what was feared by the Taliban.

These examples exhibit the way in which narrative is deeply embedded with place. The heritage of the District 6 community was deeply affected by the loss of the place of the community and in spite of the fact that the land was left undeveloped, the community's place was so radically altered that the community narrative and heritage itself suffered. Much the same holds in the case of the destruction of the Buddhist statues in Afghanistan. What we also see in these examples is the way in which the ultimate resurrection of these places of memory allows for the sedimentation of the memories of the past and multiple traditions that get carried along. We can think of the power of places in terms of two prongs of remembrance that Ricoeur identifies and which we will elaborate upon in the next chapter. One prong is testimony. The other is archive. Ricoeur describes testimony as the presence of the past while archive is described as the presence of the future. I argue that monuments take up a position between testimony and archive due to their palimpsestic character. Monuments that are erected in the place of a death or historically significant event serve that in between most effectively in the sense that they retrieve the past of that place while also projecting our preservation of that past into the future through the monument. Other monuments such as Morrison's benches or even the Vietnam Veterans Memorial weigh one of those prongs (archive) more heavily than the other since the place upon which those monuments rest lacks the testimonial power. Such places still serve the archival role, but are restricted in their testimonial role. We could think of this in much the same way that the Holocaust Memorial in Boston, as powerful as it is, pales compared to the Holocaust Memorial at Buchenwald. Buchenwald, in the place of the atrocities of the Holocaust, carries the testimonial and archival power, while the Memorial in Boston carries only the archival power. The palimpsests of memory and tradition are embedded in the palimpsest of the place. The narrative is deeply dependent upon place.

NARRATIVITY AND ITS LIMITS: THE NECESSITY OF PLACE

So, why do we make pilgrimages? What is the draw of going home? The answer lies in the undeniable connection between place and narrative. We seek out the places of our prior others, our near and dear others, the others of our own past, for the sake of our own identity, our own narrative, as well as for the sake of the communion with others that is always an uneasy communion, an incomplete union, which fundamentally reminds us of the frailty of our own being and the frailty of our community with others be they singular others or multiple, communal others. Immigrants who travel back to their homeland one last time before they die, or who request to be returned to their homeland to be buried seem to recognize that their own narrative is tied to the land of their past, to that foundational home of their own existence. To return is to embrace the uncanniness of that home in the final stage of one's own narrative.

Martin Heidegger describes the uncanny in *Being and Time* as intimately connected with anxiety. I will not rehash all the details of Heidegger's account of anxiety except to say that he claims primarily that anxiety for Dasein has to do with Dasein's own fundamental being-towards-death. In "What is Metaphysics?" he writes, "in anxiety, we say, 'one feels ill at ease'"; "one feels something uncanny."[21] For Heidegger the desire to cast ourselves away from the anxiety, into a home is always in tension with our homelessness.[22] When we question our own traditions we engage in a process that makes us uneasy. To live in this uneasiness, in the uncanny is to refuse the comfort of traditional ways of thinking and to engage in questioning. What this also means, though, is that the process of questioning is always at the same time an attempt to recover a home, to bring us back to a home where we can find comfort. To be homeless is still to be bound up with home. For, to be genuinely at home in this world, one must affirm the homelessness that is essential to us. It means to recognize the essential uncanniness of our dwelling that can only be thought in relation to a home, but it is a home that withdraws whenever we seek to secure it for ourselves. For our project, then, to be confronted with the uncanniness of the graveyard or the altered cityscape or neighborhood of our youth, is at the same time to be connected to the home. What is that connection? I would suggest that the narrative of memory allows us to mimetically represent the home through the uncanniness of our homelessness in the place of the home. The narrative attempts to capture the home of the past while at the same time knowing that any narrative is incomplete, insufficient, and uncanny.

When we endeavor to remember those who have gone before us, we seek to return to the places of importance, we seek a home. Graveyards give us places to remember. Impromptu memorials give us places to remember. We make pilgrimages to places of importance in order to call to mind the past. I would suggest, however, that it is precisely due to the place-bound nature of this type of remembering that makes the homecoming uncanny. For the places change and what we discover upon making the pilgrimage is that all is not how we expected it to be or how we remember it. The tree where we loved to meet and play has been chopped down and paved over. The house where grandpa was born has been torn down, and the school that grandma used to walk to has been added on to. With the change in place, we sense the temporal frailty of the narrative of the family and the community, we realize the transitoriness of our presence on this earth, but perhaps we also realize the great power of the narrative of self and community that is tied to these places. That narrative allows us to say "remember when this hairdresser's shop was great-grandpa's pork butcher shop? And after that it was an X-rated movie dealer?" The place in its particularity also shows to us the narrative of the community in its constantly evolving state—1940s middle-class British families gave way to fractured immigrant middle-eastern families that gave way to a strong working-class Islamic community. The narrative of self that we think of as transpiring for the sake of identity is one that cannot be separated off from place and relies, therefore upon place even while place cannot be secured from the passage of time. Narrative and place are intertwined in structuring the temporality of the subject such that a homecoming is always a narrative return to a place that is never without the uneasiness of the temporal frailty that is human.

However much a return to one's ancestral home or the graves of one's forbearers is intertwined with the narrative of one's self as well as one's community, the experience is at the same time the quiet reminder of one's loss of self and loss of world and others. For, no matter how important the places of one's past may have been, in returning to them, we note that they have not remained unchanged, they have not waited for us, they are altered and are indifferent to our memories. Even those places that have a fundamental influence upon our manner of constitution of the world such that our embodied experience is familiar in the feeling of the dry air upon our skin, or the organization of the pans in the kitchen of our childhood home, for instance, even those places have been altered in other kinds of ways such that we cannot relive our childhood in them. Those with whom we shared the streets walk on different streets and do not even know enough to miss us. We recognize that the places that are so instrumental in the formation of our knowledge and our way of being-in-the-world are oblivious to us in our particularity. While the mark of place can sometimes be quite deep upon us, our mark upon the place is erased or buried so deeply as to be unnoticeable to the everyday. This too is the uncanny.

And what does the place have to do with the work of mourning? I have argued here that mourning includes the process of recognizing the changing face of places that are deeply intertwined with the person or identity that is lost. We mourn our own past and our own loss when we return to such places. The places in which our loved one is embedded are revisited as part of the mourning process. We begin to recognize that the places, too, change—Iowa City, Iowa is not what it was when I was there as an undergraduate. The people with whom I spent my time are mourned, not because all of them are dead, but because many of them are in new places unknown to me. They were a part of my everyday life in the past, but my life too has changed and moved on.

Like Ondaatje, we may make a journey home as an act of mourning. What do we seek to find? I have suggested here that the homecoming is on the one hand an effort to fill in the narrative of self and family through experience of places of memory. At the same time, this homecoming is uncanny precisely because of the change of place and the hermeneutic process that recognizes any narrative as well as any place is always read or told anew. Narrative identity, whether we speak of an individual, a family, or a community, in part because it is associated and imbued with place, is never constant, never static, never a completely restful home. As Ondaatje muses at the end of his memoir, "[b]ut the book again is incomplete. In the end all your children move among the scattered acts and memories with no more clues."[23] The narrative and the places are always incomplete only giving a fraction of the communal identity, the communal memories, but with the places and the narratives we have no option but to be uncannily content.

Specifically in response to the issues of mourning, we begin to recognize that even in death, place becomes important to the sense of who one is. This is, of course, not strictly for one's own sense of identity, but for the narrative of one's life in its intersubjectivity. In the following section, we will explore the limitations of a theory of narrative identity in the sense that in not recognizing the role of place in the construction and maintenance of identity as well as the way in which such an identity is like a palimpsest, a theory of narrative identity alone cannot give us the truth of who we are.

Ed Casey finds this kind of talk of narrativity to be troubling. He claims that such accounts of the connection between place and narrative ultimately favor the dimension of temporality and reduce the importance of place. And while that may be the case to some degree in what we are about the see from Ricoeur, it does not mean that place is ignored altogether nor need it be ignored in discussions of narrative. Casey seems to overlook the way in which narrative makes possible an understanding of place that is dynamic, and that the dynamism of place makes possible the alterations of narrative. Where Casey wants to focus on the perdurance of place, I would argue that the notion of the palimpsest helps us to understand the complex intertwining of place and memory. For sometimes narrative helps us to make sense of the changes in a place of memory while at other times the resistance to change in a place helps to keep a narrative intact and helps us to call to mind aspects of a narrative that might otherwise have been lost. Each helps to keep the other from fading away, reinforcing the memory and tradition by covering over some aspects at some times and allowing those erasures to shine through at other times.

In his essay "Narrative Identity," Paul Ricoeur asserts three primary things. 1) self-knowledge is a matter of interpretation, 2) interpretation finds narrative "a privileged mediation," and 3) the mediation borrows from history making identity a matter of historical fiction.[24] Ricoeur claims that the "narrative constructs the durable character of an individual, which one can call his or her narrative identity, in constructing the sort of dynamic identity proper to the plot which creates the identity of the protagonist in the story."[25] Ricoeur stresses the importance of the plot since it is primarily through the plot that the discordance of concordance can be discerned. In other words, what Ricoeur is pointing to is the change through plot that is still brought to bear on the sameness of a self through narrative identity. In discussing this point further, Ricoeur makes clear that the modern literary narrative which directs itself to the self-alienation of its characters still relies upon the narrative for continuity. Without the narrative, there wouldn't be continuity and there would be no ability to recognize self-alienation of a character. At the same time, even Ricoeur recognizes that the narrative depends upon the invariant of the embodied condition of its characters. As he claims, "the presupposed embodied condition constitutes an insurpassable mediation between the self and the world . . . In other words, the imaginary variations in the literary field have for their horizon our unavoidable earthly condition."[26]

Further, as Ricoeur's magnum opus, *Time and Narrative,* would suggest, narrative is related to time, for it is through narrative that the times of the self are connected to one another and brought to identity. Ricoeur identifies time as the primary characteristic of the human condition. He sees the temporality of experience as common to both history and fiction as mediated by narrativity. We use narrative for both fictional stories that transpire through a temporality, but we also use narrative for historical accounts of the past that unfold as stories.[27] Narrative plays the role of connection between the temporality of experience both as past and as present.

We can see quite clearly here that Ricoeur in stressing temporality overlooks the fundamental role of place. Granted, he does acknowledge the embodied nature of the character/person, but he does not develop it to the extent that he develops the sense of temporality. It is odd that Ricoeur so blatantly overlooks the platial elements since even in the examples that he uses they are important. In discussing the irreducibility of numerical identity to qualitative identity and vice versa, Ricoeur offers the example of someone who must be identified in a criminal lineup as the suspect of a crime. He indicates that it is important for that person to look the same as he or she did at the moment of the crime in order to be identified as the same person and therefore as the suspect. But what is apparent in this is that the person must also be identified according to having been in the same place as the criminal activity. Who of us is not familiar with the crime story detective's question of where one was at the time of the crime? In the lineup, one compares this person here and now with the person who was there and then. The place identity is just as important as the temporal identity.

For Ricoeur, the ability to secure identity depends in large part upon a principle of permanence in time. However, he rejects attempts to reduce this to a substratum of substance. Instead, he relates it to the question "who" as opposed to "what." It is not what subsists through time that interests him, but rather who subsists. This who has to do with a permanence of character across time and this is what can be established through narrative. This is also the moment that is important for a question of permanence across place. For, it is not simply "where" that becomes important, but the bigger question of the cultural where which we might frame as "whence." This is not unlike the distinction between a kind of objective space and the subjective-cultural place that formulates our character and not just an anonymous space in which we find ourselves. Place is not simply the setting for our lives, it is constructive of the character of our lives.

Ricoeur uses narrative to conceive of both the mediation between sameness as idem and sameness as ipse that he views as character, but he also wants to stress that idem and ipse can be held at a distance from one another through narrative that allows selfhood to be free from simple sameness. This he views in terms of the responsibility for keeping one's word which is also related to one's character, but not in terms of a reductive sameness. If we then consider this on the level of place, we can see that there is a similarity. The place I am from contributes to my character is the sense of both sameness and selfhood, but it does so in different ways. In terms of sameness, I am the same character who was born in Illinois, and grew up in Nebraska. In terms of selfhood, this matters to a great degree in defining who I am, but cannot confine me since I am engaged in the process of renewal and critique as we saw in chapter 2 above.

What this draws attention to is that Ricoeur's position links any self to the heritage of tradition that comes from prior generations and to a community of others. For Ricoeur, "it is only in the telling of our individual stories, over time, that a durable character becomes recognizable as belonging to a certain family, locality, tradition and culture-all of which are enmeshed in a complex web of prior stories that make up the narrative heritage of our great works, epics, tragedies, dramas, and novels handed down to us by our culture."[28] Ricoeur goes on to describe the way in which the narrative telling of oneself provides the continuity for all the discordant elements of one's life such that one's character is developed through the stories told. Character is the sedimentation of the stories told by earlier generations as well. One's character is plot. By character, Ricoeur means, "the set of lasting dispositions by which a person is recognized."[29] In this way, the notion of character serves as a limit point. This means that it makes it possible for one to act "out of character" while still being the same self, but also allows us to identify that action as being "out of character." There is a stability that is offered through the acquisition of habits and identifications that does not eliminate the possibility of innovation. Ricoeur suggests that narrative plays a role in this position between the lasting, distinctive traits by which we recognize a person or community, and the traits which are open to change. Narrative makes possible the redeploying of historically sedimented traits for innovation. He argues that "it will be the task of a reflection on narrative identity to balance, on one side, the immutable traits which this identity owes to the anchoring of the history of a life in a character and, on the other, those traits which tend to separate the identity of the self from the sameness of character."[30]

Ricoeur raises the idea of keeping one's promises as a juncture at which the identity as sameness and identity as self diverge. He describes the identity required for the act of keeping one's word to be one that opens a polarity between two models of permanence in time which relate to identity as sameness and identity as self. He argues that the mediation between these two senses of identity is to be found in the sphere of temporality and that it is this position in between that is occupied by narrative identity. "We will not be surprised to see narrative identity oscillate between two limits: a lower limit, where permanence in time expresses the confusion of idem and ipse; and an upper limit, where the ipse poses the question of its identity without the aid and support of the idem."[31]

Again, what is stressed throughout this discussion for Ricoeur is the temporality of the connection that is maintained through the telling of stories. What is not stressed is the role of the places of those stories and the embodied way in which constitution of the world is characterized by the sedimentation of traditions that mark the places of our world. Even in Ricoeur's analysis of the paradoxical examples provided by Derek Parfit, Ricoeur stresses the fact that the person in Parfit's thought experiments is teleported and that this is an alteration of temporality.[32] But what is teleportation except an alteration of place? Identity can primarily become a problem in these thought experiments because of the change of place that expresses the change of time.[33]

When describing narrative in detail, Ricoeur stresses two things: character and plot. By now, surely we recognize that to do so is to undermine a third fundamental and necessary part of any narrative and that is setting. It is important to remember that when we speak of setting, we are not simply speaking of a place where the action of a plot transpires for the characters. Setting is much more integral to the plot and the characters than simply a place of action. It is that which contributes to the meaning of the action for the characters. It is equally as dynamic in identity as plot and character. Finally, Ricoeur does acknowledge that it is necessary to "take into account the topology underlying the change of 'place'—initial and terminal places of transfer—on the basis of which one can then speak of a 'sequence of performances.'"[34] But in this regard, Ricoeur seems to understand the role of place here as simply denoting a change between one element of action within a plot and another. He does not seem to take seriously the way in which place affects the very sense of the action and the characters.

For Ricoeur, it is the correlation between action and character that provides for "dialectic *internal* to the character which is the exact corollary of the dialectic of concordance and discordance developed by the emplotment of action."[35] What this means for Ricoeur is that the identity of the character, her singularity is drawn from the unity of a temporality that is distinct from others. The discordance is occasioned by the events yet to happen that might not be entirely in keeping with the already established unity. So the synthesis of these two provides for the identity of the character through the narrative. Again, I would suggest here that Ricoeur has completely overlooked the role of the embodiment of the character that emplaces that character within a dynamic setting that is equally at play. If, as we have seen in previous chapters, the place of home is written on the body and is carried with one in the act of constitution of both that which is conceived as normal and that which is conceived as abnormal, it gives to the narrative yet another layer of synthesis of concordance and discordance. The home as it is written on the body is not static and in its dynamism it underwrites the narrative of the action that synthesizes the concordant and discordant of the character.

Ricoeur acknowledges one level of place when addressing the importance of corporeality, but he does not dwell on it and seems to view it as more of a substructure than an active part of character. He writes, "Insofar as the body as one's own is a dimension of oneself, the imaginative variations around the corporeal condition are variations on the self and its selfhood. Furthermore, in virtue of the mediating function of the body as one's own in the structure of being in the world, the feature of selfhood belonging to corporeality is extended to that of the world as it is inhabited corporeally."[36] What Ricoeur seems to be suggesting is that the world is an extension of the self rather than the two being so deeply intertwined that they mutually write upon each other as I have been suggesting.

Ricoeur identifies "The Earth" as something more than a planet. It is, rather, "our corporeal anchoring in the world."[37] Perhaps he begins to get at the interconnection here in making the distinction between earth and world in much the same way that Husserl or Heidegger might, but Ricoeur provides no further explanation leaving us with questions about precisely what that relationship might be and how important the corporeality-world connection is to selfhood.

Ricoeur stresses the difference between a literary fiction and a science fiction. Literary fiction depends upon a notion of selfhood that requires the foundation for self in the corporeal condition that allows for the mediation between self and world. Technological fiction or science fiction does not acknowledge that necessary foundation and instead focuses on sameness where the brain is understood to be the locus of identity. So, literary fiction concerns selfhood while science fiction concerns sameness. The difference as Ricoeur sees it is that literary fiction recognizes the role of embodiment and world whereas science fiction sees those elements as alterable without significant effect. Still, Ricoeur has not underscored exactly why world would have importance to narrative other than as simply the setting for the action that supports self. He also claims that the corporeal and terrestrial conditions are invariant, thereby providing stability for a narrative identity. It is here that I would like to introduce some nuance into Ricoeur's position, for as we have seen in previous chapters through the idea of the palimpsest, neither the corporeality nor the terrestriality are invariant. There is some stability provided, but they too are overwritten and erased in ways that make them fluid. As a consequence, identity of selfhood too is fluid.

It is interesting that in summing up this discussion, Ricoeur appeals to the intertwining of the two poles of narrative identity. The first pole is that which we have spoken of as character which allows one to be identified and reidentified. The second pole is that of self-constancy which Ricoeur relates to accountability both in the sense of being counted upon, but also in being held accountable for. These two notions are united in the notion of responsibility. Ricoeur appeals here to the Levinasian claim of responsibility as response when one's response is "Here I am!" What I find so telling is that the response "Here I am!" appeals to place and not time.[38] We do not say "Now I am!" in response to a call by the Other. We say "Here I am!" and this implies our proximity to the Other—a position vis-à-vis the other in a place with the Other. Place returns us to ourselves in the midst of and in response to Others. It serves as the foundation for the narrative of self and for the communal narrative that holds the traditions that we pass along to others.

PALIMPSESTS AND HERMENEUTICS

If places of memory serve as vehicles for collective identity or social cohesion, we must consider how they function and how meaning gets transferred through them. I have already suggested that place, like memory, can be thought of as a kind of palimpsest meaning we must reread the memories in light of what has been erased, covered over, brought to light. There are, of course, differing views on how this transpires. If, as we have already suggested, places as well as memories are open to change, then collective memory cannot be simply conceived. Pierre Nora, in his work of the 1970s, stresses the complex and changing sense of social memory. Nora suggests that there is a two-fold impetus at work in contemporary memorials. On the one hand, we recognize that they are open to change while on the other, part of the motivation to erect monuments and memorials stems from a desire to forestall the change and preserve a communal tradition and identity.

For Nora places of memory provide "the presence of the past within the present" or the "administration of the past in the present," but these characterizations of places of memory are misleading in adhering to a linear understanding of temporality and history in a failure to take into account the fundamental hermeneutic activity that must transpire in any encounter with a place of memory. The memory is not transferred as a moment of the past being brought into the present. Instead, the interpretive act of the encounter ensures that the present is engaging a moment of the past, but only through the present. As Gadamer, or even Husserl, taught us, one cannot simply transport oneself to the past and recover it into the present. The present characterizes that past in a peculiar way that prevents the past from being strictly past, making it instead a kind of reflection of the present. This is the palimpsest effect. While what is written is the present, vestiges of the past or previous understandings are sometimes perceptible, never completely covered over, but making themselves felt in the contemporary interpretation. The past is sensed in the place, but also as sedimented in the experience of the place by one whose own memories and style of constitution arise from a palimpsest of traditions and history. This means that any encounter with a monument or place of memory, while it is a window onto a past, a window onto a world of values from the past, is always one that is filtered by the light of the present, through the hermeneutic gaze of the one encountering the monument.

Nora attributes this focus on the present to the rise of what he calls social consciousness. For Nora mass media have made it possible to remove the constitution of history from the exclusive hands of the historians and to place it in the hands of society. We become consumed with determining what of the present will be fixed as past. The legitimation of the past is tied up with events of the present meaning that only that which is deemed to be of consequence in the present or for the future is preserved of the past. Nora's concern is that the shift towards a social consciousness frees memory from history and gives it its own force in the social sphere in determining what of the past matters. While the authority may have shifted, however, this does not necessarily mean that memory itself functions any differently. The response to and interpretation of the meanings of the past is still and always has been a result of the encounter between the present and actors in the present and their own relationship to the past.

What also becomes apparent if we think of the way in which collective memories are supported by place is that they are not immune to relations of power by being secured "permanently" on the land. Maurice Halbwachs argues that in order to secure the memories of a group, there must be a "double focus—a physical object, a material reality such as a statue, a monument, a place in space, and also a symbol, or something of spiritual significance, something shared by the group that adheres to and is superimposed upon this physical reality"[39] But the encounter with the place also brings to the place the sedimentations of social traditions and manners of understanding that allow for the possibility of reinterpretation of the symbolic value of the place. The place is dynamic in this respect—a palimpsest being written and overwritten in each new encounter with each new generation.

We begin to see a tension arising here between the impetus to secure a moment, a value for the future, by embedding it in stone and the inevitable dynamism that inheres in any encounter with the place. This attests on both sides to the power of place in the preservation and creation of collective memories. While such places are frequently erected by governments or powerful agents to promote certain ideals and values, they also include groups of opposition to reinterpret or write over those places. As Karen Till reminds us, "Citizen groups that wish to give voice and presence to peoples, pasts, and places forgotten in national narratives often establish alternative places of memory, such as the Lower East Side Tenement Museum in New York or the District Six Museum in central Cape Town, South Africa."[40] It is important to note here that what supports the counter narrative is an alternative place of memory. Again, this is why it is so important to someone like Toni Morrison for there to be a bench by the road.

While places are not immune from the relations of power, in part because they can be understood as palimpsests, they can also be understood not to be static, not fixed in absolute space, but to be open to change and critique. Again, as Till tells us, "Although elites have had more control over the establishment of places of memory in public settings, they cannot control how they are perceived, understood, and interpreted by individuals and various social groups."[41] Moreover, for Till the increasing popularity of places of memory for tourists does not mean that those who experience those places come away from them with the same interpretation. Places like Holocaust memorials or national monuments are perceived differently by international visitors, or even visitors from different social groups within a nation. The place itself cannot be static or singular in its meaning. This does not mean that those who erect them do not sometimes work very hard to restrict and control the meaning of a monument or memorial, but this is an issue we will explore in more detail in the next chapter.

If we think about what this means for understanding places, mourning, and memory, we realize the role of the hermeneutic interweaving of horizons of the one who encounters the place and the place one encounters. The two things are intertwined in the recognition of the meaning of memory, tradition and mourning. Monuments and memorials are precisely the kinds of places that make us most attentive to the role of this hermeneutic interweaving as we will make most apparent in the following chapter.

NOTES

1. By creating places, I mean places that have markers built upon them, as well as places that perhaps remain deliberately unmarked, but take on significance for a group. See the discussion below of places in South Africa where churches and other communal buildings were destroyed under apartheid.
2. Felicia R. Lee, "Bench of Memory at Slavery's Gateway," *New York Times*, July 28, 2008.
3. See Jeremy Wisnewski, "What we Owe the Dead," *Journal of Applied Philosophy* 26 (2009): 54–70.
4. Note that what is at issue here is mourning as bearing witness. In bearing witness, we attempt to provide a final chapter to someone's narrative by expressing what that person meant to us, or to engage in public remembrance of that person. This makes mourning significantly different from grief. One may suffer the pain of loss and grieve that loss without engaging in mourning.
5. Jacques Derrida, *The Gift of Death* (Chicago: University of Chicago Press, 2007), 35.
6. See Jill Peterson Adams, "Mourning, the Messianic, and the Specter: Derrida's Appropriation of Benjamin in *Specters of Marx*," *Philosophy Today* 51 suppl. (2007): 143.
7. Jacques Derrida, *The Work of Mourning*, eds. Pascale-Anne Brault and Michael Naas (Chicago: University of Chicago Press, 2001), 2.
8. Derrida, *The Work of Mourning*, 10.
9. Derrida, *The Work of Mourning*, 225.
10. Paul Ricoeur, *Living Up To Death*, translated by David Pellauer (Chicago, University of Chicago Press, 2009), 33.
11. Albert Camus, *The Fall* (New York: Vintage Books, 1991), 34.
12. Karsten Harries, *The Ethical Function of Architecture* (Cambridge: MIT Press, 1998), 292.
13. One might object that we, in fact, don't care so much about cemeteries anymore. There is a higher frequency of cremation these days without the need for a marker which leaves us without the cemetery or any place to return to for meditation on the dead, one's own mortality, or the family heritage. Perhaps this is the case, but then what does that mean for the narrative of self and community that cemeteries have served? At the same time as there has been a possible reduction in the importance of cemeteries, there has been a rise in the roadside memorial, the marking of the place of death. With this shift, we see an attempt to re-integrate the death into the daily life of the community.
14. Michael Ondaatje, *Running in the Family* (Toronto: McClelland & Stewart, Ltd., 1982), 22.
15. Jeff Malpas, *Place and Experience* (Cambridge: Cambridge University Press, 1999), 180.

16. For some that past has been so traumatic that the place is avoided in order to avoid incorporation of the past into the self. In other cases, the place is avoided as an act of respect for those who suffered the horror and trauma that the place embodies. But in neither case is the place inconsequential.

17. Malpas, *Place and Experience*, 191.

18. Derrida, *The Work of Mourning*, 19.

19. There is a District 6 museum that offers photographs of District 6 in its heyday, artifacts from the shops and homes, street signs and a sense of what life in District 6 was like before it was bulldozed, but the central streets of District 6 are gone and nothing has been put in their place. The land has been left empty and allowed to grow fallow.

20. Even since the fall of Apartheid, the return of residences to the area has been very slow with much conflict and tension over how to preserve the integrity of the history of District 6 as it is embedded in the land.

21. Martin Heidegger, "What is Metaphysics?" *Basic Writings*, edited by David Farrell Krell (New York: HarperPerennial, 2008), 101.

22. For Heidegger the uncanny is intimately connected to homelessness since the German word "Unheimlich" literally means "homeless."

23. Ondaatje, *Running in the Family*, 201.

24. See Paul Ricoeur, "Narrative Identity," *Philosophy Today* 35 (1991): 73–81.

25. Ricoeur, "Narrative Identity," 77.

26. Ricoeur, "Narrative Identity," 78.

27. See Mark Muldoon, "Ricoeur and Merleau-Ponty on Narrative Identity," *American Catholic Philosophical Quarterly* 71 (1997): 39.

28. Muldoon, "Ricoeur and Merleau-Ponty," 40.

29. Paul Ricoeur, *Oneself as Another*, translated by Kathleen Blamey (Chicago: University of Chicago Press, 1992), 121.

30. Ricoeur, *Oneself as Another*, 123.

31. Ricoeur, *Oneself as Another*, 124.

32. For his explanation of Parfit's thought experiment, see Ricoeur, *Oneself as Another*, 134–5.

33. See Ricoeur, *Oneself as Another*, 135–7.

34. Ricoeur, *Oneself as Another*, 146.

35. Ricoeur, *Oneself as Another*, 147.

36. Ricoeur, *Oneself as Another*, 150.

37. *ibid.*

38. See Ricoeur, *Oneself as Another*, 165.

39. Maurice Halbwachs, *The Collective Memory*, translated by Francis Ditter, Jr. and Vida Yazdi Ditter (New York: Harper and Row, 1980), 204.

40. Karen Till, "Places of Memory," *A Companion to Political Geography*, edited by J. Agnew, K. Mitchell, and G. Toal (Oxford: Blackwell Publishers, 2003), 296.

41. Till, "Places of Memory," 297.

FOUR

A Hermeneutics of Monuments

In the past thirty years we have seen images of weeping mothers and soldiers at the Vietnam Veterans Memorial in Washington, DC. We have seen images of statues of Lenin toppled from their platforms in the former Soviet Union, and the destruction of Buddhist mountain carvings in Afghanistan. Monuments like these grace public squares, tower over cities, or mark quiet corners where important events transpired. We perhaps do not notice some of them and yet they can play galvanizing roles in our societies. As sites of memory they are instrumental in passing along cultural traditions with all of the complexities described in previous chapters. We consider now *how* monuments preserve memory, how they participate in the passing along of traditions, and thus how they contribute to our dwelling on this earth.

Hannah Arendt argues in *The Human Condition* that the built environment is one of the fundamental contributions of the human being to the condition in which we find ourselves.[1] The production of buildings and monuments is positive insofar as they contribute to the public sphere in their everlastingness. Because buildings and monuments that we erect are made of durable materials, they indicate our desire to produce something that outlives us, something that contributes to a cultural world that will continue. She lauds this contribution as a passing along of tradition and heritage to future generations. Monuments contribute to the creation of a world.[2]

From this and the foregoing descriptions, we can conceive of an encounter with a monument as an encounter with temporality and place. Erected in the past by a prior generation, a monument projects itself in its (pseudo)permanence into the future. In the experience of a monument we are reminded of our own transitoriness in this place in the face of the permanence of the past through the monument and its preservation of that past into the future. But perhaps, too, the monument produces in us sweet dreams of immortality, as Arendt suggests. Through the monument we can be pitted against nature—nature in its cyclicality is violated by the durability of the stone of the monument—we can think we have triumphed over the death nature brings, and the replacement of ourselves in this place by some subsequent generation.

What Arendt overlooks in her claims, however, is that while monuments are at once attempts at staving off temporality, at transcending our time, they are always caught back up within history, never escaping temporality altogether, since they are always within the (inter)subjective phenomenological experience. In spite of pretensions to immortality, or historical objectivity, monuments can only ever be experienced within a transitory present by a transitory individual, from within a certain historical, intersubjective perspective.

Drawing upon the work of Martin Heidegger and Paul Ricoeur, we can come to conceive of monuments as elements of our built environment that are not to be revered and unassailably preserved, but that are living elements of our temporality, historicity, and broader environment. Recognizing the palimpsest of place as well as the palimpsest of memory in the monument, we can also recognize that this tension between the eternality and historicality of monuments leads to the need to approach them hermeneutically. A hermeneutic approach appropriately repositions them, limiting their ideological power without denying their role in transmitting to us a tradition, and opening for us a world. But it also allows us to see the place of monuments as existing in the tension between the presence of the past and the presence of the future, between memory and history, between testimony and archive, between one and another.

In this chapter I will elaborate upon a hermeneutics of monuments in order to provide a phenomenological explication of the notion of the trifold palimpsest of memory, tradition, and place that we have been exploring throughout this book. By using Arendt's understanding of public action and Heidegger's understanding of dwelling in conjunction with Ricoeur's ideas of testimony, archive, and narrative in an analysis of a few particular monuments, my aim is to provide an image of what monuments achieve in our world and how we might evaluate the monuments we encounter. Monuments serve as examples of places of memory that require of us a kind of attentiveness we do not usually give them. Thinking through their relationship to tradition, collective memory, and embodiment will shed light on the importance of a hermeneutic approach to the places of our surrounding world.

MEMORY, PLACE, AND DWELLING: THE ROLE OF MONUMENTS

Often monuments and memorials are built for soldiers who have died in war, prominent national figures, literary and scientific heroes, or to mark places of tragedy. The word *monument* is derived from the Latin *monumentum* meaning memorial, coming from the root *monere* which means "to remind." *Memorial* comes from the Latin *memor* meaning "mindful." These definitions imply that a monument, which often serves as a memorial, is meant to call us to be reminded and to be mindful.

In addition, monuments have a privileged position among the things we build with respect to the organization of common space. They often serve as a focal point around which public space is organized. They invoke a shared past in a complex and complicated way. They contribute physically to the world, but can also make less concrete contributions in making human beings mindful of themselves and their relationships to their communities. Monuments are places of intensified meaning that construct our world and preserve and produce collective memories and traditions. But they are dynamic and therefore require the active engagement of the one who experiences them. We will elaborate on how monuments function in order to clarify the hermeneutic process necessary to make sense of the complex relationship between memory, tradition, and place that transpires in the place of the monument.

Monuments and Embodiment

In the experience of public places one experiences something bodily. The *genius locus* is embodied in the place in such a way that it can be transferred to the body of the visitor. There is an atmosphere that is bodily sensed and if habituated in the sense of repeated visits to a place, that atmosphere becomes written on the body. There is a kind of embodied memory in the very experience of walking through a place. Monuments in general are three dimensional inviting if not requiring our bodily engagement. We can walk through, past, and around monuments. We enter into them or climb up to them or even sit upon or touch them.

As I climb the steps to the Lincoln Memorial, I remember the first step to the last.[3] I remember the setting of the Washington, DC Mall that is now at my back. Upon entering the monument, I remember the flight of stairs as I turn to read the inscription on the walls inside. This is a bodily memory that formulates how I move through the place. Even as I write this, the memory of that place in its breadth and vastness is one that is available for recall. I can almost bodily feel the ambience of the place. Ed Casey explains that "the body mediates between my awareness of a place and that place itself, moving me between one place and another and taking me into the intimate interstices of any given place."[4] The body is vital to the being of the place itself. Again, Casey describes "As I come to know it, this building becomes a com-presence in my experience, and I become compresent to it. Such double withness underlies my sense of being-at-home-with a built place."[5] As we saw with the description of the way in which our originary home writes itself on the body in such a way that all subsequent constitution is characterized according to the normativity of home, we can see similar construction of an embodied way of being in conjunction with places of public, communal memory. In fact, phenomenologically speaking, it is difficult to establish a place separate from embodiment and embodiment separate from place as we saw in previous chapters. This is the very meaning of the "there" of Heidegger's Dasein or Husserl's and Merleau-Ponty's embodied self. As those phenomenologists have taught us, we are always already immediately in a world. We do not have to engage in any kind of representation of the world to ourselves in a kind of picture consciousness. Our being-in-the-world is always more immediate than any representation.

Casey, in associating this kind of embodiment with memory, suggests that it is the being-with that constitutes the togetherness of the memory of the place with the feeling of the place. Again, Casey writes, "in memory as in architecture, the things I am with help to constitute an ongoing "aura," an enveloping atmosphere, which surrounds me."[6] Aura surrounds me, and is, therefore, something that exists in a place. We can think of aura as functioning in two different ways. Aura is, on the one hand, simply the feel of a place that surrounds me. In this respect, any place with which I have a connected memory of meaning has aura. On the other hand, the connections with Benjamin's notion of aura are not coincidental. For Benjamin, as we saw in chapter 2, aura surrounds the work of art in its cult value. The same can be said of some places of memory. There are some places of memory that have cultic aura. These are places where an attempt has been made to shield the place against change, to construct the place in such a way as to preserve a unified and singular sense of its meaning. This sense of aura leads to an ideological meaning. Much of the time this is how monuments and memorials function.

Whether we are consciously aware of it or not, monuments and memorials engage our bodies in different ways and the ways in which our bodies are engaged makes a difference in the manner of our experience and what gets passed along through the monument. If we consider the Vietnam Veterans Memorial, for example, it encourages our bodily interaction. As we walk along next to the wall with the names beginning at only ankle height, the wall "grows" beside us until it eventually is above our heads, but never beyond our reach. The monument almost beckons us to reach out and touch it. In many cases people are touching the wall—making rubbings of the name of a loved one or simply touching the name. By allowing people to leave mementos at the site, it also gains in accessibility to us all. It is not meant to inspire awe by towering over us. Instead, it calls us to interact with it, to react to the names of those who were killed, and to respond to the complexity of that war with rigorous thought, not simply to allow some sense of heroism to wash over us.

On the other hand, if we consider the experience of the World War II Memorial on the Mall in Washington, DC, we realize that while it engages us bodily by inviting us to walk through it and amongst the various elements of it, at the same time, it restricts that movement and makes us feel small in comparison to its soaring domes and massive stone columns. The monument covers a vast amount of land compared to other memorials on the Washington, DC Mall, giving it a kind of pride of place. In the very middle of the monument is a pool of water with fountains. Of course, in the heat of summer the child-tourists are eager to play in the water, but it is forbidden. The monument demands reverence for "The Great Generation" rather than inspiring that reverence or even celebrating what the World War II soldiers lost their lives for—the freedom of children to play. The bodies of those who visit this memorial are restrained, minimized, overpowered by the size and heaviness of the monument.

It is perhaps not quite clear yet how it is that body memory can be intersubjective. We described body memory in detail in chapter 1, but our focus there was on individual bodily habits. It is not difficult to recognize those as individual. So, how can we claim that body memory has anything to do with collective memory. We do not have a collective body or at least not one that is obviously habitual. How, then, do we describe and explain the intertwining of body memory and collective memory?

I would like to suggest that this connection comes from the sedimentation of tradition that transpires across generations and that links any given body with both a past generation but also with contemporary bodies. Any experience is already intersubjective just as it is always already bodily and always already implaced.

One example of the way in which a kind of collective habitual body is partly created in conjunction with monuments or places, is just what might be dictated by the places encountered. If one wants to view the Lincoln Memorial, one must, like all others, climb many steps in order to step beyond the columns to read the inscriptions from speeches by Lincoln and to gaze upon the larger-than-life statue of Lincoln sitting in his chair. Likewise, the construction of the Korean War Memorial makes it clear how one is to traverse the space that the memorial takes up allowing for one to look at the faces of the statues in close proximity, but to remain separated from them at the same time. We respond to these worldly clues without thinking about them, just as we respond to the cues in the department store that send us on winding paths through the merchandise. Further examples might include the almost immediate stretching out of one's hand to rub the nose of the Albert Einstein statue which seems simply to call out for this response. Clearly, many, many people have responded to the call as the statue of Einstein has a shiny bronze nose exactly where people have rubbed it while the rest of the statue is burnished bronze. We react in part to the fact that "everyone else has done it" and that it's "what you do" when you see the statue, but also in part to the way in which the statue itself invites such interaction. We don't necessarily stop to consider it, we simply interact with the statue bodily in a way that we are comfortable doing.

But even more than this, we have more general ways of bodily carriage that have the mark of intersubjective inheritance upon them. We habitually move around people in these places with a traditional understanding of personal bodily space that dictates proper cultural distances between people. We have no need to cognitively measure these, our bodies simply know how to position themselves vis-à-vis others around us and respond pre-reflectively to the movements of those others. We were taught these things as children and those cultural inheritances are written on our bodily responses to the world.

In part, this is what monuments and memorials intend to evoke. We go there to remind ourselves of generations past, to walk on the same stones they traversed, to look out over the same views they reflected upon. For many monuments and memorials it is important that they are erected in the places where just such things occurred in the past so that they can capture those elements within the stone and earth of the monument itself. But we don't always, and can't always, erect monuments in the places that bear the memories of generations past within them. We chose not to erect the Vietnam Veterans memorial in Vietnam, for instance, because our relations with Vietnam are such that most Americans are not traveling there, nor are we perceived as heroes in that land (unlike Normandy or other European places where there are World War II memorials to Americans). So, instead, we erected the Vietnam Veterans Memorial in a place that would provide healing to the country by ascribing to those who died in Vietnam a pride of place in our national heritage. Does this mean that the experience of the Vietnam Veterans Memorial is different than it would be if it were in Vietnam, in a place of a particularly virulent battle, or the site of the loss of many? Undoubtedly, but that does not mean that the experience is lacking in the power of place.

The embodied nature of being with monuments gives them a different kind of impact than simply a narrative of heroism or nationhood, sacrifice or suffering. The physicality constructs the collective memory with that subtle embodied element that ties us to the place, each other, and the past in a very concrete way. This has important ramifications for collective memory and tradition and for our project in thinking through the palimpsest of place, memory and tradition.

Monuments and Collective Memory/Tradition

Jacques Derrida has suggested that where tradition is transferred through writing it has an ability to be repeated. Such repetition allows for the embeddedness of cultural traditions and values. Certainly this holds true of monuments and memorials in the sense that their physical manifestation allows them, like the written word, also to be replicated, imitated, and embedded in cultural institutions. Part of the power of monuments derives from this permanence and repeatability. "They overflow the present, and by their iterative power stretch out their significance into enduring strands of order."[7] But this "force[s] an unnatural conformity upon the world . . . it involves a subordination of the future to the past."[8] The ramifications of this are a limited reiteration of the same. There is no radical thought; there is little critique.

On the one hand, then, monuments and memorials take up a valued place in our built environment because of their power to interrupt the everyday and their role as places of intensified meaning where the transference of cultural values and traditions can take place. But at the same time we are confronted with the closedness of monuments and memorials in their reiteration of the values of the soldier as hero, or the memorialized event as a watershed for our society, or the tragedy as our victimization or terrorization. The Civil Rights Memorial in Montgomery, Alabama, for example, presents a picture of the civil rights movement, tells the story of the movement, and gives that epoch of American history an overriding meaning. The events listed there are not random, meaningless events, but events that have importance and meaning with a national impact. In constructing the memorial, then, the history is told, the story is ended, and the meaning is closed. The future is dominated and subordinated to the past in the place of such a monument or memorial. Or such is the attempt.

Are these two roles of the monument inevitably linked, or is there a way to erect a monument that is a place for an encounter with the past that can interrupt the complacency of the everyday, but still remain open, where the future is not subordinated, where the past is not written in stone?

Friedrich Nietzsche and Martin Heidegger offer ways to think about remembering that might give us some indication of a possibility for an openness of places of memory that the idea of the palimpsest implicitly embraces. In *Untimely Meditations*, Nietzsche suggests that "history pertains to the living man in three respects: it pertains to him as a being who acts and strives, as a being who preserves and reveres, as a being who suffers and seeks deliverance."[9] These three categories he associates with the monumental, the antiquarian, and the critical. Nietzsche's discussion of these three modes of history indicates that all three are required in equal measure and that one aspect of this history ought not rule over the others. This is informative for our discussion of monuments and memorials themselves in the sense that as a place for the transference of history and tradition across generations, the monument too must have these elements in equal measure. It cannot be only a celebration of the acting and striving of the human, but must also address the preserving and the critical aspects. For, as he argues, "If the monumental mode of regarding history rules over the other modes . . . the past itself suffers harm: whole segments of it are forgotten, despised, and flow away in an uninterrupted colourless flood, and only individual embellished facts rise out of it like islands . . ."[10] It is not that Nietzsche doesn't recognize the need for preservation, but he stresses the importance of the passage of time in order to preserve rightly. Those who are only interested in preservation have a limited field of vision. The desire to preserve a moment of the past immediately and to abstract it from life, mummifies that moment and undermines any continuing life.[11]

Likewise, the third element must be present in any relationship to the past that we might have. This is the element of critique. As Nietzsche proclaims, "the best we can do is to confront our inherited and hereditary nature with our knowledge, and through a new, stern discipline combat our inborn heritage and inplant in ourselves a new habit, a new instinct . . ."[12] If we take Nietzsche's three elements of history seriously, then we can claim that for a monument or memorial to have the possibility of being able both to preserve and transfer the past and tradition while at the same time being open to this new instinct of which Nietzsche speaks, it must not be immediately constructed and abstracted from life and it must contain both the celebration of human life and the critique of that which is being transferred. This is a difficult balance to conceive. How does a monument or memorial live up to such demands?

We turn to Heidegger's analysis of Nietzsche's views on time. Heidegger stresses that the preservation of the past and an appropriate historicity might give us an avenue by which to understand this delicate role that monuments could play in opening up our past and our present to commemorative thinking. Heidegger, in reading Nietzsche, also argues for a unity of modes of history. As Heidegger suggests, "The historiology which is both monumental and antiquarian is necessarily a critique of the 'Present.'"[13] Heidegger underscores in *Being and Time* that *Dasein* is historical and that "the threefold character of historiology is adumbrated in the historicality of *Dasein.*"[14] Its historicity is inauthentic when "it is loaded down with the legacy of a 'past' which has become unrecognizable." It understands the past only in terms of the present.[15] On the other hand, *Dasein's* historicity is authentic when it "deprives the 'today' of its character as present, and weans one from the conventionalities of the 'They.'"[16]

Heidegger's contribution, then, indicates that the monument or memorial should be something that depresentifies the viewer and does not allow the viewer to be comfortable in the "ways of the They." In other words, the monument must frustrate the propensity of the viewer to come away with an answer for what "they mean" in building the monument. It should rather provoke the viewer to take up a hermeneutic approach, to contemplate and consider for herself, while not allowing her to be front and center in this reflection. Reflections on history, tradition, community, or death are entailed in the interruption of the everyday that does not retreat into abstractions.

For both Nietzsche and Heidegger, the openness to which we should all be attentive and to which any call to history ought to remind us is the openness to the necessary possibility of mortality. This is precisely where the monumentality of monuments most often fails. The monuments to the fallen heroes or the genius heroes or the tragic events of our existence all too often encourage closedness in their approach to human existence and human thinking. Our eagerness to erect a memorial as soon as possible for any tragedy almost ensures such closedness. There are two additional kinds of memorials, other than the national memorials we have been discussing, that risk such closedness. The first is the spontaneous production of impromptu memorials at the sites of local tragedies and occasionally at the sites of national or celebrity tragedies. The second is the production of virtual memorials. We will look at each in turn to consider how they function in the creation of collective memory and tradition.

Impromptu Memorials

Impromptu memorials arise and disappear from our landscape on a local level. They are not permanent; they are not planned. They seem to arise from an outpouring of emotion, grief, pain, or anxiety at sites of tragedy. They are often composed of flowers and cards or teddy bears, or crosses and wreaths on the side of the road where traffic accidents took a life. They mark the place of the tragedy and indicate a kind of immediate pilgrimage by those of the community to the site. The impetus that inspires the erection of such monuments is different from that which drives the erection of public monuments such as war memorials or memorials to national tragedies. These spontaneous displays of grief and pain indicate a desire to be connected to the dead as well as to the living. We see this desire in the fact that the flowers and teddy bears are placed upon a pile at the site of a tragedy, they are not sent to the families of the victims. The notes on the cards are written not to the survivors and other mourners, but to the missing or the dead.[17] This exhibits a desire to show concern for the dead, to engage in community with them. It also shows a desire to be connected with the community of others affected by the loss and grief, but in a communal rather than a particular way.

Impromptu memorials may reveal an effort on the part of many to reintegrate the presence of the dead in our cities. Early monuments of the ancient Egyptians were erected out of concern for the passage of the dead to the afterworld. They were works of communal production and engaged the living with the dead. Throughout history the place of graveyards has changed many times from yards surrounding churches, to cemeteries outside the city's boundaries, but until recently concern for the dead had been constant. Karsten Harries suggests that with the nineteenth century concern with and for the dead has abated. He describes our cemeteries today as places that are neglected. So few of us live close to and care for the graves of ancestors.[18] The effect of this neglect of the dead contributes to our alienation from our communities and ourselves; an alienation that we attempt to overcome through public displays of grief that are immediate and immediately gratifying perhaps, but that lack any permanence or the on-going care that provides a lasting sense of community as connected to this place. As Harries asserts, "every grave bears witness not only to human mortality but also the historicity of life. The care that tends the grave builds tradition and thus community."[19] Impromptu memorials do provide for the interruption of the everyday that is required to make us mindful of mortality and the fragility of human existence, but the fact that they are only temporary limits that interruption to the short period of time that the flowers and teddy bears remain.

In some cases impromptu memorials lead to a more permanent, but understated memorial such as a small plaque or street-side bench, but often these memorials become so much a part of the fabric of the everyday built environment that they are overlooked and lose their impact.[20] The ephemerality of impromptu memorials is in tension with the embeddedness of memory in place. While it is reasonable to think that for those most closely affected by a tragedy, the place itself will be laden with memory of the lost loved one or the tragedy itself, for the community more generally, the intensity of the place and memory usually passes.

When we erect impromptu memorials at sites of individual human tragedy, we do indeed want to be mindful of the fragility of human existence, the inevitability, but utter inconceivability of death. We long for the reunification of our community through such mourning. But we are mistaken in this belief that such public mourning produces a sense of lasting community. This response is a false replacement for what Harries asserts above about the tending of graves. No tending of a grave is involved here. We toss our flowers onto the pile and walk away. In many cases, we feel no need to engage with any of the other mourners. Nothing more is required of us. We don't return to the site to tend the flowers, or clean a gravestone. No true connection to the dead is fostered here; no genuine community with others either living or dead is embraced beyond the moment or moments of the existence of the pile of mementos.[21]

Figure 4.1. Roadside memorial, Carroll County, Georgia. Photo by Janet Donohoe

No tradition is passed along or maintained. Such memorials ultimately fail to do all the work that we need memorials to do. On the other hand, more permanent memorials that we erect do not capture what those impromptu memorials often do. They attempt to preserve the past and celebrate communal values and traditions. They draw us into reflection about our history and our community. But, as indicated above, they often do so in an over-simplified and totalizing way.

In addition to the increasing prominence of impromptu memorials, we also can see an increasing interest in virtual memorials. These too could be viewed through Harries' lens of a reduced interest in maintaining a more permanent connection to communities of past and future in favor of a more immediate gratification of a desire to emote.

Figure 4.2. Roadside memorial, Carroll County, Georgia. Photo by Janet Donohoe

Virtual Memorials

Gregory Ulmer argues in *Electronic Monuments* that the rise of electronic media signifies a shift in communication the magnitude of which recalls the shift from an oral to a written tradition.[22] Moreover, he claims that it requires a parallel shift in our thinking from literacy to what he calls electracy. The shift from an oral to a written structure of communication had ramifications for notions of memory, collective identity, and self-identity among other things. The oral tradition can be characterized by the practice of ritual and the establishment of a collective identity by the tribe. That order was replaced by the order of literacy characterized by the institution of organized education, the nation-state as the culmination of collective print identity, and the rise of notions of selfhood. Electracy, Ulmer argues, is the emerging position that is dominated by digital media and will have ramifications for our own understanding of education, collective identity and memory.[23] While Ulmer may be right that electracy is necessary for the kind of communication that electronic media represent, its role with respect to monuments and their place in the transference of tradition and the contributions to collective memory and identity is questionable. Monuments due to their impact on the body as well as on the community have a peculiar role that cannot be so easily replaced through electronic media. To make this clear, we will consider the role of Internet monuments in comparison with other types of monuments thereby seeking to provide some insight into whether virtual monuments do the same kind of work as monuments of stone.

If one surfs the Internet for virtual memorials and monuments, the findings are extensive and varied. There are memorial sites dedicated to helping mourners construct and post an on-line memorial. There are endless memorial sites for the attacks on the World Trade Center in 2001. There are sites memorializing those who suffered from Hurricane Katrina, the Tsunami of 2004, and each type of individual human tragedy from automobile accidents, to abduction, to suicide. There are sites to the famous and the anonymous alike. The question that arises as one peruses these sites is "why?" Particularly with respect to the most personal losses, why is it that mourners feel the need to post a memorial site for their individual loved one who has departed this life? Do these electronic monuments serve a different sense of selfhood, a new notion of community? Or do they serve the same purpose that the physical marking of the earth serves in our mourning, transference of tradition, and collective memories?

One Internet site called "Virtual Memorials" provides some insight into these questions. It is a site founded in 1996 that tracks the kinds of memorials that families, friends and groups or fans have set up to honor their loved ones. This not-for-profit site provides links to pet memorials, links to support groups, graphics and sound options for creating memorials, links to the most recently created memorials, and more. There are hundreds of memorials posted on the site dating back to its inception and representing all kinds of personal loss as well as loss of very public figures. Most sites have at least a picture and a narrative of the person who has died as well as messages that have been posted there by friends and family. The site is searchable by name, by date of death, or by age. The site declares that "Your loved one's Virtual Memorial captures the essence of who they were and provides a place to share your cherished memories."[24]

Yet another site, the "Virtual Memorial Garden," explains that

> [it] is not a place of death, but somewhere people can celebrate their family, friends and pets; to tell the rest of us about them and why they were special. People's attitude to death in Europe and North America has undergone a radical change in the last one hundred years. Death is no longer the commonplace event that it was when we were less healthy and medical care was not as effective.[25]

Even if we grant that death is not what it was one hundred years ago, that does not provide an explanation for why such memorials are becoming more common. It seems that by posting a narrative about a loved one who has died, one can indefinitely celebrate that person's life. This is perhaps something more than what we expect of a gravestone or a short-lived funeral.

At first, it might seem that virtual memorials are more like the impromptu memorials that spring up at the sites of tragedy than they are like more permanent memorials of stone. Virtual monuments serve a more personal and individualized function than national memorials to soldiers or to national tragedies such as the Oklahoma City bombing, or the 9/11 Memorials. Like impromptu memorials, we could say virtual memorials are more private, less public than national memorials. Virtual memorials like impromptu memorials indicate a desire to be connected to those who have died and to others who mourn their loss. In both cases, however, the connection is a virtual connection since leaving a teddy bear at the site of a tragedy, placing a cross on the roadside, or digitally creating a website does not require any real-time communion with others. It often transpires anonymously.

Virtual and impromptu memorials allow us to express a moment of grief or solidarity, but they also allow that moment to be fleeting, without any continued responsibility to those who are suffering or to those who have died. It might be possible to say that for the virtual memorial, at least, one is in the position to update the web site and certainly there are some that do. There are also sites that have not been updated in years. There is no maintenance of the site required. Unlike monuments that are written in stone and will most likely last several generations, virtual memorials merely give the illusion of permanence.[26] Existing in cyberspace, they don't have a place at all. They cannot be bodily experienced.[27] They cannot become a part of embodied memory.

Virtual memorials can be the sites for a different kind of community, however. They can create a kind of community that does not depend upon spatial proximity or common friends. Rather, they provide an opportunity for those who share in a type of loss to form a community. Most virtual memorials have a function whereby visitors to the page may leave comments. One can electronically communicate with others anywhere in the world who have lost loved ones in similar ways. A community can form around those who have died in automobile accidents, or from stomach cancer, or suicide, or the like.

Such global communities can offer solace and advice. But, while these communities can provide such comfort, they function in a rather exclusive way. One is not specifically excluded, but the community is for those like us, not those who have suffered differently, or who have not suffered loss at all. In other words, these communities function according to a foundation of sameness that is quite limited, but also according to egoistic choice. I can choose my community in a way that is more specific than my neighborhood, my church, or my city. These internet communities are less pluralistic, inclusive, or expansive. Their global reach does not make the users of them immediately any more open to difference or diversity. They do not necessarily create community with those who are other because their focus is only on those aspects that bring its members together. There is no need to recognize the difference of those with whom one shares the internet community—I needn't know anything more about someone other than the loss that we share.

This leaves us with the explanation that these kinds of memorials are personal coping mechanisms. They allow one to publicly display one's grief in the same way that leaving mementos at the Vietnam Veterans Memorial might do. However, unlike the leaving of mementos at the Vietnam Veterans Memorial, these public displays, in being virtual, do not engage one with the expanded and pluralistic community. They lack the truly public nature of place. They seem, then, to be places for a kind of insular and slightly narcissistic expression of selfhood. In serving the self and entailing the risk of narcissism in the same ways that we saw of mourning in chapter 3, the production of virtual memorials does not challenge us to think what we are doing. It does not encourage our engagement in the renewal and critique that remains the promise of monuments and memorials that interrupt our daily lives, impose upon our bodies, and cause us to consider our humanity.

Perhaps it is the possibility for narrative that makes virtual monuments compelling. Here, one can tell the story of one's loved one. As the memorial site indicates, one can represent the "essence" of the person. Whether one really can represent the essence is beside the point; clearly, people think that such can be the case. So, is it a matter of swapping the narrative for the *genius loci*? If this is the case, then what Ulmer is calling a shift from literacy to electracy only functions due to the narrative qualities that can be more universally present on the internet. This means that in fact, electracy still depends deeply upon literacy, but is separated from the co-foundation in place that makes narrative so effective in the production of both communal and individual identity due in part to its role in the transference of tradition and the preservation of the palimpsest of memory.

There is also the sense that virtual memorials can be more egalitarian and more open, or less ideological than monuments of stone. Anybody can post a memorial. Most of the sites allow one to post a memorial for free. Further, anybody can comment on a memorial. It is just as possible for me to post my own feelings and comments about the death of Michael Jackson as it is about my own parent or sibling. There are also many ways in which one can produce a more elaborate site with more photos, or more video footage or audio, but these additional elements often cost something. With this kind of commercial element, even the egalitarian nature of the sites is drawn into question. The Internet itself is seen as an open forum, but each individual site certainly is not. Sites themselves can be just as ideological as party politics. Again, this indicates that the communities they foster are limited.

If we consider for a moment how global or national virtual memorials differ from the more personal virtual memorials, we are confronted with a different set of questions. There is still perhaps the appeal to the desire for public grieving. But since these memorials are more likely to be visited by those who were not directly affected by the loss, the grieving *seems* to have a more communal appeal. It is possible, however, that those who leave messages at such sites do so out of some desire to be part of a national media circus, those who want some connection to the "big deal" that is being made over what is for others a very personal tragedy. More generously, we could say that the 9/11 memorials, for instance, offer an opportunity for Americans to join together as a community of mourners. This might mean that the memorials offer the possibility for genuine community. While many of the national memorials, specifically the memorials to 9/11, have a place for comments from others, the content of the memorials is unreflective and unambiguously represents the events of 9/11 as tragedy, and those who died as heroes.[28] Again, the lack of plurality and diversity is worthy of consideration.

Virtual monuments have an element of what Hannah Arendt might associate with our desire to rocket to the moon.[29] They reveal the ongoing struggle to escape this earth, and attempt to release ourselves from the burden of tradition that is written on this earth. In Arendt's discussion of the launch of Sputnik, she suggests that it represents a human longing to escape our earth-bound existence. It is a desire to live, not in the world as we have found it, but in a world of our own making, a world that we have created. The launch of Sputnik is the first step towards this desire. Perhaps virtual memorials are yet another step on this path. They are a step to control the death of our loved ones. We endeavor to "keep them alive" on the Internet until we decide that we are ready to let go. They thus run the risk of the kind of narcissism in mourning that we encountered in our discussion of Derrida in chapter 3.

What virtual memorials are lacking is the permanence and deliberately placed nature of memorials that are written in stone and occupy places in our more physical world, thereby affecting our embodied being. Many will argue that the Internet is also composed of places. But there are significant differences that allow us to see how each kind of memorial has its strengths and weaknesses.

Embodiment is missing in a virtual place. Virtual places are not only disembodied, but are places that must be mediated by the already embodied immediate experience. A virtual place is one that is represented to me through the computer screen, but it is the computer screen itself that is bodily present. The chair I am sitting on is the immediate embodied experience. As Jeff Malpas has suggested, "things may be brought near visually, through a computer screen, through a mouse, through a set of speakers, but the things are not brought 'near' in the way that the computer screen, the mouse, or the set of speakers themselves are near."[30] Unlike a visit to the Lincoln Memorial, a virtual place is one that I may have stumbled across in surfing the web. I may not have any idea how many links, or which links I followed in order to get there. There is no bodily memory imbued in a virtual place. The Internet is not devoid of places, but those places don't and can't surround me. They cannot become embodied places where my life transpires and which become the places of my memory. The places of the internet are second level representations that are grounded upon a more immediate bodily engagement with the place in which I find myself. The embodiment of place is immediate. It is neither something that must be represented to me, nor something that is mediated.

As we learned from Husserl, the body cannot be made peripheral. It is the immediate encounter and there is no avoiding it. Merleau-Ponty reminds us that it is only by the intervention of the body that anything appears to us. Even that which appears to us virtually can only do so due to the immediacy of our body. As Casey says, "the lived body is a center which refuses to be decentered, a central boundary that will not become peripheral, precisely because this body already encompasses the marginal within its own arena of activity."[31] Moreover, this body is always inextricably tied up with memory and place. We have seen already how memory and place are written upon the body layer upon layer upon layer, covering over some aspects while uncovering others. As new layers are added and different aspects are covered and uncovered, the body is still always the palimpsest upon which the memories and places are written. Again, Casey says, "The lived body is always in the thick of things; and as remembered, it continues to be concentric for the world which it has come to inhabit. What Merleau-Ponty calls the 'Memory of the World' is very much the memory of being bodily in the world, being a central memorial presence there."[32]

So, in final opposition to Ulmer's argument about the shift taking place from literacy to electracy, I'd like to suggest that in fact there is a sense in which any kind of shift to electracy is a move back towards a Modern view of the subject as being divorced from the world, separated from its bodily experiences in such a way that it can preserve an illusion of control and an illusion of self-contained experience. What happens in the representation of the electronic media is a kind of narcissism of selfhood that deludes itself into believing that it can take control of suffering, can separate itself from the world and can leave the body behind. This is a kind of cognitive dissonance that phenomenology seeks to overcome. It is also a kind of dissonance that the recognition of the embeddedness of memory and tradition in place can overcome.

In looking carefully at the experience of virtual memorials, we question the role that they can play in the preservation of memory, the establishing of community, and the production of place. In many ways it may seem that virtual memorials can serve these functions, but their virtual places fail to establish the kind of embodiment that is necessary for the transference of tradition and the production or preservation of memory. Their lack of a thoroughly public nature limits their impact, and they become in many respects a very personal coping mechanism that sometimes serves commercial interests. What this means is that Ulmer is right that a shift from literacy to electracy would have deep ramifications for issues of memory, collective identity, and personal identity. But his claim that electracy indicates the supplanting of literacy through the rise of digital media does not go far enough in recognizing the fundamental nature of embodied memory, and the role of place in the preservation of tradition and the establishment of community.

MONUMENTS AND THE PRODUCTION OF NATIONAL NARRATIVES: IDEOLOGY OR POETRY

We have given monuments and memorials a lot of power in their role as the locus of transmission of tradition and preservation of memory. They are places that are delimited, marked off from the surrounding world. The erection of monuments alters the world. When a monument interrupts the space of the surrounding world it collects the horizon of space to itself as place. In so doing, it creates a place of intensified meaning. The intensification of meaning, which the monument effects, calls us to reflect upon a moment or moments of the past and to relate those moments to our sense of who we are and what our community values. The monument is a created place that is a deliberate way of transferring tradition across generations, and of writing history on the world.[33] But in so doing it often simplifies that past for a unified meaning. Author and critic William H. Gass suggests that as "more than a marker, a monument literally stands for something; it speaks to a community, a city, a state; but monumentality, as a quality which only a few objects . . . possess, exceeds speech. It moves to make and solidify the society it addresses, actually drawing toward and even taking into itself a public which its significance then shapes."[34] It often functions as the "last word" on a period of a collective past.

Not all monuments are equally successful at these tasks, however. We must distinguish the monuments that call us to be mindful of the complexities of our existence and the relationships that we have to our communities and our history, on the one hand, from those monuments that do not inspire us to address those issues thoughtfully, on the other. Some monuments not only are not successful, but can be destructive of these aims. Some monuments are more open to the hermeneutic horizons than others.

Monuments have long been seen as instruments of totalitarian regimes that have a coercive or manipulative force. For example, consider the Stalinist architecture in Moscow, or the many monuments to the motherland that are scattered throughout the provinces of the former Soviet Union. These monolithic, metal statues of a victorious woman with a sword raised over her head stand on hillsides towering over such cities as Kiev, Volgograd (formerly Stalingrad), and Ashkhabad among others.

The statues representing the motherland are visible from virtually any point in each city. They were erected by Stalin after the Second World War to celebrate the victory of the Soviet Union, to honor the dead soldiers, and to remind the Soviet citizens of their "required" loyalty to the motherland and to their leader whose watchfulness one could not escape. They are awesome and dominate each city. They have a coercive force in making the people of these cities fearful of their leader's power, or any act that might betray the required loyalty. Coercive monuments often aim to foster fear and awe, and to elevate a dictator to the position of a

Figure 4.3. Motherland Russia Monument, Kiev, Ukraine. Photo courtesy of Ken and Bernadine Clark. Taken 7/25/2007.

saint or hero. Again, consider the many statues to Lenin that can be found in any city of the former Soviet Union or Eastern Europe.

Is there any foundation, however, for believing totalitarian monuments to be more coercive than other kinds of monuments? It is difficult to distinguish between such monuments that are coercive or inspire fear and monuments that do not. So how are we to know the difference? A hermeneutic process is required, one that is attentive to the possibility of the many levels of meaning, the palimpsest of memory, tradition, and place that monuments represent.

In order for monuments to resist tyranny they must avoid offering us an escape from the anxiety of our own individual death. The tyranny of a monument is achieved by its promise of immortality through the glorification of death for the state or by promising the unyielding protection and power of a ruler. Only some monuments are capable of avoiding this. Following Harries, I propose the Vietnam Veterans Memorial in Washington, D.C. as one such monument. The Memorial designed by Maya Lin and dedicated in 1982, is a black marble slab that cuts into the earth. It is etched with the names of those who died during service in Vietnam. The names, unlike previous war memorials, are not etched in alphabetical order, but instead follow a chronological order of the date of each soldier's death. Each panel of marble, then, represents a year, giving the viewer the sense of the rise and decline of the war. As you approach the wall is low, at ankle level, but as you walk past the names, the wall begins to rise above you and then descends again as you near its far end. The shiny, black marble reflects the faces of those looking at it. Maya Lin says of it that she wanted to create something that viewers "could relate to as on a journey, or passage, that would bring each to his own conclusions . . ."[35]

The monument resists order, resists ideology, and inspires the telling of personal histories as it is strewn with messages to and mementos of those whose names are listed there. Tom Carhart labeled the memorial a "black gash of sorrow,"[36] suggesting that it presents the sorrow of the war, not valorizing the war effort, not presenting those who died as national heroes, but presenting the complexity and ambivalence surrounding that war. In so doing, the Vietnam memorial calls us to reflect upon the fragility of human existence, the complexity of our relationships with others, and the United States' relationship to other communities. The memorial does not elevate an abstract state ideology over the fragility of human existence. It does not present us with idols. In this way, it helps us to be mindful of our own individual death and frees the monument to be what it is, allowing a meaning to come forth or not for each viewer, rather than imposing a particular reading on each visitor. The success of the monument can in some way be measured by the response of those who visit it. When you approach the memorial there is a spontaneous quiet that descends. There is no need to demand silence here as there is at other monuments, the tomb of the Unknown Soldier in Arlington cemetery in Arlington, Virginia, for instance. Personal artifacts are placed by visitors at the base of the Vietnam Veterans Memorial, each with its own message and own contribution to make to the monument. Such personal artifacts could hardly be laid at the feet of the controversial, nameless, idealized statues that were added off to one side of the memorial.

The controversy surrounding the addition of the statues reveals how we often think of war memorials and monuments: that they must be patriotic. In an effort to silence the complaints from some quarters that the Vietnam Veterans Memorial was not patriotic enough, a sculpture of three soldiers was added to the Memorial.

This risks making the memorial something ideological. It is meant to cover over the questions that the wall poses with certainty about the heroism of dying as a soldier. It challenges Heidegger's notion of dwelling by giving a false impression of immortality and allowing us to avoid the anxiety of individual mortality. It denies soldiers an individual death by giving a mere representation in the form of nameless, ideal soldiers. Those who view the statues are confronted with ideals, not with individual, human death.

Those monuments that attempt to provide certainty, offer us visions of ideals, and appease our anxiety about death, distract us from the fragility of life, and prevent our attentiveness to the human condition. Monuments that do not present idols, or unified, totalizing meaning, challenge us to be mindful of our own mortality and do not allow us to become comfortable in the mundanity of everyday existence.

Beyond robbing the individual of death, some monuments of totalitarian regimes and democratic regimes alike fail in allowing the world to be open to us. In Heidegger's terms, they fail to be poetic. In other words, monuments that resist interpretation and instead present an ideological perspective close off our ability to be mindful and to be reminded in a way that is conducive to active and open public discussion of their role and purpose in our social and political life. Monuments, because they have such great potential to organize public space, and because they invoke our past and inspire us to address our future, can be extremely important in public discourse. But just what they say has to be determined through an appropriate hermeneutic process.

As we noted earlier, a monument is public insofar as it preserves the many perspectives through which it is understood. In other words, if the monument can evoke a multiplicity of interpretations in varied experiences of it, then it can be considered public. This gives us a starting point for thinking about a hermeneutics of monuments. For Arendt, it is important for those who experience a monument to recognize that we perceive it differently, but that we all still perceive the same monument. The monument can evoke different responses from those who view it (e.g., sorrow, anger, anxiety), but still at the same time represent the same thing (e.g., those who died in the Vietnam War) to the viewers. This capacity to evoke multiple interpretations can be associated with what Heidegger terms the poetic. Like poetry, for something to be part of the public is for it to be open to multiple interpretations. When the common, public world is only understood, or only presents itself through one perspective, it has come to an end. This does not mean that there is nothing that is common. Clearly, the public realm must have a certain commonality, something around which we can all participate. However, this commonality is diverse. As Lea Caragata has suggested "the public is a diverse realm in which all of the sectors of a society have an opportunity or, even better, a compelling purpose to engage in a discourse about the forms, structures and nature of their city, in whatever ways these issues arise for them."[37] The monument that contributes to the public realm would resist a singular meaning and instead would provide space for discourse and a multiplicity of meanings. Such a monument calls for a hermeneutic approach.

Martin Heidegger's concept of dwelling which we explored to some degree already in chapter 1 from such phenomenological works as ". . . Poetically man dwells . . ."[38] and "Building Dwelling Thinking,"[39] may shed some light on possible distinctions between kinds of monuments. In these works, Heidegger suggests that humans have forgotten what it means to dwell. We are so wrapped up with the mundane concerns of our everyday lives that we fail to give any thought to what human existence on this earth is about. To give heed to existence is to begin to recognize that to be human is to be mortal. This recognition of mortality is essential to authentic dwelling. But, humans must not make death the goal, nor "darken dwelling by blindly staring toward the end."[40] To make death the goal either as a projection of existence into an afterlife or as a desired release from this life denies that death *is* death. It fends off death by proposing the continuation of life and allows one to escape facing the finality of death. Instead of such a denial, Heidegger suggests that it is more properly human to feel anxiety in the face of such finality. He asserts that this anxiety draws us away from our constant concern for the mundane activities of everyday life. Our familiarity with things is interrupted, our reliance upon the common understanding of the world is disrupted, and each of us must face our own death. We come to recognize that death is the one thing that no one can do for us. It is inevitable, yet ineffable and indeterminate. When we grasp these things, we begin to understand what it means to dwell on this earth.

The other aspect of dwelling that Heidegger stresses is a way of allowing the earth to be what it is rather than imposing a structure upon it. We most often approach our world with presuppositions about what the things around us mean and what they are used for. Things in our world are built to serve useful purposes and they have certain meanings. This imposes upon us and upon our surroundings a structure that limits our ability to think beyond those useful purposes or certainties. Heidegger encourages us to approach the world rather like a poet.[41] The poet tries to reveal things in a way that is uncommon and perhaps even surprises us in its ability to evoke something from a perspective we would not normally consider. This is a way of allowing the thing to open itself to us without presupposing its purpose or meaning. It is a way of being mindful of the world around us in an open way.

Monuments, in contributing to our dwelling, would be most effective if they served these two prongs of dwelling. They must keep us mindful of our own death and must remind us of an open relationship to the world that resists presuppositions or the imposition of meaning.

Consider again monuments of totalitarian regimes. Often such monuments that celebrate the heroes of tyrannies foster fear and awe by elevating a dictator to the position of a saint or hero. They fail to make us mindful of our own death since, as Karsten Harries suggests, any monument of such a regime "promises to liberate the individual from the burden of his or her individuality, which means also from the fear of death, as it is in keeping generally with the appeal of totalitarianism."[42] Relieving someone of the burden of individuality robs that person of her or his own death. This is also something that is encouraged by coercive monuments that create a sense of fear of the regime. The watchful eyes of a dictator, whose power is pervasive, can be supported by the monuments erected in his or her honor. The dictator's power is a power to kill that keeps a populace in fear. The fear is a fear of not being able to die a human death but to be killed like an animal. It denies one the ability to go through what is essential about one's own death. It replaces that death with a systematic process that is blind to individuality and could be satisfied with a substitute. In other words, it is a process of eliminating an anonymous offender, rather than its focus being the death of a particular human.

Heidegger compares this to what happened to the Jews during World War II. Those who were systematically gassed were not murdered as humans, but exterminated anonymously like animals, thus denying them a human death. This is what Heidegger finds to be most atrocious about the Holocaust. So, whether the monument of the totalitarian regime offers the promise of liberation from death through a god-like dictator, or the fear of death from a despot's power to kill, both eliminate the particularity and specificity of individual human death, thereby denying one of the proper aspects of dwelling.

We cannot, however, rest assured that the monuments of democratic cultures avoid such messages. Many "democratic" monuments fail in much the same way. Most war memorials in the United States valorize those who gave their lives for democracy to protect the rest of us from death or slavery. In their attempt to make us secure in our own society, and in their valorization of the war hero, they create idols that provide the illusion that death is not individual. The war hero depicted is usually faceless and nameless, not an individual. Such monuments do not invoke the past for its own sake. They invoke the past as a way of directing us to ideals of the state, or ideals of a life beyond this life. The war memorial often honors collective ideals through the glorification of death for a cause, unquestioningly placing the collective in a position of priority over the individual.

Yet, as I have argued above, memorials are important for the transference of traditions across generations. They present to future generations what elements of our society are valued and worthy of representation in monuments and memorials. So we are left to wonder how we can approach memorials in such a way that any totalitarian inclinations are limited while not destroying the important work of transference of traditions for which monuments are partly responsible.

In understanding monuments through the phenomenological approach presented here, we can comprehend the role they play in our dwelling. Monuments are not easily categorized as those that are the products of "totalitarian" or "democratic" regimes. By understanding those categories through an understanding of dwelling, we possess different criteria that can be used to comprehend the role monuments play in our world. Monuments which encourage us to be mindful of the human condition of mortality and remind us of the multiple perspectives on the world are those that have the most to contribute to our dwelling.

When we come to understand the relationship of place to memory and tradition in terms of the sedimentation of layers of meaning, as with the image of the palimpsest, we begin to recognize that even the places of monuments are not immune to change and reinterpretation. The meaning of monuments, even ones that might at first seem the most ideological, can change. One way such change happens is through the counterproduction of memory that transpires in the created place of memory. In other words, we can think of occasions when place has represented the re-production of memory in a new light. Take for instance the civil rights rallies that took place in the 1960s in the United States on the steps of the Lincoln Memorial in Washington, D.C. These rallies re-produced the national memory of Lincoln in conjunction with the struggle for civil rights in America. The site of the Lincoln Memorial would be forever altered by this reproduction. It is a place where the conjunction of present and past can be seen in the production of collective memory. The Lincoln Memorial was selected no doubt because of the traditional view of Lincoln as a hero of rights for the African American population through his struggle to abolish slavery. But this is further underlined and this image made even more concrete in the selection of this place for the rallies. The place of the Lincoln Memorial holds the collective memory of an aspect of the civil rights movement in America that it did not hold before.

There are many other examples of the creation of collective memory through the creation or recreation of place. Holocaust memorials across the United States, Europe, and Israel attempt to create a sense of the horror and pain suffered by millions at the hands of the Nazis. The Vietnam Veterans memorial in Washington, D.C. creates a national memory in an attempt at healing a divisive time of the American past. The Clothesline Project that temporarily appears during rape awareness week on many campuses throughout the United States is a display of very personal memories of individuals who have suffered sexual abuse, but very deliberately takes on a role in the creation of a national memory. These three examples represent a history that is not accepted by all and are in fact representations of history that some would want to ignore, but those who have suffered have insisted on the need for a place for the memorialization of this difficult and painful part of their, and thus our, past.

In South Africa in the 1940s, the African National Congress party called for the erection of monuments that would celebrate the heroes of African history and thus create a strong national memory.[43] However, during the ensuing years of apartheid in South Africa, many places of memory were destroyed. Churches were bulldozed; schools and missions were closed and destroyed. What became apparent was that even without the buildings that were sacred, many of the places retained their importance for the collective memory. "The architecture of memory in South Africa [that] connected people to specific places—a home, a school, a church—[that] were not merely "property" but sacred sites where memory gathered . . . Linking human beings with place, therefore, the architecture of memory can reconstruct even what the state destroyed."[44] As we saw with the example of District 6 in Cape Town, the places that support a community can arise through the simple living of daily life. The bodily habits and communal interactions that compose that life are embedded in the place such that the place itself becomes the foundation for the community, even when the community is dispersed, and the place destroyed. In spite of the differing views on the place by those of the apartheid government as opposed to the inhabitants of the neighborhood, the place of District 6 was recognized as fundamental to the community's coherence, traditions, and memories.

Considering monuments in light of Arendt's definitions of public, private, and social and also with respect to Heidegger's concept of dwelling, it is possible to distinguish between two types of monuments: those that encourage us to dwell authentically and contribute to the public realm, and those that allow us to dwell inauthentically and remain in the social or even private realm. To allow us to dwell inauthentically is to accommodate the desire to flee the anxiety of the human condition by finding comfort in ideology. Such monuments do not disrupt our concern for the mundane aspects of everyday life. They also do not accommodate multiple perspectives of public discourse, but offer instead an ideological and unified meaning, closing off opportunities for discussion. In encouraging us to dwell authentically, monuments disrupt our satisfaction in daily life with a sense of anxiety about our own mortality and confront us with space for public discourse. We are called to be mindful of our own mortality and to be reminded of those whose perspectives are different from our own and with whom we must engage if we are to participate in the public realm. They do not allow us to settle into conformity because they resist an easy unified meaning. The memories and traditions that are transferred through such places cannot be singular and monolithic because they are overlaid with layers of meaning that are uncovered differently in different eras and by different generations.

Arendt's categories allow us to say that some monuments elevate the soldier to protector of our national family and restrict the importance of the soldier to a laboring role, something that transpires in the private realm. In other words, they fail to preserve the distinction between private and public. They also have a tendency to elevate the soldier to the position of god, to immortalize the soldier as ideal soldier, not as a particular human being. The effect of this type of monument is to distract us from the mortality of an individual human being and to impress upon us an ideological perspective on the value of life with respect to the nation. An example of such a monument is the United States Marine Corps War Memorial more commonly known as the Iwo Jima Monument in Arlington, Virginia. This famous bronze monument, sculpted by Felix deWeldon and dedicated in 1954, presents six soldiers struggling to raise an American flag on Iwo Jima.

The sculpture is based upon a photograph taken by Joseph J. Rosenthal during an actual flag raising. Although the statues are very life-like, and are based upon actual men, they are utterly depersonalized by the sheer size of the monument. It towers above the viewers at a total height of seventy-eight feet. Their historic act is aggrandized and they "assume a propagandistic function upholding national triumphalism."[45] Even the specificity of the act itself is denied because of the inscription at the base of the sculpture, which lists all conflicts in which the Marines have participated. The monument is, then, not to honor specific men for a specific action, but as President Richard Nixon declared at the dedication, it stands as a "symbol of the hopes and dreams of all Americans and as a testimonial to the 'freedom-loving' philosophy of Americans who engage in foreign battles."[46] The soldiers have lost their identity in becoming representatives of a collective and heroic act that stands as a symbol of American patriotism. This monument defies the deaths of these men and replaces it with idealism and patriotism.

In opposition to such death-defying monuments, the main force of a monument like the Vietnam Veterans Memorial is its refusal to idealize, and instead its encouragement of our recognition of our own mortality. It also has a public force in that it does not present an ideological message about the Vietnam War, but encourages public discourse and varied perspectives on that part of American history. It does not deny those soldiers their death by representing a nameless hero. Even now, thirty years after the wall was dedicated and in spite of the controversial addition of the statue of three soldiers, people go to the wall and have very profound experiences. There are still veterans who gather at the monument and who use it as a backdrop for political discourse about veteran's issues. This is the mark of a truly public space. Certainly the juxtaposition of the "patriotic" sculpture of nameless soldiers detracts from the openness of the wall to multiple perspectives, but has not destroyed that effect altogether.

The Role of Forgetting

What has been underscored here is the importance of monuments as deliberate places of collective memory that are instrumental in the transference of tradition from generation to generation. Another structure of their function is the role of forgetting that transpires in the built environment, particularly with respect to monuments. Why forgetting? Forgetting is inseparable from remembering. It is impossible to remember without forgetting. Every memory requires the forgetting of something for it is not a reliving of the event, but a memory of the event that lacks something. It does not share in the fullness of the original experience. In elevating something to the position of being worthy of remembrance, remembering allows that which is not worthy to slip away, to become forgotten. In many cases this is deliberate, in others, a mere consequence of the process of remembering.

One cannot remember every detail of an event, so we focus on the most salient features and other details are seen to be less important, thus less worth remembering. The salient features are most prominent in memory, while other features may require some work on our part to recollect and still others disappear from memory altogether. While we may accept this as a matter of course for any given individual, it may have disturbing ramifications for collective memory because, of course, questions arise about exactly what is being transferred to future generations, what image of the past is evoked by the built environment and from what or whose perspective. No locus of transference of a communal event can capture every aspect of that event. It cannot provide for a reliving of the event, nor would we necessarily want it to, but that means that decisions must be made about what aspects to forget and what aspects to memorialize. Any such decision will never be interestless. The result of this is that no monument or memorial can be completely objective, providing an external view of an event, or person. Each monument presents a simplified version that is given from a particular perspective.

When a monument elevates an aspect of an event and thus covers over other aspects, thereby causing a forgetting of those, it secures a particular story or version of the past. It, in part, closes the past to other meanings or other aspects allowing them to slip into oblivion. The timing of when monuments are erected is important, particularly so with respect to war monuments, since they serve as physical acts of closure to a period of time. They allow us to make the past past, to consider an event, an era or a movement to be over. In many respects time is controlled by place through the production of a monument or memorial.

Following World War I, war memorials were erected quickly in many small towns across the United States and Europe. National War memorials went up within the space of a couple of years. The American tomb of the Unknown Soldier in Arlington Cemetery in Washington, D.C. was dedicated in 1921 a mere three years after the end of the war. The British Cenotaph in Whitehall in London was first erected of wood in 1919 for the first anniversary of the armistice and was rebuilt in stone and dedicated in 1920. These monuments commemorate the soldiers who died defending their country. They provide reassurance that the soldiers' sacrifice was worthwhile. They give closure through assurances and provide certainty of the values that have been defended.

But such monuments, in their glorification of soldierly sacrifice, cover over the dehumanizing aspect of war, the internal national conflicts caused by those who refuse to fight, and the role of those who labor on the home front in support of the war. The Cenotaph in Whitehall, a simple stone plinth with the inscription "The Glorious Dead," indicates a forgetting of the complexity of wartime, the horrors of the loss of life under conditions of war, the internal conflict for the returning British soldiers who were not always given the treatment and jobs they had been promised. Instead, it provides a simple and simplified vision of the glorious soldier. By elevating the Unknown Soldier to the position of hero, the monument attempts to cause us to forget the millions of unidentified, "eternally anonymous and unheroic dead" or the ignored and aching wounded who have returned to their homeland.[47]

William Gass claims that for a memorial to war to be honest "it would contain the muddy trench, the bloated corpse, the stallion lying by its bowels, blown-apart buildings, abandoned equipment, recordings of outcry."[48] While one might be sympathetic to Gass's claim, what such "honesty" forgets is that this representation of war also provides a simplified view. The monument needs to disrupt and call into question in a way that struggles against the penchant most viewers have for easy answers. It needs to be open to the possibility of the multiple perspectives on the issues of war and heroism, to recognize that there are many ways to be heroic, many ways to respond to war and conflict, many things to think about when contemplating the past and its challenges.

Monuments to national heroes such as Lenin for the Russians, or Thomas Jefferson for Americans, have a similar role in covering over the complexities of the characters of those "heroes." The monuments to Lenin, in presenting him as the young man of ideals, the hero of communism, cover over the complexities and violence that placed Lenin in the role of a leader in the first place. Likewise, the monument to Thomas Jefferson in Washington, D.C. makes no mention of Jefferson's role as a slave owner. It is not meant to be a part of the collective memory of this hero of American nationhood. The role of forgetting in these cases points out the constructed nature of these collective memories, this tradition.

The Civil Rights Memorial produced by Maya Lin and located in Montgomery, Alabama calls attention to many of the events and important people of the civil rights movement in the United States in the 1950s and 1960s.[49] The monument, dedicated on November 5, 1989, is comprised of two pieces of polished black granite. A slightly convex wall rises behind a circular-top table that looks as if it is precariously balanced upon its pointed base. Both pieces of granite are inscribed. The wall has an inscription quoting Dr. Martin Luther King, Jr.'s paraphrase of a Biblical passage from Amos 5:24, while the table is inscribed with the dates of important events in the civil rights movement including the "names of forty men, women and children who gave their lives for freedom."[50] The memorial is covered by a thin film of water that flows down over the wall from a reflecting pool on an upper plaza. The table's water comes from a source that bubbles up at a point off-center of the tabletop.

Although the Memorial sits facing the sidewalk of a downtown street at the entrance to the Southern Poverty Law Center, it disrupts the texture of the business and government district surrounding it. The place itself is separated from the surrounding, everyday world in that it is a place of intensified historical, communal meaning linking one to a past that is shared with others precisely because of the monument. The memorial calls us to be mindful of our past, not simply due to the quotation from Martin Luther King, Jr. that graces the black granite wall, nor due to the dates of events important to the civil rights movement that are etched into the black granite tabletop balanced on its off-kilter pedestal. The history of the surrounding world is gathered together at the place of the monument. It is that place that invokes a different time and frames the surrounding world differently.

The experience of the Civil Rights Memorial is interactive between the person who approaches the memorial and the memorial itself. Since the flowing water and the black granite together form a slightly reflective surface, anyone who is reading the words from Martin Luther King, Jr., or the inscribed dates of the selected civil rights events spanning the years 1955 to 1968, has his or her own face reflected in the surface. The monument, in evoking a shared history, is a place where collective memory can be reflected and reflected upon. For those of another generation who did not experience the civil rights movement within their own personal history, this is a place where that collective memory can be transferred, where the intensification of the history provides for the passing along of the importance and meaning of those events.

The Civil Rights Memorial presents a picture of the civil rights movement that focuses entirely on the non-violent protests of those fighting for freedom and justice. But Malcolm X, probably the second most prominent leader in mobilizing the American Black population during the civil rights era, is not mentioned or listed on the tabletop inscriptions. Thus, his more militaristic, separatist approach is ignored, devalued and excluded from the account of the civil rights movement. What does the absence of this side of the story, or the absence of acknowledgement of conflict within the movement, do to the tradition of the civil rights movement that is passed along to future generations? The history, events, and meaning have become simplified in their transference.

Given the foregoing analysis of monuments that encourage us to dwell publicly as opposed to those that do not, we are faced with a question of whether we should make our judgments and do away with those monuments that do not call us to dwell authentically, those that give a totalizing view of our world, those that do not allow for honest public exchange. There is no easy answer to such a question. Monuments in Eastern Europe were torn down by the mobilized populace. This political response on the part of the populace is an action that many in the West and around the world might be inclined to condone. Yet recently, as we saw in chapter 3, Taliban destroyed Buddhist idols on a mountainside in Afghanistan. This action is one generally condemned by much of the world. How do we evaluate these actions with respect to monuments?

Due to their historical nature, monuments are not static, but dynamic. By force of the public space they inhabit, and the use of that space, the impact of any monument can be altered. Its impact can shift from political to cultural or emotional impact over time. A monument to a fallen dictator can often take on the characteristic of a reminder, not a reminder of a past hero, but a reminder of repressions that have been overcome. We see this in the communist monuments that remain in Russia. The Russian people recognize a change in monuments that present the communist heroes. Those monuments now serve as a reminder of a difficult past that the Russian people have the ability to acknowledge and live with.[51] It is a part of their cultural past that they choose to preserve. Monuments can be treated as a reminder of the dead, but can also cause us to be mindful of what has been overcome and what repression marks our past. Many Holocaust memorials have much the same role in serving as reminders of those who died, but also in making us mindful of the horrors that can happen if we are not attentive to our past and our culture. Monuments can cause us to question our history and our ideals.

The dynamism of monuments and traditions, their openness as language, places the viewer in a position of responsibility with respect to their interpretation. To be mindful of the role of place and of monuments in our collective memory should make us mindful of how our collective memory is in part created. What is required in our approach to monuments is a hermeneutic process that allows us to make sense of the depths of the monuments we encounter. Monuments, in linking tradition and collective memories to place, call us to engage in more than a narrative account of our collective past. They call us to come to that past through renewal and critique that recognizes the role of place in the transference of the past to the present and the future. We need to explore in more detail what the hermeneutics of place looks like and how monuments take on their role within that hermeneutics.

MONUMENTS AND A HERMENEUTICS OF PLACE

So far we have looked at the ways in which monuments establish public places in the built environment, thereby assisting in the activity of mourning, the production of collective memory, and passing along of tradition. We need, however, to be more explicit about how this happens as a movement towards understanding how we should interpret monuments. To that end, we will examine monuments in their role as both testimony and archive.

Monuments and the Presence of the Past: Memory and Testimony

On a general and fairly surface level, we can speak of monuments as narratives written in stone—both literally through the inscriptions on many monuments, and figuratively through their bas-relief elements, the sculptures associated with them, the symbols of the state, or cultural references that grace many of them. But we recognize, too, that this narrative must be encountered by one who comes to it with a forestructure out of a cultural horizon that shares elements with it, while at the same time coming to the narrative from out of her or his own era of history. The monument in its transference of tradition across generations appeals to a shared tradition and produces a collective cultural memory. Unlike other elements of the built environment, monuments set themselves off from the everyday, encouraging us to reflect upon a collective history. I have elaborated on the way in which the sedimentation of layers is embedded in the monument. But here, I would like to raise a further issue with respect to the relationship between collective memory, tradition, and monuments that arises when we consider monuments in their productive role. As place-embedded narratives, they produce memory and history.

In production of collective memory, monuments function as testimony in recording the experience, in giving image or shape to something that frequently cannot be thought or remembered otherwise, and in making that memory available to the community as a whole. They serve as living reminders that appeal to us to remember. The monument, as W. James Booth suggests, is a "signifier, pointing to a past event, and sometimes also a call to remember, latent and awaiting a witness's voice to cast light on it."[52] It illuminates and shapes the meaning of the past. A monument bears witness to the past by preserving it within the present. Booth also suggests that bearing witness is a gesture of defiance and resistance. Monuments, in being built of stone, marble, or other durable material, put up a resistance to the passage of time and have pretensions to immortality. But they are also acts of resistance against the fragility of memory and the silence of the past by ushering that past and those memories into the present.[53]

Take, for example, the small memorial placed on the spot where Amy Biehl was killed by a mob in Cape Town, South Africa on August 25, 1993. Amy Biehl was a Stanford University graduate and anti-apartheid activist in South Africa on a Fulbright fellowship. She was giving three South African friends a ride home to the Gugulethu Township when she was pulled from her car by an angry mob and stabbed to death. The simple stone cross memorial serves as a reminder of Amy Biehl's tragic and violent death in that particular place, but it also serves as a historical marker of a period of 1990s South African history marked by many such killings and violent unrest.[54]

The memorial stands between the historical past and the call to remember. It is historical and archival in that it sits on the spot where Amy was killed. But it also testifies to her death and life. It sits barely off the road near a busy gas station in the middle of the township. It does not have a lofty position, was not erected by the State, but serves as a constant presence of the past in the lives of Cape Town citizens in a way that many more exalted monuments do not. The monument serves as a salve to free the members of the township from a past that threatens it with shame or conflict. But it also serves as a call to remember a particular individual.

Preserving memory against those who would otherwise be inclined to erase it altogether out of guilt or indifference, is to bring that which is immemorial, other, and which surpasses us, into a manageable sphere where it can be accommodated, experienced, grasped. This is after all what we must do—we must place into narrative that which cannot be spoken. We must accommodate that which is radically other.[55] The monument serves as a command: "Remember this!" It speaks of shared re-

Figure 4.4. Amy Biehl Memorial, Gugulethu Township, Cape Town, South Africa. Photo courtesy of Steve Gish. Taken 2001.

sponsibility, of a debt to the past. Yet the process of understanding that past is always at the same time memory of the present, in the present, through the present. It is only we who can interpret the experience of the monument for ourselves and our time, through the lens of our own traditions and prejudices. Thus, our interpretation of the monument always runs the risk of reduction, sameness, hubris, elevation of our time and our meaning. As Booth notes, commemoration "can yield silence by replacing one memory with another."[56] It perhaps replaces the testimony of the witness with our memory now. We question, then, whether it is utterly self-serving, now-serving, anti-frailty to place into stone that which we remember.

Ultimately, the meaning of the memorial or the monument can only be determined by those who encounter it. This does not mean, however, that we are at liberty to use monuments simply to reflect ourselves back to ourselves. The monument serves as a point of contact between present and past and as such it shows forth the ongoing life of a community. It serves to call us to responsibility for preserving the memory and inscribing us within the history of the community. Booth argues that it calls us to bear witness and "bearing witness can be understood as a 'reciprocal obligation' between generations of a community and an affirmation of their deep identity."[57] The place of the monument provides the foundation for the memory and responsibility of the community. And the place is particular. The Amy Biehl memorial is effective because it is in the place where Amy Biehl's killing happened. The past is embedded in the world at that place. A call to remember and to responsibility could not be as effective if the memorial were randomly erected without connection to the world of Amy Biehl.

Booth's analysis of the function of the preservation of concentration camps and the memorials that have been erected there can also be useful to us here. He argues that such places have become central in the recollection of European Jewish life in and of the twentieth century insofar as they "rescue the hour of their destruction from the silence of the rustic settings that might have shrouded Auschwitz and other killing centers."[58] The preservation disrupts the silence that might otherwise ensue in the growing over of a site of an atrocity. However, preserving this site of victimhood also leaves untold and forgotten the civilization and the culture that had been established prior to the destruction of millions. Extrapolating from Booth's position, we could say the same of Amy Biehl and perhaps of monuments generally. In the testimony to Amy Biehl's violent and untimely death, she has become a symbol of resistance to apartheid and of the power of reconciliation due to the circumstances surrounding her death and her parents' subsequent reconciliation with the four men convicted of her murder. But what of Amy Biehl, the Stanford student? What of Amy Biehl, the California child? These are shadowed by the monument itself, by the testimony, which necessarily entails a certain level of forgetting.

Thus, if we only view monuments in terms of our duty to remember, we run the risk of reducing the historical to the testimonial. Instead, the monument holds both testimony and history in tension in order not to run the risk of either idolatry of the dead or ideology of the state. In spite of the shadow on Amy Biehl's early life, the memorial to her death does seem to balance the tension between testimony and history by its placement in the midst of the everyday lives of the people of the township, and its human-scale presence that serves as both a reminder and as a historical marker.

In their role as markers of events of the past and representations of the past through the interruption of the everyday, then, monuments can serve as testimony. Annette Wieviorka argues that testimony is more than simply the recounting of facts or even a narrative that provides objective knowledge of the past. Instead, testimony attempts to keep the meaning of the past alive through a presentation of the truth of the past not as objectively and scientifically determined, but as remembered through narrative, through symbolic representation, and I would add, through place. And as Booth elaborates, testimony "seeks to guard the truth against effacement or oblivion. But it is a relationship to the truth about the past that is part of a mesh of identity, justice, and debt. Its governing imperative is a mix of debt to the now voiceless past, to preserve the voice of justice against forgetting or falsehood, and to the needs of continuity in identity."[59] Monuments cannot, however, be reduced to testimony, for they also serve as archives and as projections of the now into the future. They draw together temporality and become the locus for the meeting of past and future, I and Other, testimony and archive.

Monuments and the Presence of the Future: History and Archive

If we consider Arendt's position again, she suggests that the production of monuments is important for the transference of a story to future generations to allow for the survival of history. She writes "acting and speaking men need the help of *homo faber* in his highest capacity, that is, the help of the artist, of poets and historiographers, of monument-builders or writers, because without them the only product of their activity, the story they enact and tell, would not survive at all."[60] Arendt places stipulations on how this needs to happen by suggesting that the monuments need to be "fit for action and speech." She writes that they must be appropriate "for activities not only entirely useless for the necessities of life but of an entirely different nature from the manifold activities of fabrication by which the world itself and all things in it are produced."[61] She acknowledges that the projection into the future by the monument is not necessarily projection into a certainty, since it risks reinterpretation by the future, the re-valuation of the stone marker by a generation that cannot be controlled or foreseen. What becomes clear from these passages from Arendt, and is underscored by Ricoeur's reading, is that the world is made for humans during their life on earth. Monuments are produced for the living, not for the dead. Perhaps we are called by the dead to produce the monument as testimony, but it is erected in the world of human living. The living read and understand the story of the monument. Its message is for the living. It may direct us to that which is not of the living, to that which is radically other, but it must direct *us* and those to come, not those who are no longer. Its focus, then, is on the future. It is archival preservation for future generations.

Ricoeur views the archive as written to be consulted as the deposited testimony that is itself the narrative of a declarative memory.[62] The physical place of the archive is a shelter for the trace of memory. This shelter, this preservation of the trace, however, is not entirely innocent. Because it takes up its position within the social and the public, it is open to whoever approaches it. Without a designated addressee, the monument as archive takes on a certain authority over those who view it. It is most frequently seen to be giving us the truth of the event or the person it glorifies or represents. Like the process of producing an archive, decisions are made as to what is to be represented in monuments and memorials. Such decisions are made with the expectation of future interpretation. How we in the present want an event to be remembered in the future, or even determining which events shall be remembered, are the motivating desires for the production of the archive that is the monument.

And if we think of the power of the monument with respect to its surrounding world, we can see that it organizes the surrounding world, with itself as a focal point such that the other elements fade into the background. It conquers the landscape in a very physical sense; its substance (usually cement or marble) withstands nature, does not allow for the growth of anything in its place, puts up resistance to the winds and the weather. In its physicality, it is future oriented, erected for the future, meant to carry a tradition and meaning to the future.

In the encounter with the kinds of monuments that Arendt's passage evokes, we might be tempted to view monuments as primarily productive in creating an environment of national power, collective ideals that attempt to persuade the individual of the priority of the nation or the culture over the individual. We kill in the name of the United States, for instance, and can rest assured that our names will ultimately be glorified in a war monument. War memorials easily come to mind as creating the national archive of participation in violent conflicts.

If we think of the typical glorifying monument to soldiers in war, we experience a moment that contributes to the ongoing narrative of a nation. What transpires in this kind of monument is an abstraction. We are not to pay attention to a particular soldier. The soldier represented in the monument is frequently anonymous. It is not a soldier, it is representative of soldierliness. It is an abstraction that allows us to view war as glorious and is about heroes as opposed to being about the horrors of the destruction of flesh, the gruesomeness of mutilation and the death of particular individuals. In this respect the abstraction goes hand in hand with the ideology of the monument. This is not historical narrative, telling the story of what happens in battle; this is production of a narrative of a nation as war-winners, as gloriously on the right side of the battle. But it is precisely in the abstraction that distortion takes place and the particular deaths, the particular victims, are put aside, forgotten, or dismissed.

Even those monuments that bring into question the glorious war have been opposed and limited, their narratives restricted. In France, for instance, after World War I, there was a movement to erect pacifist war memorials not celebrating or honoring the fallen soldier, but pointing to the horrors of war through the presentation of widows and orphaned children, the grieving and the lost. One of the most famous of these is at Gentioux-Pigerolles with its inscription "Maudite soit la guerre" (Cursed by war).

This memorial, made of stone with a sculpture of an orphaned boy, standing cap in hand, fist raised toward the inscription of names of the dead, was only officially inaugurated in 1990 after many, many years of obstructionist behavior on the part of the French military. In the effort to preserve the power to shape and produce the archive as desired by the state, the testimony to the effects of war was to be covered over. The monument in its testimonial power was to be denied in favor of a constructed history.

It seems, then, that what monuments and memorials can do, in holding the past and the future in tension, in speaking as both archive and testimony, is to provide a foundation for a narrative of the past, to bring it into the present, and to project for the future the memory of those who are no more. In order to achieve this, monuments cannot be restricted to archive and the archival element cannot be strictly anonymous history, but must include the testimony of the other within its narrative. The monument as a place of memory can do this in its bodily effect and through the fulfillment of the narrative with the aura of the place.

If places like monuments can be ideological as we have seen above, then how do we allow for the testimony in light of the ideological dimensions and the ideological decisions necessary for archives? As Ricoeur points out, ideology is "linked to the necessity for a social group to give itself an image of itself, to represent and to realize itself, in the theatrical sense of the word."[63] Among the characteristics that Ricoeur attributes to ideology is one that is particularly apt for monuments: ideology is "simplifying and schematic." It gives an overall view of a group and that group's history in relation to the world as a means of justifying not only the group itself, but many of the group's actions. "For it is through an idealized image that a group represents its own existence, and it is this image that, in turn, reinforces the interpretative code. The phenomena of ritualization and stereotype thus appear with the first celebrations of the founding events."[64] This ritualization itself is a necessary element in the cohesion of a group and is not of itself negative. When ideology becomes something to beware, we recognize that it functions at the level of formulating thought rather than inspiring it. It is uncritical and unreflective in its opacity.[65] Monuments in their inherent temporality are in some respects automatically tied to a certain level of ideology. As Ricoeur reminds us, "All interpretation takes place in a limited field, but ideology effects a narrowing of the field in relation to the possibilities of interpretation which characterized the original momentum of the event. In this sense we may speak of ideological closure, indeed of ideological blindness."[66]

Ultimately, for Ricoeur, "Ideology is the error that makes us take the image for the real, the reflection for the original."[67] The ideological role here, however, is not necessarily negative. It becomes negative when it is narrowed and fails to incorporate an element of critique. With regard to monuments, then, if the monument is instrumental in securing a social bond, it is ideological, but it can secure that social bond in ways that are open to the reinterpretation of the past as well as to creative projection into the future. It is that position in between that must be preserved for monuments and that we intend to explore below.

Ricoeur on the Between

We adopt Ricoeur's understanding of the twofold use of the word "history" here as "the set of events (facts) past, present, and to come, and as the set of discourses on these events (these facts) in testimony, narrative, explanation, and finally the historians' representation of the past."[68] Ricoeur suggests that our making of history is something that comes about because we ourselves are historical. Monument-making is just one way among many that we make history. It is in this way, too, then, that we justify our continued monument-making in spite of the difficulties that monuments pose for the transmission of culture across generations. This does not eliminate the possibility that monument-making could happen in a very different fashion in the future. We should consider how human temporality and historicality contributes to our role as monument-makers.

Ricoeur raises concerns about Heidegger's use of the fundamental structure of care and its temporality as a way into a revised understanding of the temporality of humans. For Ricoeur, Heidegger is mistaken when he conflates the totality and the mortality of the human being. In spite of Heidegger's claim regarding the openness of Dasein to its possibilities, the insistence upon Dasein's ownmost possibility as being that of death seems to have the effect of closing off Dasein. Ricoeur finds that focusing on the imminent threat of dying masks "the joy of the spark of life."[69] Instead he, like Hannah Arendt, wants to stress the theme of natality. He describes it as underlying the three Arendtian categories that compose the *vita activa*: labor, work, and action.[70]

Moreover, Ricoeur asks "Does not the jubilation produced by the vow—which I take as my own—to remain alive until . . . and not for death, put into relief by contrast the existentiell, partial, and unavoidably one-sided aspect of Heideggerian resoluteness in the face of dying?"[71] As a response to this question, Ricoeur finds value in the dialogue between the historian and the philosopher regarding death. It is also at this juncture that I find the role of the monument.

Initially, Ricoeur wants to explore the relationship between the embodied desire for life and its association with death. He suggests that in fact, this knowledge of death, as promoted by biology, is still heterogeneous to the desire to live. "It is only at the end of a long work on oneself that the entirely factual necessity of dying can be converted, not to be sure into the potentiality-of-dying but into the acceptance of having to die."[72] For Ricoeur, even when an acceptance of death has taken place, it does not replace the anguish or the fear of death precisely because of the "radical heterogeneity" of death with respect to the desire for life.

The second tack for Ricoeur is in the plurality of death. He challenges Heidegger's lack of attention to the death of the other as having the same impact as the angst of one's own being-towards-death. For Ricoeur, "What it is important to plumb instead are the resources of veracity concealed in the experience of losing a loved one, placed back into the perspective of the difficult work of reappropriation of the knowledge about death."[73] Unlike Derrida's claim that mourning is impossible, Ricoeur thinks that through the death of the other we learn loss and mourning. With respect to the loss of someone close, Ricoeur likens it to a loss of an integral part of one's self-identity. The loss of the other with whom we communicated constitutes a step towards the loss of self. So, like Derrida, Ricoeur sees our own self-concern in mourning. In mourning the loss of the other, we anticipate the mourning that others will go through at our own future death. This redoubles the anticipation of one's own death with which we struggle to reconcile ourselves.

Ricoeur recognizes, however, that this is only on the order of the loss of someone close. How, then, do we accommodate the loss of the strangers whose names we frequently read on monuments. Do monuments play a role in this process? The answer to this question is a decisive yes. Ricoeur draws upon Levinas too when he thinks through the way in which the death of another, not a close other, but an Other reflects my own fear of death back to me. For Ricoeur, as for Levinas, the most extreme example of this is the violent death of murder. What we have in the form of a war memorial or monument in particular is the presentation of the violent death of countless others in war. It is death by the state, or death by the national enemy, but violent death all the same. Ricoeur refers to this as the problem of death in history.

By recognizing a role for places of remembering the death and loss of others as a way of reflecting our own fear of death back to us, we have a way of understanding the role of monuments vis-à-vis memory and history that can be helpful in shattering the ideological pretensions of monuments. Some monuments are successful in bringing us to mind of our own being-towards-death while other monuments represent an attempt to allow us to escape that grasp. Part of the success of such monuments is their role in making us feel the death of the other in its particularity. This brings us face to face with our own death, but also face to face with our own life—as Ricoeur says drawing upon Levinas, our "being against death."[74]

The monument to Amy Biehl calls us to remember her violent death at the hands of fellow human beings. In such a memory is also the shadow of life. This simple confrontation on a dusty street corner in a township brings one to mind of one's own mortality, life cut short, but also brings one to mind of the very aliveness of one's living with the dust in one's eyes and the heat on one's neck. It is testimony to Amy Biehl and her violent death. But as testimony, it is also confrontation with the death of the other that calls to mind one's own death. At the same time it testifies to one's own being alive since the monument was placed as a reminder to the living. In its archival element as a reminder in the township of an era of violence, but also of reconciliation, it serves also as a call to continue that heritage of reconciliation. There is a power in the monument that calls us to such reflection.

The attention to life as well as death marks the value of the monuments at the individual level of memory. But what of the other side of the equation, the value of the monument at the historical, communal level? Ricoeur attempts to reconcile individual temporality and history through, on the one hand, the concept of attestation as discovered in Heidegger, and on the other hand, the concept of "heritage-debt." On Ricoeur's reading, attestation in Heidegger is the locus of the unity of our historical condition through its three temporal phases. It is the testimony of the past, the anticipation of our historical condition, and the "I can" of the present that is felt in the capacity for speech, action, and narrative. Heritage-debt likewise "constitutes the existential possibility of standing for" which remains dependent on the retrospective orientation of historical knowledge.[75] These are the two prongs between which monuments can be understood to mediate. Both of these prongs are an effort to exist in the tension between the absence of the past and the representation of that past in the presence of history. What Michel de Certeau attributes to the writing of history, I likewise attribute to the monument (not unlike what he calls the sepulcher). He identifies two different movements in this writing. It "exorcizes death by inserting it into discourse," while in the same moment it "performs a 'symbolic function' which 'allows a society to situate itself by giving itself a past through language.'"[76] For Certeau, Ricoeur asserts, the writing plays the role of the past. Ricoeur also refers to Ranciere who indicates that death in history is not usually the death of anonymous people, but is the death of the king or other important personages. The writing of these deaths attempts to make the deaths redeemable by history. We need only look at a brief history of monuments themselves to see this.

Early war memorials, in particular, honored great military leaders and their victories. The Romans imported obelisks from Egypt to celebrate their victories. Common soldiers, however, were not among those honored and celebrated. It was not until after World War I that monuments and memorials became more democratic, honoring the common soldier. These monuments were often erected to unknown soldiers—the ones whose remains were never recovered, or whose remains were recovered but were unidentifiable. Only in the most recent past have the names of the known, common soldiers been included in the commemorative process. The victims of atrocities, too, have only recently been commemorated or marked by a monument.

The duty to remember does not ensure that memory is put to effective use. Tzvetan Todorov suggests that it is not easy to determine the good uses of the past from the bad ones, but that this does not mean that we should give up only in favor of the particularities of the past.[77] Todorov makes a distinction between literal use of memory and exemplary use of memory. Literal use of memory preserves an event in memory as fact; it is never moved beyond regardless of whether it is true or not. In such cases, an initial event is associatively connected to subsequent events, but leads "nowhere beyond itself."[78] Exemplary use of memory, on the other hand, opens the event in question, trauma for instance, to generalization thereby distancing it from oneself, using it as a principle for present action, and making it an example from which to learn. Todorov upholds exemplary memory due to its ability to generalize and bring justice, which is impersonal law, impartial judgment. In arguing for exemplarity, he charges that one must move beyond victim to fight against injustice. Monuments to the victims of atrocities can be seen as one attempt to do just that: to provide a foundation for a narrative that acknowledges the injustice, that serves as testimony and witness for the victims, and attempts to bring justice by using their memory against obscurity through time and as a reminder of a lesson to be learned. This is why so frequently such monuments are located in the place of the atrocity or the tragedy. The place fulfills the narrative with its aura. There is a fine line here, however. In making an event an example, one must guard against the shadow that can cover the particularity of the experience of the victims. Thus, the conservation of the memory for history can only truly be effective, I would argue, if in the experience of the monument one is confronted with the particularity of the event and of the particular deaths in such a way that one is allowed to see beyond this particularity to the example they represent. This is the position 'in between' that the monument takes up.

This fine line is accomplished through the place of a successful monument that supports a mimetic narrative. While monuments them-

may not be fully developed narratives, they share the qualities of mimesis as outlined by Ricoeur. In brief, they contribute to the narrative identities of the groups who erect them, as well as the groups for whom they are erected. They contribute to narratives in their symbolic depictions of victims or heroes, and in the use of cultural symbols that emphasize the valor or the pain they commemorate. In this way, they are instrumental in promoting a prefigurative understanding of one's own nation, for instance, as a certain kind of player on the world stage. They also contribute to the emplotment of a national story by enveloping a particular event into the general story and helping to refigure the event within our own lives, perhaps allowing us to walk away from a monument or memorial with a different perspective on that which it commemorates.

This commemorative narrative, however, cannot be a reduction of history to memory, nor can it be a reduction of memory to history. Instead, narrative, as transfigured in monuments, is obligated to hold memory and history in tension with one another. If we view the monument as merely archival, we could see monuments as simply an injunction to remember a particular event of the past, leading to the ready question of how one could be required to remember something that was not even of one's own generation. How could I be expected to remember the Holocaust when it happened before I was born? How can memory be involved here? Memory and history are held in tension through the physical manifestation of the place of the monument and its role as both archive and testimonial.

And what precisely is one being called to remember through any particular monument? Are we to remember only those who were killed? Or are we to remember the perpetrators as well? How much can we know about the event that could be transmitted through the monument? We know names, perhaps. We have numbers, perhaps. But what do they mean? How do we remember the untold millions who died on The Middle Passage, whose names were unrecognized and unrecorded and who no longer have a place?

Ricoeur describes the duty to remember as a duty of justice where justice is understood as related to a component of otherness. It is, in other words, a call to do justice, through memory as both archive and testimony to those who are other than the self. As he writes, "we are indebted to those who have gone before us for part of what we are. The duty of memory i[...]t restricted to preserving the material trace, whether scrip-
t[...]of past events, but maintains the feeling of being obligated
[...]these others of whom we shall later say, not that they are
[...]t they were."[79]

[...]v argues that this imperative to remember has been too
[...]om history in the sense that it has been taken up as a
[...]orate. If we simply divorce the duty to remember from
[...]e end up with a rush to memorialize that lands us in

an ideological position that is not about the duty to the other, but is about securing our own place as victim. The duty of memory, then, might more properly be understood to involve the duty to remain in the tension between memory and history. This is where commemoration must reside, but it is a point that monuments and memorials so frequently fail to find.

Monuments as places imbued with meaning are responsible for making the dead speak, for bringing the past into the present, and for projecting that past and our present into the future. As the monument is always experienced in the now from the perspective of a current generation, its interpretation is the transmission of a dynamic meaning across time. The monument takes up a position between past and future, between I and other, between temporality and history, between testimony and archive, and it does so by providing a place of remembering.

Of course, any encounter with a monument must recognize the need to be open to the traditions, the history, and the memory that the monument evokes. And in that openness is the responsibility of the experiencer to recognize the relationship between history and temporality that makes the experience possible in the first place. As Ricoeur reminds us, "the temporal constitution of the being that we are proves more fundamental than the simple reference of memory and of history to the past as such. In other words, temporality constitutes the existential precondition for the reference of memory and of history to the past."[80] Successful monuments take up the position in between allowing for us to experience both the possibility of testimony, as memory of those who were, while at the same time allowing for the possibility of archive and projecting that history and tradition for the future. To reduce the effect of a monument to testimony is to misunderstand its position within history, but to reduce the monument to archive is to misunderstand its role in bringing us to be mindful of the other and of ourselves with respect to the absent other. The monument's position in between makes it complex in its meaning and allows us to take on a position of critique of its possible ideological and historical assertions. In calling both of these aspects to mind in the experience of a monument, we are ever more aware of our own historicality and our own position in the in between of the present.

Memory, History, and Critique

A monument or memorial always runs the risk of creating a place of closure where the past is evoked in a way so determined and certain that it discourages critique, discourse, and thinking. To guard against such discouragement, we must be cautious in erecting memorials and controlling places of memory. For places of monuments to be open to thought, they themselves must be open to the aspects of a tragedy or an event that might otherwise run the risk of being forgotten. Such openness requires an active engagement of the individual in the process of remembering within the place of the monument.

As a cautionary tale, we can consider the eagerness on the part of many Americans to erect memorials to the September 11, 2001 attack on the World Trade Center Towers in New York City. Just two years after the attack, a plan was approved for a memorial to those who died. The plan received much attention. It was praised by some, and criticized by others, but the eagerness to erect a memorial so quickly was questioned by very few.

For permanent national memorials or regional memorials, the eagerness to memorialize reveals a desire for immediate closure, whether to release us as a nation or a community from the pain of a tragedy, or to allow us to control the way a tragedy is understood in the future and ultimately to cover over mortality by creating eternal heroes of the dead. The very fact that this manifests itself as a desire to quickly erect a memorial points to our unspoken understanding of the power of place to undergird a narrative and to control time.

The rush to memorialize reflects a desire to control the perspective, to make certain that the event is understood in a way that puts us and our suffering at the center. Derrida's claims of our own narcissism rear their heads again here. Perhaps we are afraid that history will belittle our suffering. Perhaps we want to make sure that future events do not affect the way we view the events of September 11, for example. In any case, the rush to memorialize eliminates the necessary historical distance that allows for a perspective on the event and allows for the dialogue that helps us determine what values should be celebrated in a memorial to an event of magnitude.

Nietzsche criticizes the rush to memorialize in saying that "art flees away" in any effort to immediately preserve events as history.

> He who wants to understand, grasp and assess in a moment that before which he ought to stand long in awe as before an incomprehensible sublimity may be called reasonable, but only in the sense in which Schiller speaks of the rationality of the reasonable man: there are things he does not see which even a child sees, there are things he does not hear which even a child hears, and these things are precisely the most important things: because he does not understand these things, his understanding is more childish than the child and more simple than simplicity.[81]

Nietzsche claims that the individual engaged in this immediacy ends by sinking into his own interior, which has no outward effect and cannot become life. Immediately to memorialize is to limit the outward effect. It seals a meaning of immediacy without allowing for an effect of the event on life and action. It creates imperviousness to anything other than the status quo.

We might read the rush to memorialize as a struggle to connect with a past. But rather than truly look at the past in order to come to terms with who we are, we would prefer to create a past quickly that can be referred to readily without the distance for reflection or renewal and critique that otherwise would be required. Unlike monuments that engage us with our past like the Civil Rights Memorial in Montgomery, Alabama, many more contemporary monuments have arisen out of the frenzy to commemorate and do not call us to reflect upon our past or call us to a community that transcends national borders. Instead, we prescribe events in terms of our own victimization since we have yet to have a perspective, and since history has yet to give us the distance to reflect upon events and determine their long-range impact.

In the rush to memorialize, monuments lose their ability to connect us to the past and to prior generations and history. They restrict our ability to approach any tradition from a perspective of preservation and critique. Instead, they become an attempt to glorify our own generation, to determine the meaning and value of our own time as opposed to reflecting thoughtfully upon the generations who have bequeathed to us a world and traditions.

The rush to memorialize indicates our unwillingness to grapple with complex issues, or unwillingness to think about and engage in discourse about who we are and what we value. It is a desire to close the book on a tragedy that could have and should have a resounding impact on our society. Memorials can function and should function as a call to renewal and critique.

Nietzsche's balance of three modes of history acknowledges the need to retrieve and monumentalize, while at the same time recognizing the imperative to critique. Again, Nietzsche suggests: "If you acquire a living knowledge of the history of great men, you will learn from it a supreme commandment: to become mature and to flee from that paralyzing upbringing of the present age which sees its advantage in preventing your growth so as to rule and exploit you to the full while you are still immature . . . Satiate your soul with Plutarch and when you believe in his heroes dare at the same time to believe in yourself."[82] The role of critique that is made possible in some monuments due to their openness is that which allows us to believe in ourselves without taking ourselves, our suffering, or our epoch too seriously.

While it can be said that all monuments and memorials run the risk of presenting our past in a simplified and closed manner, I would argue that the rush to memorialize is at more of a risk for this limitation. For the rush to memorialize reduces or even eliminates the lapse of time that might give us perspective on an event, allowing us to be more self-reflective as to the meaning of the event, and thus, might allow for a less politicized transference of its meaning to subsequent generations.

In spite of the fact that the palimpsest of memory and the palimpsest of place mean that meanings are shifting, the ability of a monument to evoke the past and provide a connection for us to the past can only arise with historical distance. It is only through that distance that the connection to a prior generation and a tradition that spans generations can be achieved.

NOTES

1. Hannah Arendt, *The Human Condition* (Chicago: University of Chicago Press, 1958).
2. See Hannah Arendt, *The Human Condition*, 19, 55, 173.
3. I use the term "remember" here to stress that this is a part of memory, but it is clearly not recollection, it is what Husserl would call retention, meaning it is something that is retained in the present experience and is not re-presented to oneself as it would be if recollected.
4. Edward Casey, *Getting Back into Place* (Bloomington: Indiana University Press, 1993), 128.
5. *ibid.*
6. Casey, *Getting Back into Place*, 129.
7. George Allan, *The Importances of the Past* (Albany: SUNY Press,1986), 200.
8. *ibid.*
9. Friedrich Nietzsche, *Untimely Meditations* (Cambridge: Cambridge University Press, 1997), 67.
10. Nietzsche, *Untimely Meditations*, 71.
11. Nietzsche, *Untimely Meditations*, 75.
12. Nietzsche, *Untimely Meditations*, 76.
13. Martin Heidegger, *Being and Time*, trans. J. Macquarrie and E Robinson (New York: Harper & Row, 1962), 449.
14. Heidegger, *Being and Time*, 448.
15. Heidegger, *Being and Time*, 443.
16. Heidegger, *Being and Time*, 444.
17. Margaret Olin notes that most of the cards and letters left at the impromptu memorial sites for Princess Diana were addressed directly to her, not to her family or other mourners. See Nelson, Robert and Margaret Olin, eds. *Monuments and Memory, Made and Unmade* (Chicago: University of Chicago Press, 2003), 146.
18. Karsten Harries, *The Ethical Function of Architecture* (Cambridge: MIT Press, 1998), 294.
19. Harries, *The Ethical Function of Architecture*, 297.
20. Such memorials can be seen in Israel. Plaques are often placed on trees near places where terrorist attacks have taken place.
21. We can imagine situations where a spontaneous or impromptu event could foster community—such as a flash mob where people come together to dance or sing or protest, or even holding a vigil at a place of tragedy, but this is different, I think, than the rather anonymous and isolated response of placing flowers or a teddy bear on a pile where there is not necessarily any interaction with others.
22. Gregory L. Ulmer, *Electronic Monuments* (Minneapolis: University of Minnesota Press, 2005).
23. Ulmer, *Electronic Monuments*, xxiii.
24. Virtual Memorials, Inc., http://www.virtual-memorials.com (Last accessed 8/12/2013).

25. Lindsay F. Marshall, http://www.memorial.to/vmg/vmg3.html (Last accessed 8/12/2013).
26. Clearly monuments of stone are not truly permanent either, but they do give a sense of permanence in spite of their ultimate giving way to the elements or to social change.
27. More will be said below about the role of the body in experience of place as opposed to cyberspace.
28. Michael Shepp, http://www.mshepp.com/20010 911.htm (Last accessed 8/12/2013). Voices of September 11, http://www.911livingmemorial.org (last accessed 8/12/2013).
29. Arendt, *The Human Condition*, 1.
30. Jeff Malpas, "Acting at a Distance and Knowing from Afar: Agency and Knowledge on the World Wide Web," *The Robot in the Garden*, ed. Ken Goldberg (Cambridge: MIT Press, 2000), 114.
31. Edward Casey, *Remembering: A Phenomenological Study* (Bloomington: Indiana University Press, 2000), 179.
32. Edward Casey, *Remembering*, 180.
33. By creating places, I mean both places that have markers built upon them, as well as places that perhaps remain deliberately unmarked but take on a significance for a group.
34. William Gass, "Monumentality/Mentality" *Oppositions* 25 (1982): 133.
35. Maya Lin, "America Remembers" *National Geographic* 165 (1985): 557.
36. Quoted in Nicholas Capasso, "Vietnam Veterans Memorial" *The Critical Edge: Controversy in Recent American Architecture*, ed. Tod A. Marder (Cambridge: MIT Press, 1985) 191.
37. Lea Caragata, "New Meanings of Place: The Place of the Poor and the Loss of Place as a Center of Mediation" *Philosophy and Geography* 3 (1998): 221.
38. Martin Heidegger, ". . . poetically man dwells . . ." *Poetry, Language, Thought*, trans. Albert Hofstadter (New York: Harper & Row, 1971).
39. Martin Heidegger, "Building Dwelling Thinking" *Basic Writings*, trans. David Farrell Krell (San Francisco: Harper Collins, 1977).
40. Heidegger, "Building Dwelling Thinking," 329.
41. See Heidegger, ". . .poetically man dwells. . ."
42. Harries, *The Ethical Function of Architecture*, 306.
43. David Chidester, "Monuments and Fragments: Religion, Identity, and Spaces of Reconciliation" *Emory Humanities Lectures* 1 (2001): 53.
44. Chidester, "Monuments and Fragments," 52.
45. Albert Boime, *The Unveiling of National Icons* (Cambridge: Cambridge University Press, 1998), 208.
46. Boime, *The Unveiling of National Icons*, 214.
47. Samuel Hynes, *A War Imagined: The First World War and English Culture* (New York: Maxwell Macmillan International, 1991), 281.
48. William Gass, "Monumentality/Mentality," 140.
49. It is interesting to note that this is called a memorial. In conducting research on monuments and memorials I discovered that the words are not used systematically at all. The uses of "monument" and "memorial" seem to be idiosyncratic according to the artist/architect of the piece. Increasingly, there is a penchant for calling public commemorations "memorials" as opposed to monuments.
50. "The Civil Rights Memorial" tourist brochure published by the Southern Poverty Law Center, Montgomery, Alabama.
51. For specifics see Laura Mulvey, "Reflections on Disgraced Monuments" *Architecture and Revolution*, ed. Neil Leach (London: Routledge Press, 1999), 222.
52. W. James Booth, *Communities of Memory: On Witness, Identity, and Justice* (Ithaca: Cornell University Press, 2006), 73.
53. Booth, *Communities of Memory*, 74.

54. The Amy Biehl foundation has recently erected a new memorial to Amy that is a larger marble cross elevated on a marble base, so higher than the original. The new memorial also includes an inscription that valorizes Amy's life and her commitment to racial equality.

55. Like Derrida, many discuss this duty to remember in terms of the paradox of remembering the immemorial. I side with Richard Kearney in this debate in that I think we must not remain silent even in the face of the paradoxicality of speech. This is part of the reason why the narrativity of monuments to victims has taken on such a prominent role. Monuments in such cases are not for the sake of glorification but are an additional way of attempting to narrate which interrupts or disrupts more documentary or direct historical narrative.

56. Booth, *Communities of Memory*, 79.

57. Booth, *Communities of Memory*, 103.

58. Booth, *Communities of Memory*, 79.

59. Booth, *Communities of Memory*, 94.

60. Arendt, *The Human Condition*, 173.

61. Arendt, *The Human Condition*, 174. I fully recognize that there are ways in which Arendt's position is problematic and have addressed those elsewhere.

62. Ricoeur, *Memory, History, Forgetting*, 166.

63. Paul Ricoeur, *From Text to Action: Essays in Hermeneutics II* (Evanston, IL: Northwestern University Press, 2007), 249.

64. Ricoeur, *From Text to Action*, 251.

65. *ibid.*

66. Ricoeur, *From Text to Action*, 252.

67. Ricoeur, *From Text to Action*, 254.

68. Ricoeur, *Memory, History, Forgetting*, 349.

69. Ricoeur, *Memory, History, Forgetting*, 357.

70. *ibid.*

71. Ricoeur, *Memory, History, Forgetting*, 357. This notion is one that is elaborated upon by Ricoeur in one of his last works *Living Up to Death*, trans. David Pellauer (Chicago: University of Chicago Press, 2009).

72. Ricoeur, *Memory, History, Forgetting*, 358.

73. Ricoeur, *Memory, History, Forgetting*, 359.

74. Ricoeur, *Memory, History, Forgetting*, 361.

75. Ricoeur, *Memory, History, Forgetting*, 363.

76. Ricoeur, *Memory, History, Forgetting*, 367.

77. Tzvetan Todorov, "The Abuses of Memory" *Common Knowledge* 5 (1996): 6–26.

78. Todorov, "The Abuses of Memory," 14.

79. Ricoeur, *Memory, History, Forgetting*, 89.

80. Ricoeur, *Memory, History, Forgetting*, 347.

81. Nietzsche, *Untimely Meditations*, 83–4.

82. Nietzsche, *Untimely Meditations*, 94–5.

FIVE

Conclusion

I have brought places into remembrance in this book, but I have also focused on places of remembering and commemoration. In so doing, I have tried to restore place to its rightful position as foundational and central to the process of remembering. I have repeatedly suggested that the palimpsests of memory, body, tradition, and place are interwoven and that any effort to understand any one of the four requires that we grapple with the other three as well. To this end, I have focused on monuments and memorials as places of intensified meaning where tradition and memory become focused and where the place of the monument can either be open to the complexity of the palimpsest, or can attempt to shut it down by covering it over with ideology. I have stressed also that our approach to monuments and memorials, given this tension, must be a hermeneutic process.

Places are so close to us that we overlook them, are inattentive to them, and frequently close them off without thinking. They hide themselves as the invisible foundations that make the events, temporality and things of our lives our focus. To be attentive to places of remembering is to recognize the layers upon layers of meaning that surround us in the world and to which we so frequently bodily respond. It is to recognize that we are implaced and that places not only trigger layers of memory, but hold layers of memory as a palimpsest. By approaching places of memory hermeneutically, we can uncover the erasures and the overwritten layers to disclose meanings that still permeate and inform our own cultural understandings. In bringing the multiple layers to light, we come to recognize the complexity of meaning, and the multivalence of traditions. We also come to reflect upon our own way of taking up those traditions and meanings.

I have stressed the role of the body in connecting us to places that carry forth the past. While the body carries places in its habitual constitution of the world, places also reflect the body in their organization, and in their role of layering the past upon bodies. Memories are written upon the earth as well as upon the body. The image of the palimpsest helps us understand the way in which memories can be layered upon the body in such a way that they are constantly shifting in value and prominence. It also helps us understand how places have shifting value and prominence due to the interaction of the body with memories that are layered in any one place. We are reminded that there are reasons why monuments and memorials are the venues we use to honor the dead. They mark the earth allowing for a physical presence in the absence of those long gone. They engage us bodily and fulfill the rather empty memories of the Other. They are more than simply mnemonic devices. We can walk around monuments and touch them, place flowers on graves, and do rubbings of stone. These bodily interactions are rich with the testimonial memories of what has transpired in the place or the archival memories of what will be projected into the future or both as the place itself fulfills an otherwise empty memory.

We have also reflected upon the ways in which the individual bodily response is not that of an isolated self, but is imbued with intersubjectivity. Our memories of place and in place are not strictly our own, but connect us with a community that has helped us to characterize what is worth remembering and has engaged us narratively in the production of an identity. I have appealed in the foregoing chapters to Ricoeur's sense of narrative as the method by which we establish identities, both individual and collective. For Ricoeur, the notion of emplotment as a synthesis of disparate elements is the mediation between a multiplicity of events and a unified story. Ricoeur suggests that plot

> organizes together components that are as heterogeneous as unintended circumstances, discoveries, those who perform actions and those who suffer them, chance or planned encounters, interactions between actors ranging from conflict to collaboration, means that are well or poorly adjusted to ends, and finally unintended results; gathering all these factors into a single story makes the plot a totality which can be said to be at once concordant and discordant.[1]

For Ricoeur narrative understanding is neither static, nor complete. It is characterized by sedimentation and innovation, and the dynamism of tradition. Ricoeur stresses in the narrative identity of an individual that our aim in telling stories and reading stories about our lives is not to impose identity upon ourselves, but to discover our identity as it develops and changes and yet as it is embedded within cultural traditions. The richness of Ricoeur's account is that it moves beyond a myopic focus on the individual's being-towards-death to encompass the fully public and communal sense of the self that we find by being in the world, through the mediation of place. I have also relied on Ricoeur because of his ability to carve out a space 'between,' which is fundamental to the interpretation of any monument or memorial, or any place of remembering.

Ricoeur's notion of narrative is important for a third reason which is that it recognizes the role of sedimentation vis-à-vis tradition. For him, the "phenomenon of traditionality is the key to the functioning of narrative models and, consequently, of their identification. The constituting of a tradition indeed depends on the interaction between two factors, innovation and sedimentation. It is to sedimentation that we ascribe the models that constitute, after the fact, the typology of emplotment which allows us to order the history."[2] I have added to Ricoeur's account the Husserlian language of recognition of the need for renewal and critique in taking up the stories of the past. Ricoeur's acceptance of the role of sedimentation means that in taking up the past, we are taking up the manifold layers of that past. Ricoeur argues that there is a dynamic circularity between life and narrative such that the narratives into which we are born are part of the life we take up which then feeds back into the revelation or the *poiesis* of narrative that again reveals life. We have the sense of the palimpsest here.

Still, how is it that we engage in the renewal and critique of a place of remembrance? For Ricoeur, drawing initially upon Gadamer, the sense of a narrative is derived from the "intersection of the world of the text and the world of the reader."[3] For us, this means that the sense of a monument or memorial, like that of a text, transpires in the intersection of the world of the monument and the world of the person experiencing the monument. This equally applies to places of remembrance be they homes or schools or neighborhoods. The world of the monument "opens before it a horizon of possible experience" and thus to experience the monument is to "unfold the world horizon implicit in it which includes the actions, the characters, and the events of the story told."[4] Even though Ricoeur is speaking of texts, it is not a far stretch to apply his words here to monuments and places of remembrance. Heidegger too conceives of the hermeneutic activity as one of the opening of horizons. In this case, we speak of horizons of the past. The one experiencing a monument or memorial "belongs at once to the work's horizon of experience in imagination and to that of his or her own real action. The horizon of expectation and the horizon of experience continually confront one another and fuse together."[5]

Why have I been speaking of monuments and memorials, or places of remembering, as providing a foundation for narratives rather than as being narratives themselves? I do not want to discount the way in which place itself can serve a narrative function, but I also want to stress that narratives that are part of our cultural heritage are enriched by places of memory that fulfill those narratives. The places themselves contribute something different to the narratives making them richer and more alive than they would otherwise be. In spite of my appreciation of and reliance upon Ricoeur's notion of narrative as a method of interpreting places of remembering, I have also stressed that Ricoeur fails to account for the role of place in such narratives. One cannot have plot without setting and setting is not simply something which surrounds plot or makes a place for plot. Setting is fundamental to plot in the manner in which it informs constitution, informs bodily interactions in the world, and informs and holds memory. Narratives of history are phenomenologically empty until we fulfill them through place. Place engages our body and thus our imagination in ways that narrative alone cannot.

It is one thing to think of monuments and memorials, or places of remembering as narratives. We recognize that through a monument someone is attempting to say something to someone about something. As with any narrative, there is an author, a reader, and a reference. But I have tried to go one step further here in suggesting that places of remembering provide a slightly different foundation that is supportive of narrative insofar as places provide the somewhere where the communicators come together. In such places we are bodily responsive to a multiplicity of meanings that are not just on the surface of a narrative or a memory, but are brought into proximity in the place. The propinquity of history to the present takes place in the place of monuments and memorials and places of remembering that involves us in the interpretation of that history. Hannah Arendt sees narrative as amplifying the circle of selfhood into an 'enlarged mentality' capable of imagining oneself in the place of the other. I am pushing this to extend narrative not simply to the Other of the present of the monument in the sense of the multiple Others who might engage in the present narrative of the monument with me, but to include the past Others of history who are accessible through the place of remembering.

And yet, we still must wonder how this transpires. Heidegger speaks of this hermeneutic of place as having a soteriological quality. In our contemporary age when modern technology dominates, there is a poverty of place. In its calculative approach modern technology relates to locations in space that are demarcated by coordinates and quantitative descriptions. Such a calculative approach cannot accommodate places. They are not accessible. Places cannot be distinguished one from another on such an account. The locations that modern technology identifies cannot reveal the truth of the world for we do not dwell in coordinates. Our lives do not transpire simply in locations. We live in a world of different places, the differences of which are incalculable. Those differences are sensed bodily and experienced in changing traditions and through varying intensities of memory.

If we recognize that place is not just the setting for events of our lives, we can allow place to speak of our traditions and histories in such a way that we hear the past and can more responsibly take it up through the process of renewal and critique. This Husserlian notion of renewal and critique is vital to an approach to place that helps us to find that position 'in between' narcissism and ideology. It allows us to take up traditions as they are handed down to us through places of monuments and memorials, for example, but allows us to take them up through the interpretive lens of the present thereby revealing the many layers of sedimented meaning. The statues of Lenin in Eastern European countries are not just symbols of Communist Power. Now they are symbols of the fall of Communism and the power of the peoples of Eastern Europe in overcoming Communism. They are many more things as well. Attentiveness to the experience of the monument helps to make us aware of the multiplicity of those meanings in such a way that we critique them at the same time that we take them up.

Some argue that memorials and monuments no longer have a place in our society. Since we are incapable of mourning, and incapable of remembering, all monuments are failures.[6] They fail insofar as they are always caught up in political machinations. Those with the political will and the political clout can erect monuments that serve their own perspective on events thereby shutting down other possible perspectives. They fail insofar as monuments as acts of mourning cannot truly honor a person in her singularity. They fail in that our rush to erect them destroys their possibility for bringing the past into the present. They fail insofar as they glorify death covering over any need to be attentive to our own mortality. In the previous chapters I have, in fact, shown these failings to be true of many monuments. However, there is a tension between how places of remembering function and how they ought to function. There is also a tension between the way in which place is fundamental and foundational, and the ways in which constructed places may fail to do what we construct them to do. Recognizing the fundamental importance of place as I have described and explained in the foregoing chapters, allows us also to recognize the palimpsest character of place, memory, and tradition. Only then can we begin to understand places of remembering.

I have broached the narcissism of mourning and memorialization on the one hand, but have also addressed the ideological tendencies of memorializing on the other. What I have stressed is that the role of places of remembering puts us in an 'in-between.' It calls to mind the overlapping sections of a Venn diagram, where one circle of the diagram is the past embodied in the place of the monument and the other circle of the diagram is the present of the experience of the monument. Like the horizons of Gadamerian hermeneutics, each experience of the monument brings a different overlapping of the circles. The meaning shifts as we shift, the present overlaps differently with the past in each era. If we are attentive, we can be 'between' the present and the past and projecting towards the future in the erection and experience of monuments. We can be between the narcissism of our own time and our own concerns through the approach of renewal and critique of the traditions that are embedded in monuments and memorials. We can be 'between' the hermeneutic of affirmation and the hermeneutic of suspicion which should work together in the experience of a monument as we uncover layers of meaning in our encounter with a place of remembering.

Finally, we see that monuments and memorials are between art and history. They are aesthetic objects that grace our landscapes, but as aesthetic objects, they are also windows into a world that we take up repeatedly and bring into the world of the present. In so far as they are capable of opening a world of the past to us, they have a certain aura as Benjamin might have it. That aura, however, is not, as Benjamin reminds us, one that is to be viewed from a distance and with reflective awe. It rather calls us to have a heightened state of consciousness as we attempt to understand the tradition it arises from and to engage in the critique of that tradition and our own present in the encounter.

As we draw this investigation to a close, we find ourselves situated at this juncture 'in between.' We as the interpreters of monuments and memorials, as the ones who return to places of our past, as those who reinvigorate our memories through pilgrimages to places of remembering, stand between past and present, between present and future, between art and history, between narcissism and ideology, between self and Other, between testimony and archive, and between permanence and change. From that position 'in between,' we struggle for balance which requires of us a heightened state of consciousness, an attentiveness to the power of place, a necessity for thinking about what we are doing, and a rigorous engagement in a hermeneutic process. It calls us to remembering places.

NOTES

1. Paul Ricoeur, "Life in Quest of Narrative," *On Paul Ricoeur: Narrative and Interpretation*, ed. David Wood (London: Routledge , 1991), 21.
2. Ricoeur, "Life in Quest of Narrative," 24.
3. Ricoeur, "Life in Quest of Narrative," 26.
4. *ibid.*
5. *ibid.*
6. See for instance, Michael P. Levine, "Mediated Memories: The Politics of the Past," *Angelaki* 2 (2006): 117–136.

Selected Bibliography

Abram, David. *The Spell of the Sensuous: Perception and Language in a More-than-Human World*. New York: Vintage Books, 1997.

Adams, Jill Petersen. "Mourning, The Messianic, and The Specter: Derrida's Appropriation of Benjamin in *Specters of Marx*." *Philosophy Today* 51 suppl. (2007): 140–147.

Allan, George. *The Importances of the Past: A Meditation on the Authority of Tradition*. Albany: State University of New York Press, 1986.

Ambrosio, Francis. "Gadamer and Aristotle: Hermeneutics as Participation in Tradition." *Proceedings of the American Catholic Philosophical Association* 62 (1988): 174–182.

Arefi, Mahyar. "Non-Place and Placelessness as Narratives of Loss: Rethinking the Notion of Place." *Journal of Urban Design* 4 (1999): 179–193.

Arendt, Hannah. *The Human Condition*. Chicago: University of Chicago Press, 1958.

Babich, Babette. "The Essence of Questioning After Technology: Techne as Constraint and the Saving Power." *Journal of the British Society for Phenomenology* 30 (1999): 106–124.

Bachelard, Gaston. *The Poetics of Space*. Translated by Maria Joals, Boston: Beacon Press, 1994.

Backhaus, Gary, and John Murungi, eds. *Lived Topographies: And their Mediational Forces*. Lanham, MD: Lexington Books, 2005.

Barash, Jeffrey Andrew. "Martin Heidegger, Hannah Arendt and the Politics of Remembrance." *International Journal of Philosophical Studies* 10 (2002): 171–182.

Benjamin, Walter. "The Work of Art in the Age of Mechanical Reproduction." *Illuminations*. Edited by Hannah Arendt. Translated by Harry Zohn, New York: Harcourt, Brace & World, Inc. (1969): 217-251.

———. *The Arcades Project*. Translated by Howard Eiland and Kevin McLaughlin, Cambridge: Harvard University Press, 1999.

Bloomer, Kent C., and Charles W. Moore, eds. *Body, Memory, and Architecture*. New Haven: Yale University Press, 1977.

Boime, Albert. *The Unveiling of National Icons*. Cambridge: Cambridge University Press, 1998.

Booth, W. James. *Communities of Memory: On Witness, Identity, and Justice*. New York: Cornell University Press, 2006.

Boyer, M. Christine. *The City of Collective Memory: Its Historical Imagery and Architectural Entertainments*. Cambridge: MIT Press, 2001.

Brocki, Marcin. "Landscapes of Memory—Narratives of Past Places." *Place and Location: Studies in Environmental Aesthetics and Semiotics VI*. Edited by Eva Näripea, Virve Sarapik, and Jaak Tomberg, Talinn: The Research Group of Cultural and Literary Theory, Estonian Literary Museum Institute of Art History, Estonian Academy of Arts Estonian Semiotics Association (2008): 219–225.

Brown, Charles S., and Ted Toadvine, eds. *Eco-Phenomenology: Back to the Earth Itself*. Albany: State University of New York Press, 2003.

Buttimer, Anne and David Seamon, eds. *The Human Experience of Space and Place*. New York: St. Martin's Press, 1980.

Camus, Albert. *The Fall*. New York: Vintage Books, 1991.

Carr, David. *Time, Narrative, and History*. Bloomington: Indiana University Press, 1986.

Caragata, Lea. "New Meanings of Place: The Place of the Poor and the Loss of Place as a Center of Mediation." *Philosophy and Geography* 3 (1998): 215–238.

Carrier, Peter. "Places, Politics and the Archiving of Contemporary Memory in Pierre Nora's *Les Lieux de mémoire*," *Memory and Methodology*. Edited by Susannah Radstone, Oxford: Berg (2000): 37–57.

Casey, Edward. "Levinas on Memory and the Trace." *The Collegium Phaenomenologicum: The First Ten Years*. Edited by John Sallis, Giuseppina Moneta, and Jacques Taminiaux, The Hague: Martinus Nijhoff (1988): 241–255.

———. *The Fate of Place*. Berkeley: University of California Press, 1997.

———. *Getting Back into Place*. Bloomington: Indiana University Press, 1993.

———. *Remembering: A Phenomenological Study*. Bloomington: Indiana University Press, 2nd ed., 2000.

———. "Smooth Spaces and Rough-Edged Places: The Hidden History of Place." *Review of Metaphysics* 51 (1997): 267–296.

———. "J.E. Maplas's *Place and Experience: A Philosophical Topography*. Converging and Diverging in/on Place." Philosophy and Geography 4 (2001): 225–230.

Cataldi, Suzanne L., and William S. Hamrick, eds. *Merleau-Ponty and Environmental Philosophy*. Albany: State University of New York Press, 2007.

Caygill, Howard. "Benjamin, Heidegger and the Destruction of Tradition," *Walter Benjamin's Philosophy*. Edited by Andrew Benjamin and Peter Osborne, London: Routledge (1994): 1–31.

Chamberlain, Jane. "Thinking Time: Ricoeur's Husserl in *Time and Narrative*." *Journal of Philosophical Research* 27 (2002): 281–299.

Charlesworth, Andres. "Contesting Places of Memory: The case of Auschwitz." *Environment and Planning D: Society and Space* 12 (1994): 579–593.

Chidester, David. "Monuments and Fragments: Religion, Identity, and Spaces of Reconciliation." *Emory Humanities Lectures* 1 (2001): 49–58.

Connerton, Paul. *How Societies Remember*. Cambridge: Cambridge University Press, 1989.

Crang, Mike and Penny S. Travlou. "The City and Topologies of Memory." *Environment and Planning D: Society and Space* 19 (2001): 161–177.

Cresswell, Tim. *Place: A Short Introduction*. Oxford: Blackwell Publishing, 2004.

Crowell, Steven. "Spectral History: Narrative, Nostalgia, and the Time of the I." *Research in Phenomenology* 29 (1999): 83–104.

Dacres, Petrina. "Monument and Meaning." *Small Axe* 16 (2004): 137–153.

DeArmitt, Pleshette. "The impossible incorporation of Narcissus mourning and narcissim in Derrida." *Philosophy Today* 44 (2000): pp. 84–90.

de Certeau, Michel. "Practices of Space," *On Signs*. Edited by Marshall Blonsky, Oxford: Blackwell Publishing (1985): 122–145.

Derrida, Jacques. *The Gift of Death*. Chicago: University of Chicago Press, 2007.

———. *On the Name*. Stanford: Stanford University Press, 1995.

———. *The Work of Mourning*. Edited by Pascale-Anne Brault and Michael Naas, Chicago: University of Chicago Press, 2001.

Donohoe, Janet. "Dwelling with Monuments." *Philosophy and Geography* 5 (2002): 235–242.

———. "The Place of Home." *Environmental Philosophy* 8.1 (2011): 25–40.

———. "Where Were you When?: On the Relationship Between Individual and Collective Memory." *Philosophy in the Contemporary World* 16.1 (2009): 105–113.

———. "Rushing to Memorialize." *Philosophy in the Contemporary World* 13 (2006): 6–12.

Drummond, John. "Time, History, and Tradition." *The Many Faces of Time*. Edited by John Brough. Dordrecht: Kluwer Academic Publishers, 2000.

Elden, Stuart. "Heidegger's Holderlin and the Importance of Place." *Journal of the British Society for Phenomenology* 30 (1999): 258–274.

Eliade, Mircea. *Cosmos and History: The Myth of the Eternal Return*. Translated by Williard Trask. New York: Harper & Row, 1959.

———. *The Sacred and the Profane*. Translated by Williard Trask. New York: Harcourt, Brace and Co., 1959.

Entrikin, J. Nicholas. *The Betweenness of Place: Towards a Geography of Modernity*. Baltimore: Johns Hopkins University Press, 1991.

Foltz, Bruce. *Inhabiting the Earth: Heidegger, Environmental Ethics, and the Metaphysics of Nature*. Amherst, NY: Humanity Books, 1995.

Foote, Kenneth E. *Shadowed Ground: America's Landscapes of Violence and Tragedy*. Austin: University of Texas Press, 1997.

Foucault, Michel. "Of Other Spaces." Translated by Jay Miskowiec. *Diacritics* (1986): 22–27.

Gadamer, Hans-Georg. *Truth and Method*. Translated by Joel Weinsheimer and Donald G. Marshall, New York: Crossroad Publishing, 1992.

———. *Philosophical Hermeneutics*. Translated and edited by David E. Linge, Berkeley: University of California Press, 1976.

———. "The Artwork in Word and Image—"So true, so full of Being!" (Goethe)." *The Gadamer Reader: A Bouquet of his Later Writings*, edited by Richard Palmer (Evanston: Northwestern University Press, 2007): 108–120.

Gallagher, Winifred. *The Power of Place*. New York: HarperCollins, 2007.

Gass, William. "Monumentality/Mentality" *Oppositions* 25 (1982): 126–144.

Gesell, Arnold, et al. *Vision: Its Development in Infant and Child*, New York: Paul B. Hoeber, 1950.

Gonzalez, Francisco. "Dialectic and Dialogue in the Hermeneutics of Paul Ricoeur and H.G. Gadamer," *Continental Philosophy Review* 39 (2006): 313–345.

Halbwachs, Maurice. *The Collective Memory*. Translated by Francis Ditter, Jr. and Vida Yazdi Ditter, New York: Harper and Row, 1980.

Harries, Karsten. *The Ethical Function of Architecture*. Cambridge: MIT Press, 1998.

Heidegger, Martin. "The Age of the World Picture." *The Question Concerning Technology and Other Essays*. Translated by William Lovitt, New York: Harper and Row (1977): 115–154.

———. "Art and Space." Translated by Charles H. Seibert. *Man and World* 9 (1973): 3–8.

———. "Building Dwelling Thinking." *Basic Writings*. Edited by David Farrell Krell, New York: HarperPerennial (2008): 343–363.

———. *Being and Time*. Translated by J. Macquarrie and E Robinson. New York: Harper & Row, 1962.

———. "Modern Science, Metaphysics, and Mathematics." *Basic Writings*. Edited by David Farrell Krell, New York: HarperPerennial (2008): 267–305.

———. "The Origin of the Work of Art." *Basic Writings*. Edited by David Farrell Krell, New York: HarperPerennial (2008): 139–211.

———. ". . . poetically man dwells . . ." *Poetry, Language, Thought*. Translated by Albert Hofstadter, New York: HarperCollins (1975): 209–227.

———. "The Question Concerning Technology." *Basic Writings*. Edited by David Farrell Krell, New York: HarperPerennial (2008): 307–341.

———. "What is Metaphysics?" *Basic Writings*. Edited by David Farrell Krell, New York: HarperPerennial (2008): 89–109.

Hobsbawm, Eric and Terence Ranger, eds. *The Invention of Tradition*. Cambridge: Cambridge University Press, 1983.

How, Alan R. "Hermeneutics and the 'Classic' Problem in the Human Sciences" *History of the Human Sciences* 24 (2011): 47–63.

Husserl, Edmund. *Cartesian Meditations*. Translated by Dorion Cairns, The Hague: Martinus Nijhoff, 1977.

———. *The Crisis of European Sciences and Transcendental Phenomenology*. Translated by David Carr, Evanston: Northwestern University Press, 1970.

———. *Ideas for a Pure Phenomenology and a Phenomenological Philosophy*, Vol. 2, Translated by R. Rojcewicz and A. Schuwer. The Hague: Martinus Nijhoff, 1989.

———. *Analysen zur passive Synthesis. Aus Vorlesungs-und Forschungsmanuskipten 1918–1926*, ed. M. Fleischer. The Hague: Martinus Nijhoff, 1966. Husserliana Vol. XI.

———. *On the Phenomenology of the Consciousness of Internal Time (1893–1917)*. Translated by John Brough. Dordrecht: Kluwer Academic Publishers, 1991.

Huyssen, Andreas. *Present Pasts: Urban Palimpsests and the Politics of Memory*. Stanford: Stanford University Press, 2003.

Hynes, Samuel. *A War Imagined: The First World War and English Culture*. New York: Maxwell Macmillan International, 1991.

Irwin-Zarecka, Iwona. *Frames of Remembrance: The Dynamics of Collective Memory*. New Brunswick, NJ: Transaction Publishers, 1994.

Jacobson, Kirsten. "A Developed Nature: A Phenomenological Account of the Experience of Home." *Continental Philosophy Review* 42 (2009): 355–373.

Janz, Bruce. "The Terror of the Place: Anxieties of Place and the Cultural Narrative of Terrorism." *Ethics, Place and Environment* 11 (2008): 191–203.

Johnson, Nuala. "Cast in Stone: monuments, geography, and nationalism." *Environment and Planning D: Society and Space* 13 (1995): 51–65.

Jusidman, Yishai. "Un-ending Yad-Vashem: Some Notes Towards and Aesthetics of Monuments and Memorials." *Art Criticism* 12 (1997): 48–56.

Kearney, Richard and James Williams, eds. "Narrative and Ethics," *Proceedings of the Aristotelian Society* 70 suppl. (1996): 29–45 and 47–61.

Kenny, Michael. "A Place for Memory: The Interface between Individual and Collective History." *Comparative Studies in Society and History* 41 (1999): 420–437.

Knizek, Ian. "Walter Benjamin and the Mechanical Reproducibility of Art Works Revisited." *British Journal of Aesthetics* 33 (1993): 357–366.

Koshar, Rudy. *From Monuments to Traces: Artifacts of German Memory, 1870–1990*. Berkeley: University of California Press, 2000.

Krell, David Farrell. *Of Memory, Reminiscence, and Writing: On the Verge*. Bloomington: Indiana University Press, 1990.

———. "Phenomenology of Memory from Husserl to Merleau-Ponty." *Philosophy and Phenomenological Research* 42 (1982): 492–505.

Lamarche, Pierre. "Tradition, Crisis, and the Work of Art in Benjamin and Heidegger." *Philosophy Today* 45 supp. (2001): 37–45.

Landzelius, Michael. "Commemorative dis(re)membering: erasing heritage, spatializing disinheritance." *Environment and Planning D: Society and Space* 21 (2003): 195–221.

Lawlor, Leonard. *Derrida and Husserl: The Basic Problem of Phenomenology*. Bloomington: Indiana University Press, 2002.

Lefebvre, Henri. *The Production of Space*. Translated by Donald Nicholson-Smith. Oxford: Blackwell Publishing, 1991.

Legg, Stephen. "Contesting and Surviving Memory: Space, Nation, and Nostalgia in *Les Lieux de Mémoire*." *Environment and Planning D: Society and Space* 23 (2005): 481–504.

Le Goff, Jacques. *History and Memory*. Translated by Steven Rendall and Elizabeth Claman. New York: Columbia University Press, 1992.

Levine, Michael. "Mediated Memories: The Politics of the Past" *Angelaki* 2 (2006): 117–136.

Lin, Maya. "America Remembers." *National Geographic* 165 (1985): 557.

Lipsitz, George. *Time Passages: Collective Memory and American Popular Culture*. Minneapolis: University of Minnesota Press, 1990.

Lotz, Chrisitan. "Recollection, Mourning and the Absolute Past: Husserl, Freud and Derrida." *The New Yearbook for Phenomenology and Phenomenological Philosophy* 4 (2004): 121–141.

Makkreel, Rudolf. "Tradition and Orientation in Hermeneutics." *Research in Phenomenology* 16 (1986): 73–85.

Malpas, Jeff. *Place and Experience: A Philosophical Topography*. Cambridge: Cambridge University Press, 1999.

———. "Acting at a Distance and Knowing from Afar: Agency and Knowledge on the World Wide Web." *The Robot in the Garden*. Edited by Ken Goldberg, Cambridge: MIT Press, 2000.

———. "Comparing Topographies: Across Paths/Around Place: A Reply to Casey" Philosophy and Geography 4 (2001): 231–238.

———. "Finding Place: Spatiality, Locality, and Subjectivity." *Philosophy and Geography III* (1998): 21–44.

———. *Heidegger and the Thinking of Place*. Cambridge: MIT Press, 2012.

———. *Heidegger's Topology: Being, Place, World*. Cambridge: MIT Press, 2007.

Mann, Barbara. "Tel Aviv's Rothschild: When a Boulevard Becomes a Monument." *Jewish Social Studies* 7.2 (2001): 1–38.

Manzo, Lynn. "Beyond Home and Haven." *Journal of Environmental Psychology* 23 (2003): 47–61.

Merleau-Ponty, Maurice. *Phenomenology of Perception*. Translated by Colin Smith, London: Routledge Press, 1962.

Mitscherling, Jeff. "Philosophical Hermeneutics and 'The Tradition'." *Man and World* 22 (1989): 247–250.

Moore, Jeanne. "Placing *Home* in Context." *Journal of Environmental Psychology* 20 (2000): 207–217.

Morley, David. *Home Territories: Media, Mobility and Identity*. New York: Routledge Press, 2000.

Mugerauer, Robert. *Interpretations on Behalf of Place*. Albany, NY: State University of New York Press, 1994.

———. *Interpreting Environments: Tradition, Deconstruction, Hermeneutics*. Austin: University of Texas, 1995.

Muldoon, Mark. "Ricoeur and Merleau-Ponty on Narrative Identity." *American Catholic Philosophical Quarterly* 71 (1997): 35–52.

Mulvey, Laura. "Reflections on Disgraced Monuments." *Architecture and Revolution*. Edited by Neil Leach, London: Routledge Press, 1999.

Naas, Michael. "History's Remains: Of Memory, Mourning, and the Event." *Research in Phenomenology* 33 (2003): 75–96.

Nietzsche, Friedrich. *Untimely Meditations*. Edited by Daniel Breazeale. Cambridge: Cambridge University Press, 1997.

Nelson, Robert and Margaret Olin, eds. *Monuments and Memory, Made and Unmade*. Chicago: University of Chicago Press, 2003.

Nora, Pierre. "From Lieux de mémoire to Realms of Memory." *Realms of Memory*. Edited by L. D. Kritzman, New York: Columbia University Press (1996): xv–xxiv.

———. "General Introduction: Between Memory and History." *Realms of Memory*. Edited by L. D. Kritzman, New York: Columbia University Press (1996): 1–20.

Olberding, Amy. "Mourning, Memory, and Identity: A Comparative Study of the Constitution of the Self in Grief." *International Philosophical Quarterly* 37 (1997): 29–44.

Ondaatje, Michael. *Running in the Family*. Toronto: McClelland & Stewart, Ltd., 1982.

Piercey, Robert. "Ricoeur's Account of Tradition and the Gadamer-Habermas Debate." *Human Studies* 27 (2004): 259–280.

Popescu, Monica. "Translations: Lenin's Statues, Post-communism, and Post-apartheid." *The Yale Journal of Criticism* 16 (2003): 406–423.

Price, Joshua M. "The Apotheosis of Home and the Maintenance of Spaces of Violence." *Hypatia* 17 (2002): 39–70.

Rauch, Angelika. *The Hieroglyph of Tradition: Freud, Benjamin, Gadamer, Novalis, Kant*. Cranbury, NJ: Associated University Presses, 2000.

Reagan, Charles. "Reflections on Paul Ricoeur's *Memory, History, Forgetting*." *Philosophy Today* 49 (2005): 309–317.

Relph, Edward. *Place and Placelessness*, London: Pion, Ltd., 1976.

Reynolds, Jack. "Possible and Impossible, Self and Other, and the Reversibility of Merleau-Ponty and Derrida." *Philosophy Today* 48 (2004): 35–48.

Ricoeur, Paul. *From Text to Action: Essays in Hermeneutics II*. Evanston, IL: Northwestern University Press, 2007.

———. "Life in Quest of Narrative." *On Paul Ricoeur: Narrative and Interpretation*. Edited by David Wood, London: Routledge Press, 1991.

———. *Living Up To Death*. Translated by David Pellauer, Chicago: University of Chicago Press, 2009.

———. *Memory, History, Forgetting*. Translated by Kathleen Blamey and David Pellauer, Chicago: University of Chicago Press, 2004.

———. "Narrative Identity." *Philosophy Today* 35 (1991): 73–81.

———. *Oneself as Another*. Translated by Kathleen Blamey, Chicago: University of Chicago Press, 1992.

Risser, James. "Interpreting Tradition." *Journal of the British Society for Phenomenology* 34 (2003): 297–308.

Rosen, M. "Benjamin, Adorno and the Decline of the Aura." *Cambridge Companion to Critical Theory*. Edited by Fred Rush, Cambridge: Cambridge University Press (2004): 40–56.

Rossington, Michael and Anne Whitehead, eds. *Theories of Memory*. Baltimore: Johns Hopkins University Press, 2007.

Sallis, John. "Daydream." *Revue Internationale de Philosophie* 3 (1998): 397–410.

———. *Delimitations: Phenomenology and the End of Metaphysics*. Bloomington: Indiana University Press, 1995.

Sack, Robert. "The Power of Place and Space." *Geographical Review* (1993): 326–329.

Schama, Simon. *Landscape and Memory*. New York: A. A. Knopf Publishers, 1995.

Schuman, H. and J. Scott. "Generations and Collective Memories." *American Sociological Review* 54 (1989): 359–381.

Schwartz, Barry. "Social Change and Collective Memory: The Democratization of George Washington" *American Sociological Review* 56 (1991): 221–236.

———. "The Social Context of Commemoration: A Study in Collective Memory." *Social Forces* 61 (1982): 374–402.

Seamon, David, editor. *Dwelling, Place and Environment*. New York: Columbia University Press, 1989.

Sherratt, Yvonne. "Aura: The Aesthetic of Redemption?" *Philosophy and Social Criticism* 24 (1998): 25–41.

Shils, Edward. *Tradition*. Chicago: University of Chicago Press, 1981.

———. "Tradition." *Comparative Studies in Society and History* 13 (1971): 122–159.

Simms, Eva. *The Child in the World*. Detroit: Wayne State University Press, 2008.

Steinbock, Anthony. *Home and Beyond: Generative Phenomenology After Husserl*. Evanston: Northwestern University Press, 1995.

Tate, John. "Dead or Alive? Reflective versus Unreflective Traditions." *Philosophy and Social Criticism* 23 (1997): 71–91.

Till, Karen. "Places of Memory." *A Companion to Political Geography*. Edited by. J. Agnew, K. Mitchell, and G. Toal, Oxford: Blackwell Publishers (2003): 289–301.

Todorov, Tzvetan. "The Abuses of Memory." *Common Knowledge* 5 (1996): 6–26.

Trigg, Dylan. *The Memory of Place: A Phenomenology of the Uncanny*. Athens: Ohio University Press, 2012.

Truc, Gérôme. "Memory of Places and Places of Memory: for a Halbwachsian socio-ethnography of collective memory." *International Social Science Journal* 203–4 (2011): 147–159.

Tuan, Yi-Fu. *Space and Place*. Minneapolis: University of Minnesota Press, 1977.

Tyman, Stephen. "The Phenomenology of Forgetting." *Philosophy and Phenomenological Research* 44 (1983): 45–60.

Ulmer, Gregory L. *Electronic Monuments*. Minneapolis: University of Minnesota Press, 2005.

Van Reijen, Willem. "Breathing the Aura—The Holy, the Sober Breath." *Theory, Culture & Society* 18: 6 (2001): 31–50.

Vycinas, Vincent. *Earth and Gods*. The Hague: Martinus Nijhoff, 1961.

Wagner-Pacifici, Robin and Barry Schwartz. "The Vietnam Veterans Memorial: Commemorating a Difficult Past." *The American Journal of Sociology* 97 (1991): 376–420.

Wieviorka, Annette. "Memorials and Collective Memory." *Revue Francaise d'Etudes Americaines* 51 (1992): 55–62.

Wisnewski, Jeremy. "What we Owe the Dead." *Journal of Applied Philosophy* 26 (2009): 54–70.

Wood, David. ed. *On Paul Ricoeur: Narrative and Interpretation*. London: Routledge, 1991.

Wright, Kathleen. "The Place of the Work of Art in the Age of Technology." *Southern Journal of Philosophy* 22 (1984): 565–582.

Yates, Frances. *The Art of Memory*. Chicago: University of Chicago Press, 1966.

Young, James E. *The Texture of Memory: Holocaust Memorials and Meaning*. New Haven: Yale University Press, 1993.

———. "The German Counter-Monument: Memory Against Itself in Germany Today." *Critical Inquiry* 18 (1992): 267–296.

Zerubavel, Eviatar. *Social Mindscapes: An Invitation to Cognitive Sociology*. Cambridge: Harvard University Press, 1997.

———. *Time Maps: Collective Memory and the Social Shape of the Past*. Chicago: University of Chicago Press, 2003.

Ziarek, Ewa Plonowska. "Encounters Possible and Impossible: Derrida and Butler on Mourning." *Philosophy Today* 50 (2006): 144–155.

Ziarek, Krzysztof. "The Work of Art in the Age of its Electronic Mutability." *Walter Benjamin and Art*. Edited by Andrew Benjamin, London: Continuum Publishing (2005): 209–225.

Index

About the Author

Janet Donohoe received her Ph.D. from Boston College and is currently professor of philosophy at the University of West Georgia. She is the author of several articles about place and memory, and monuments and memorials, as well as a book titled *Husserl on Ethics and Intersubjectivity* (Humanity Books, 2004). She serves as book review editor for *Environmental Philosophy*. Her main areas of teaching and research include phenomenology, hermeneutics, and ecophenomenology.